Death Anxiety

A Volume in MSS' Series on Attitudes Toward Death

Papers by
Canon H. W. Montefiore, Joseph R. Cautela,
Robert N. Butler et al.

MSS Information Corporation
655 Madison Avenue, New York, N. Y. 10021

Library of Congress Cataloging in Publication Data
Main entry under title.

Death anxiety: normal and pathological aspects.

(Attitudes toward death, v. 3)
A collection of articles previously published in vari-
ous journals.
 1. Death--Psychology--Addresses, essays, lectures.
2. Anxiety--Addresses, essays, lectures. 3. Aged--
Psychology--Addresses, essays, lectures. I. Montefiore,
Conon H. W. II. Series. [DNLM: 1. Anxiety--
Collected works. 2. Death--Collected works.
BF789.D4 1973]
BF789.D4D37   616   73-12942
ISBN 0-8422-7147-3

TABLE OF CONTENTS

CREDITS AND ACKNOWLEDGEMENTS

Arsenian, John, "Situational Factors Contributing to Mental Illness in the Elderly," *Geriatrics*, 1962, 17:667-674.

Bruhn, John G.; A. Eugene Thurman; Betty C. Chandler; and Thomas A. Bruce, "Patients' Reactions to Death in a Coronary Care Unit," *Journal of Psychosomatic Research*, 1970, 14:65-70.

Butler, Robert N., "Toward a Psychiatry of the Life-Cycle: Implications of Sociopsychologic Studies of the Aging Process for the Psychotherapeutic Situation," *Psychiatric Research Report*, 1968, 23:233-248.

Cautela, Joseph R., "A Classical Conditioning Approach to the Development and Modification of Behavior in the Aged," *Gerontologist*, 1969, 9:109-113.

de Wind, E., "The Confrontation with Death," *International Journal of Psycho-Analysis*, 1968, 49:302-305.

Dudley, Donald L.; Joseph W. Verhey; Minoru Masuda; C.J. Martin; and Thomas H. Holmes, "Long-Term Adjustment, Prognosis, and Death in Irreversible Diffuse Obstructive Pulmonary Syndromes," *Psychosomatic Medicine*, 1969, 31:310-325.

Hackett, T.P.; and A.D. Weisman, "Denial as a Factor in Patients with Heart Disease and Cancer," *Annals of the New York Academy of Sciences*, 1969, 164:802-817.

Handal, Paul J., "The Relationship between Subjective Life Expectancy, Death Anxiety and General Anxiety," *Journal of Clinical Psychology*, 1969, 25:39-42.

Harari, A.; H. Munitz; H. Wijsenbeek; J. Levi; M. Steiner; and M. Rosenbaum, "Psychological Aspects of Chronic Haemodialysis," *Psychiatria, Neurologica, Neurochirurgia*, 1971, 74:219-223.

Montefiore, H.W., "Ethical Problems of Geriatrics," *Gerontologia Clinica*, 1969, 11:65-74.

Norton, Charles E., "Attitudes toward Living and Dying in Patients on Chronic Hemodialysis," *Annals of the New York Academy of Sciences*, 1969, 164:720-732.

Pandey, R.E.; and Donald I. Templer, "Use of the Death Anxiety Scale in an Inter-Racial Setting," *Omega*, 3:127-130.

Payne, Edmund C.; and Melvin J. Krant, "The Psychosocial Aspects of Advanced Cancer," *Journal of the American Medical Association*, 1969, 210:1238-1242.

Templer, Donald I., "The Construction and Validation of a Death Anxiety Scale," *The Journal of General Psychology*, 1970, 82:165-177.

Templer, Donald I., "Death Anxiety: Extraversion, Neuroticism, and

Cigarette Smoking," *Omega*, 1972, 3:53-56.

Templer, Donald I., "Death Anxiety as Related to Depression and Health of Retired Persons," *Journal of Gerontology*, 1971, 26:521-523.

Templer, Donald I., "Death Anxiety in Religiously Very Involved Persons," *Psychological Reports*, 1972, 31:361-362.

Templer, Donald I., "The Relationship between Verbalized and Non-verbalized Death Anxiety," *The Journal of Genetic Psychology*, 1971, 119:211-214.

Templer, Donald I., "Relatively Non-Technical Description of the Death Anxiety Scale," *Archives of the Foundation of Thanatology*, 1971, 3: 91-94.

Templer, Donald I.; and Elsie Dotson, "Religious Correlates of Death Anxiety," *Psychological Reports*, 1970, 26:895-897.

Templer, Donald I.; and Carol F. Ruff, "Death Anxiety Scale Means, Standard Deviations, and Embedding," *Psychological Reports*, 1971, 29:173-174.

Tietz, Walter, "School Phobia and the Fear of Death," *Mental Hygiene*, 1970, 54:565-568.

Tolor, Alexander; and Marvin Reznikoff, "Relation between Insight, Repression-Sensitization, Internal-External Control, and Death Anxiety," *Journal of Abnormal Psychology*, 1967, 72:426-430.

Wijsenbeek, H.; and H. Munitz, "Group Treatment in a Hemodialysis Center," *Psychiatria, Neurologica, Neurochirurgia*, 1970, 73:213-220.

Williams, Robert L.; and Spurgeon Cole, "Religiosity, Generalized Anxiety, and Apprehension Concerning Death," *The Journal of Social Psychology*, 1968, 75:111-117.

Zampella, A.D., "A Sampling of Attitudes toward Aging," *Journal of the American Geriatrics Society*, 1969, 17:488-492.

PREFACE

Anxiety caused by conscious and unconscious fears of death and dying is the subject of this volume. Attitudes among the aged, death anxiety in the general population, and death anxiety in chronically ill or dying patients are the major topics discussed.

Attitudes toward aging reflect many of our underlying fears of death. Death is taboo, unproductive, "failure" in the victim and a source of guilt to those who survive him. Resulting from this attitude in the general population are many ethical problems in the treatment of the aged. These problems are examined in the opening section. A sampling of attitudes towards aging, sociopsychological implications of the aging process, and situational factors contributing to mental illness in the aged are also discussed.

Templer's Death Anxiety Scale (DAS) is discussed in the following section, in terms of means, standard deviations, and embedding. The construction and validation of DAS, its use in an interracial setting, and DAS scores among religiously-involved individuals are also examined. Other papers cover death anxiety and neuroticism, death anxiety among concentration camp victims, the relation of death anxiety to depression in retired persons, the relation between insight, repression-sensitization, internal-external control and death anxiety, and the relationship between subjective life expectancy, death anxiety, and general anxiety.

The final section deals with death anxiety in chronically ill and terminal patients. Papers examine such topics as the psychosocial aspects of cancer, reactions to death in a coronary care unit, psychological aspects of chronic hemodialysis, and the role of denial in patients with fatal diseases.

Attitudes Toward Aging

Ethical Problems of Geriatrics

Canon H. W. MONTEFIORE

Let me start by saying that I am an amateur at this subject; and although I must admit that a recent illness made me feel like a geriatric patient, I do not yet qualify by years for that status. And when I see the formidable array of specialists that you have gathered for this course, I feel even more amateur than before. My only acquaintance with geriatrics has come through contacts with elderly members of my own and my wife's families (and here of course there are always emotional factors which cloud one's judgement); and through my pastoral work as a Vicar of a city parish (and here again one is always so conscious that as a Vicar one often sees only one side of the picture). I can claim no special acquaintance with the problems of geriatrics, and it is against this background of ignorance that you must judge all that I have to say. But let me add another point. I do not regard it as the job of a clergyman to be an expert in all the different fields of human experience. If he did make these expert claims, he would usually only be betraying his ignorance. So far as I understand my job as a clergyman, it is rather to stimulate and help lay people to do their jobs. Many of the ethical decisions – I would indeed say most of the ethical decisions concerning geriatrics – can only be taken by the experts, because they alone have the expert knowledge to decide them. There are of course a few ethical decisions which can be painted in black and white – and we shall have to examine our field this afternoon to see whether we have any such. But mostly ethical decisions involve a choice between different tones of grey. And here expert knowledge is tremendously important. We hear a lot these days about situation ethics: that is, instead of a cut and dried system of casuistry, which tells us clearly what is right and what is wrong, we are to have situation ethics, in which each individual decides in a particular situation what is the most loving action he can take. Since no two situations are exactly alike, the practitioners of this kind of ethic say that there can be no rules at all. Now I am not one of these who go along with situation ethics. I believe that rules are of the greatest assistance when we make ethical decisions, so long as they do not gain the mastery of us, lest we become slaves to them. There are always times when some rules should be broken, but rules serve a most useful purpose in allowing us to make quick decisions; they prevent emotional factors from swaying us and inclining us to make softer but less just decisions; they save us the necessity of thinking out each problem on its own merits. This would not merely take up an immense amount of our time and emotional energy, but it would be quite impractical in some of the instant decisions that face doctors and all who work in the medical field. Yet, having said all that against situation ethics, let me also say that just because situations do differ, the application of rules will differ, and that is why knowledge of the particular person is so essential to anyone making a decision about that person. Some people think that ethical decisions can be made by means of a sort of telegram from heaven. I am not one of these people myself. I think that one must know as many of the relevant facts about a case as possible before making any ethical decision about that case.

Now I would divide up the ethical problems of geriatrics into three main types. The first of these is what I call the national questions. The second I call the medical questions. And the third are what I would call the family questions. It would be interesting to know whether you, as experts in the subject, would agree with this division.

Let us first look at the national questions. How much money should be set aside from the national exchequer for health services at all? I do not know the answer to this question. It is easy enough to say that we should set aside as much as we can afford: this kind of answer gets us nowhere. I have seen in print that the U.K. sets aside a smaller proportion of the national income than other countries in Western Europe: I do not know whether this is true, but I rather think it is. And then of this money how much should be set aside for geriatric purposes? Again it is no good saying that we should set aside as much as is required. Required for what? And required for whom? At what standard of geriatric care is it right to aim? This is a particularly difficult problem with an ageing population. (I rather think that the expectation of life has not increased in recent years as much as had been expected; but nevertheless it has increased greatly within the lifespan of our present elderly age-groups, and so the proportion of elderly will continue to increase for some time ahead.) Presumably our needs are, so far as geriatrics are concerned, a bottomless pit. There is always room for more care, more doctors, more nurses, more ancilliary services and also more professional help for home cases. There is always room for more money. It is an accepted maxim that every department fights for a larger share of the cake. I must confess that even in my own subject, this same rule prevails. A divinity faculty in a university fights as much as any other faculty for a larger share of the money available for teaching and research. No doubt in the field of national health, geriatrics does the same. Is this ethical? What criteria should we have for deciding the extent of geriatric help that we should make available? Has the state a duty to make life tolerable for those in the eventide of existence if this means that younger people will lack the care that would restore them to mental or physical health more quickly? Should it do so if schools are to suffer, thus robbing the younger generation of opportunities? These are very difficult ethical problems, and it would be stupid if I pretended to know the answers. I do not. But I do think that they are important, and I do not often see them publicly argued out. And this is not only a question of money and resources. It is also a question of social service. Here is a very practical problem even in Cambridge. We have here something we call Youth Action Cambridge, a clearing house for young people who volunteer to do social work, to help in the community. Some of them go to Fulbourn Mental Hospital. Some befriend an old person and visit him or her through the Cambridge Task Force, which is run from Great St. Mary's, the church where I serve. Others have helped in the wards of Chesterton Old Peoples Hospital. At the moment each good cause tends to compete against the other. This produces a kind of equilibrium, but it means that the less rewarding work tends to attract less people. What call on voluntary work ought geriatrics to have? What weighting should be given to it? I find it difficult to answer; but I am sure once again that this is really an ethical problem, although it is not often aired.

This leads me to a further ethical problem. There are families who have an aged member, probably a mother or a father, who for some reason or another is not able to go to a state home or hospital in old age, or for whom such facilities are not, for one reason or another, really suitable. For such people there are privately run homes for the elderly. It so happened that my wife had to go into all this last year for her mother, although a merciful providence in the end took the matter out of our hands. It became plain that there are some homes which are recommended, and others which are definitely not recommended by local authorities. Now this raises ethical problems which are seldom investigated. How much value is it right to give for money? Presumably people who run these homes are doing so for profit – if they were not gainfully employed in this way, they would have to find some other way of earning their living. But few people might choose this particular way unless for a good reason. There are peculiar difficulties in looking after old people: physical problems such as incontinence and debility, and administrative problems such as staffing, nursing, etc. Is it not reasonable that people who work in such apparently disagreable fields should earn a higher profit? Here is an ethical problem concerning those who live off the elderly, or rather, those who live off those who support the elderly. When does exploitation end and fair profit begin? How can you define exploitation? I can see that you can differentiate private homes on the grounds of standards of nursing or kindness to patients, but so far as fees are concerned, I have not got the expert knowledge to offer you any solution.

There are many ethical problems of geriatrics which concern the family exclusively, and of course the family are a consideration in most problems concerning the elderly. In particular I am thinking of the problems concerning care of the elderly, and the gratification of the old people's wishes. Most old people prefer to live at home, or with their children or grandchildren. It is very difficult indeed to know at what point a family insists on a geriatric parent being taken into care, or insists that he or she comes and lives with them, or, more difficult still, insists that he or she goes into a home, when the needs are beyond the family's resources. And then of course there is the difficult problem – what kind of home? If the family can afford it, should it be a private home, or a public institution? In point of fact the nursing is often better in a public institution, but this is not the only consideration. And the question of what the family can afford is not always easy to answer: there is the ethical problem of how much a family should economise in order to find the money for a home.

I think that these problems often resolve themselves through the good sense of the people involved, but often not without a lot of agonizing, and frequently considerable inconvenience. There is the ethical problem of a family neglecting the children because of care of the elderly; the housewife reduced nearly to breaking point by the extra care involved. The family plainly have a real responsibility. If our parents looked after us for so many years when we were helpless and unable to look after ourselves, it seems not a matter of charity but of ordinary justice that we in turn should look after them when they become helpless.

But in this kind of justice more than two people are involved, and this is what complicates matters. If we lived in the kind of extended family that is the pattern in more primitive cultures, then the situation would be different. Here a person is given additional status by reason of age, and it is normal, almost expected, for granny or granpa to stumble round the house, even if they are in a state of great decrepitude. But we cannot put the clock back. Our society is not like that. By and large we live in two generation units, and what is more our housing is built to this requirement. I do not think that there can be any rule for the family in deciding whether or not to keep a geriatric parent at home, other than the condition of the patient, the resources of the family and the nursing facilities available. When a patient does leave home, I think that the family has a moral duty to visit as often as is practicable. Even if the visit is not long, it does allow a patient to feel still attached, and still tied by emotional bonds to kith and kin. I can imagine nothing so cruel as the dereliction of a geriatric patient by the family: I say that as a result of pastoral visiting. There is a kind of hopelessness and despair that results. It is small things that keep alive interest and affection; small presents, little bits of news, and especially visits by younger members of the family. The idea that young people should be shielded from geriatric patients seems to me wrong on two counts: first, it is shielding young people from reality, and secondly it is depriving the elderly of one of their chief sources of pleasure. Old people love the young.

To what extent should families give in to the wishes of the elderly? The oncome of senility means usually a breakdown of defences, and a person's real character, often hidden during active life by self-control, or imprisoned by the 'censor' in the unconscious, breaks into the open with the onset of old age. Saints become saints; but this is given to few. Most people are more demanding, more self-centred, more querulous, more childish than when they were in their prime. It is often a source of considerable embarrassment and even pain to their families that this should be the case. Is it right, in such a case, always to give in to

14

the wishes of an elderly person? Here I think the ethical problem is akin to that of dealing with a child, although the actual way of dealing with an elderly person will of course be very different. But the ethical problem is the same. Children should not be met with blank refusals: things should be explained. Children's wishes should be respected wherever this is reasonable. I believe that it is the same with the elderly. I know a person who keeps in her house an elderly aunt. She is very old, and has become very difficult. She is very cross indeed if, when the person goes out, she does not come and see her as the very first thing that happens when she re-enters her home. This is not always possible. If this woman did not take care, this geriatric patient would eat up her niece, who would find that she neglected her husband. It is necessary both to be kind and considerate, and at the same time to be firm and clear about the right priorities.

Many of these ethical problems are not peculiar to the family. They effect those in homes who have the care of the elderly. And so I turn now to that aspect of geriatric ethics which must affect you most – what I have called the medical problems.

Let us consider the most important problem of all: the right to life. I am not suggesting that this is an easy problem, still less that I have the answers. Here, as in so many fields, it is very easy indeed to lay down principles, and a very difficult effort of judgement to translated principles into action in any particular case.

I put on one side the ethics of suicide in geriatric cases. I do not think that they are strictly relevant to you as members of the nursing profession: but I must confess in passing that I do not always find this particular ethical question of suicide easy to resolve. But euthanasia does concern you. I am one of those who believe that we do not have the right to take active and positive steps to terminate a person's earthly life. (I know that it happens during warfare, but I do not consider the situations exactly parallel, nor is the question of penal execution exactly the same either.) The authority to carry out euthanasia is, in my judgement, too dangerous for any doctor or nurse to have. It is too difficult to draw lines. The patient may not be able to be consulted or if consulted may not be in a proper frame of mind to give a balanced answer. Let me say that I do not regard as euthanasia the administration of anaesthetizing drugs which have the result of hastening the end of a terminal illness. The drugs are given to anaesthetize pain, and not to hasten death. The intention behind their administration is not death but freedom from pain. It would be cruel

to withold such drugs when they are required. It would, in my judgement, be unethical to refuse them.

But euthanasia is one thing: whereas the witholding of special
efforts to restore health is quite another. Here I must reaffirm some
fundamental principles:

1. *Death is not always a disaster.* I am sure that it is not necessary to
emphasise this in such a company as this; and yet there are sections of
the medical profession who by their training are brought up to believe
that death is always a failure. In the Christian view of life, our existence
on this planet is the training ground for eternal life. This world is the soil
in which the tender plant is to grow up which will fruit and flower in
the life to come – or be stunted and barren, as the case may be. The
tragedy, in my judgement, that besets so many people, and especially
families who are concerned with the elderly, is that they do not
believe that there is anything beyond death. As the Latin poet said,
Mors est nox perpetua dormienda – death is a night of perpetual
sleep. If people really believe that, then they will want to hang on to
life at all costs – or rather not at all costs but at least where there is not
overwhelming pain. A cabbage-like existence is better than no existence, they think. This, in my judgement, is a warped perspective.
Death is universal, at any rate at the moment. It is not necessarily a
disaster, but it ends a chapter, naturally and properly.

2. *Grief is right and proper.* It is natural that anyone should grieve
over the loss of loved ones. In making decisions that concern the life
and death of the elderly it is proper to take into consideration the
family and their reaction. But it is wrong, in my judgement, to take a
step concerning A because of the effect on A's family – that grief
would be insupportable, etc. The syndrome of grief has been well
studied by the Tavistock Clinic. Acute grief usually passes, whether in
a short or long time. In taking a life-or-death decision about a geriatric
patient, the attitude of the family may properly sway a decision, but it
should never be the dominant factor.

3. *Man is made in the image of God.* What is it that distinguishes man
from the beasts? Traditional Christianity has said that he is made in
the image of God, while the beasts are not. Further research has modified the difference to one of degree rather than kind; but the distinction still stands. What does it mean to be made in the image of God?
As I understand it, it means that there are three inherent characteristics
which man has in virtue of his humanity: without these he is sub-
human. These three are (1) Communicability, that is, the ability of man

16

to have personal relationships with other people and so also with God. Man is a person, because he can have personal relationships. (2) Responsibility, that is, the ability to be responsible for his actions. Man may as a matter of fact act responsibly or irresponsibly: but the very fact that we say that he acts irresponsibly implies that he could be responsible. (3) Intelligence, that is the power to reason, to ratiocinate, whether logically or intuitively. This is found rudimentarily in the beasts, but man's brain ensures that he alone can properly exercise intelligence.

4. *Man has a natural term of life.* Here I must express myself with some caution. I put the proposition in the present. It may not always be true; but it is still true. It may be that future biological research may be able to make us immortal. I hope not. The prospect of endless life on this planet fills me with horror. It is rather like being condemned to spend the whole of one's life in a junior school. The length of our term of life differs for individuals. It is a matter for thankfulness when this natural term is longer rather than shorter: but it still remains a term. If you agree with my earlier propositions, namely that death is not always a disaster, but rather the close of the first chapter of life, and if man is made in the image of God, then perhaps you will further agree that there is little to be said for artificially extending a life for its own sake. While I have already argued that it would be wrong to take active steps to end a life, this is very different from artificially extending a life. I have suggested earlier than extreme pain should be anaesthetized, even if it means an earlier termination of life than would otherwise have occurred. What about the case when age or debility has removed, or seems to have removed, the distinctive characteristics of man made in the image of God? What about persons apparently permanently condemned to a cabbage-like existence, without the gifts of communicability, intelligence or responsibility; i.e. those who are absolutely without responsibility for their actions, unable to communicate with others or to use their intelligence? It would seem to me almost unethical to take steps artificially to keep such people alive, such as intensive care and the use of resuscitation techniques, if there was no hope at all of these people recovering these basic human characteristics. 'Thou shale not kill: but needs not strive officiously to keep alive' would seem to me proper ethical advice in such cases. But of course in the case of most geriatric patients the issue is not so clear cut. And here the decision is so much harder. Who knows how much a geriatric patient may recover from a stroke? Who knows what may be the chance of full recovery from a broken limb? – a fractured femur

17

or a broken thigh? I remember that my mother-in-law died from an operation which was carried out on her broken thigh. Without the operation there was no chance that she would ever leave her bed again: with the operation there was a slight chance of recovery, but still to a very limited geriatric life with mental decay and fairly acute diverticulitis. In fact she never recovered from the operation; and one is bound to ask: was is right that it should take place? And the answer surely is Yes: better the chance of a reasonably normal life or death, rather than a cabbage-like existence permanently in bed. But not all cases are so easy than this. Senility may not always be permanent, so far as the mind is concerned; and depressions can lift. Here I think the clergyman can give little advice, save to enunciate general principles. It is the task of the doctor, together with the nurses and all the vital ancillary services, and of course the family, to come to a decision about the course that should be taken – a job of course they do now with great responsibility. It is no good shrinking from these decisions: they must be taken, especially with limited resources; and doctors will have on their hands more and more life and death decisions than they have had in the past.

I warned you at the outset that this lecture would be sadly deficient and now you see that I am right. Perhaps I may end by reminding you of some important ethical factors:

.1. We all have a duty to follow our conscience, even if this means acting differently from other people. But we also have a duty to have an informed conscience, especially if we tend to reach conclusions different from those of other people.

2. As for any responsible decision we make, if we act in good faith, we have no need whatever to reproach outselves. If consequently we find that we have acted wrongly or foolishly, it should not be guilt that we feel, but perhaps something more egocentric called remorse. For if we act in good faith, although we may afterwards feel we acted wrongly, we were at the time right to take the decision that seemed right to us.

3. Each case must be judged on its merits, especially if it involves one of those difficult decisions where it is not easy to know that we are right. Rules are immensely useful, especially when there is no time to think out a difficult case when an immediate decision is required; but still each person may be different, and there may be always an occasion when a rule should be broken.

4. Normally in making an ethical decision, three factors need to be

born in mind; first, the intention of the agent; secondly the nature of the act; and third, the probable consequences of the act. It is impossible to lay down a hard and fast rule about the weighting which should be given to each factor in arriving at a decision.

Summary

Ethical decisions in geriatrics need expert knowledge and insight into particular situations. Problems fall into three kinds; national, affecting use of resources, etc.; family, concerning the relationships of the elderly to the rest of the family; medical, of which the most important concerns the right to live. Some principles can be stated. Death is not alway a disaster. Grief is unavoidable in bereavement. Man is made in the image of God. He has a natural term of life.

In any ethical decision, there is a duty to follow conscience. We are not blameworthy if we act in good faith. Each case is unique. An ethical decision involves the intention of the agent, the nature of the act and its probable consequences.

A Classical Conditioning Approach to the Development and Modification of Behavior in the Aged[1]

Joseph R. Cautela, Ph.D.

THE characteristics of the aged can be classified into the following three categories:

1) Low Behavioral Output—
   a) behave more slowly,
   b) engage in fewer behaviors,
   c) show a decreased variety in their behavior repertoires,
   d) act less vigorously upon the physical and social environments,
   e) devote themselves to the conservation of their resources.

2) Faulty Learning and Retention—
   a) exhibit more defects in memory,
   b) learn less readily,
   c) perform less readily on conventional tests of intelligence,
   d) cling to familiar objects and routines (avoidance of poor performance).

[1] Paper presented at the American Psychological Association Annual Convention, San Francisco, August 30, 1968.

3) Perceive Themselves as Rejected and Near Death—
   a) contemplate the prospect of death,
   b) either accept more negative statements about themselves or deny they are old,
   c) give the impression that they have lost their direction or purpose in life, feeling adrift or disenfranchised.

Of course, we all realize that such characteristics do not necessarily apply to all elders and can be applied to younger adults as well.

From the vast amount of speculation and extensive empirical work done by Pavlov in his lifetime, it is surprising to note that he made relatively little direct mention of the aged. It has been necessary, as a result, to obtain data and make references of the application of Pavlov's model to the aged from three sources: 1) Pavlov's experimentation with aged animals, 2) Pavlov's studies of the effect of extirpation of the cortex on the development and extinction of conditioned reflexes, and 3) Pavlov's speculation on personality types.

In this paper I will discuss the first two categories (Low Behavioral Output and Faulty Learning and Retention) within the framework of the Pavlovian Classical Conditioning model and the third category (Perceive Themselves as Rejected and Near Death) in terms of the respondent or Reciprocal Inhibition methods of Wolpe (1958). As will be evident, our knowledge of methods for the modification of behaviors is much more specific than our knowledge of how the behavior developed originally.

Low Behavioral Output

Pavlov (1928) characterizes the aged individual as one declining in activity and in the process of inhibition. He observed (1928, 1957) that very weak excitability is present in the cortex of aged animals. From the typology developed by Pavlov based on properties of the nervous system, some aspects have relevance in the discussion of the characteristics of the aged.

One aspect of Pavlov's typology concerns the balance of excitation and inhibition in the nervous system. Individuals can be classified on a continuum from total inhibition (sleep) to an excitable stage in which conditioned reflexes are formed rapidly and it is difficult to obtain negative reflexes (extinction). The nature of the cortical cells determine the amount of excitability the cortex can tolerate. The cortical cells possess a certain limit of efficiency, and beyond this point there arises inhibition which results from excessive functional exhaustion of the cell. The limit of efficiency is not constant; it undergoes both acute and chronic changes under certain conditions such as hypnosis, brain damage, excessive stimulation, and old age. According to Pavlov, the development of old age is a process in which the efficiency of the cortical cells is reduced to such an extent that these cells can be easily exhausted. When monotonous stimulation is presented (as is often the case with the aged in institutions and with the daily living habits of the non-institutionalized aged), such stimulation will be repeatedly affecting the same cortical cells. This results in exhaustion of the excitatory substance and inhibition occurs. Since the cortical cells have already lost some efficiency due to the aging process, aged individuals develop inhibition more rapidly than younger adults under conditions of monotonous stimulation. Also, with old age the mobility of the nervous system declines. Mobility is determined empirically by the ease of transition from positive conditioning (acquiring conditioned reflexes) to immediately being placed in a situation where previous conditioned reflexes (not necessarily the ones just acquired) are to be inhibited. Mobility can also be determined by the ease with which an organism can go from a situation where inhibition is required to a state where positive conditioned reflexes are to be elicited. This is seen behaviorally in the lack of ability of the aged population to adjust rapidly to change. Pavlov's observations of brain-damaged animals also demonstrated rapid exhaustion of cortical cells and poor mobility. His observations concerning the effects of brain damage are quite relevant here, since many investigators believe that most geriatric individuals who exhibit maladaptive behavior have brain syndromes (Corsellis, 1962; Epstein & Simon, 1967; Gellerstedt, 1933; Goldfarb, 1962; Rothchild, 1937; Simon, 1968).

When an animal exhibited lethargic or sleepy behavior during an experimental session, Pavlov (1928) used various procedures to increase activity. He found that stroking or slapping was suitable for that purpose and, furthermore, seemed to facilitate the conditioning process. These techniques can be applied to aged individuals in the form of such tactile stimulation as hugging and kissing, and should produce a higher rate of activity. Theoretically, the performance of aged individuals in a learning task should be facilitated if they were stroked or petted immediately before the task. The results of Doty (1968) lend support to this assumption. She found that by handling old animals the conditioning process was facilitated to an extent greater than that of rats handled at an early age.

Pavlov also observed that presentation of reinforcement (increased excitability of the cells) tended to increase activity. An aged population usually obtains very little reinforcement from the physical or social environment. Some elderly persons obtain reinforcement from occupational endeavors or hobbies; for others, such reinforcements are not sufficient to overcome the inhibitory processes. For these latter individuals it would first be necessary to discover the stimuli that have reinforcing properties for them before designing a behavior modification program. Kastenbaum and I have developed a Reinforcement Survey Schedule that can be useful for this purpose (Cautela & Kastenbaum, 1967). Ss are required to indicate on a 5-point scale the amount of pleasure they feel for certain stimuli ranging from food to such abstract things as being praised, being perfect, etc. The results of this schedule can then be made available to ward personnel, therapists, or relatives, who can systematically present specific reinforcers for any behaviors desired.

At Dejarnette State Hospital in Virginia we are establishing a behavioral conditioning ward, in which half the population is 65 years or over. The other half varies in age from 18 to 45. We intend to give all Ss on the ward an RSS and use this information to increase activity and shape behavior.

Pavlov also found that varying the stimuli for an organism increased activity. Since different cortical cells would be stimulated, there is less probability of cortical exhaustion. Applying this procedure to the elderly, it means that they should not just be kept busy, but that planned stimulus variability is needed. Finally, Pavlov found it necessary to use stronger conditioned stimuli and more intense unconditioned stimuli to modify the behavior of the inhibitory personality types. Sometimes this observation is neglected in attempts to engage geriatric individuals in some activity and when comparing behaviors of elders and young adults in experimental situations.

There is one important note of caution. According to Pavlov, the cortical cells of aged individuals can easily be overloaded by excessive stimulation or inhibition. Care must be taken to determine the amount of stimulus intensity and variability that can be tolerated by the elderly without increasing disorganization. Pavlov himself (1957) and other investigators (Gantt, 1964; Teplov, in Gray, 1964) have developed methods of determining the nervous system toleration levels of particular individuals to excessive stimulation. A modification of these procedures can be used in systematic research and plans for individual treatment.

2) *Faulty Learning and Retention*

In the aged organism, according to Pavlov (1957), individual reflexes, previously produced in a regular stereotyped way, become irregular and chaotic. Also in the aged personality, conditioned reflexes in the process of acquisition are easily disrupted by extra stimuli (Cautela, 1966; Pavlov, 1957) which then put a strain on the excitatory capacity of the cells. Since brain pathology is considered in some way responsible for the maladaptive behavior of aged individuals, Pavlov's observations concerning the effect of cortical damage on behavior is especially relevant here. In general, Pavlov (1957) observed that by fully or partially extirpating the cerebral hemispheres, either all or certain groups of conditioned reflexes (habits) disappeared. He also observed a great impairment in the ability of Ss to form conditioned reflexes. Gantt (1964) has observed the same results in human beings. As a result of possible brain damage and the poor inhibitory process characteristic of an aged individual, it is difficult to extinguish old habits that interfere with the adjustment of the aged to new demands brought about by reduction of physical capability and new social adjustment.

Treatment

Pavlov's empirical findings concerning learning and retention can be useful in establishing procedures to facilitate these processes in the elderly.

Pavlov found that paced learning was more resistive to extinction than massed learning. Eisdorfer (1965) and Talland (1967) also concluded that it is important to pace learning for elderly Ss. Taking on too much information at one time can interfere with learning. (Since the aged individual's attention span is often poor, learning will be facilitated if he is given tasks to learn in small bits.) Programmed teaching can be especially useful for this purpose, as well as for providing a setting in which the aged can proceed at their own pace. As mentioned previously, some kind of tactile stimulation can be helpful if it is applied just prior to learning.

Since the elderly are easily distracted (external inhibition is readily formed), learning should take place for the elderly in conditions where extra stimuli have been reduced to a minimum. Perhaps the best setting for learning is a soundproof room with only the teacher (therapist, trainer, etc.) present. In fact, if at all possible, the S should be in the room by himself, learning from a programmed text. Once habits are well established, external inhibition is less likely to occur.

Strong CS and US are necessary to obtain well-established conditioned responses. Pavlov observed that when an older person is given sensory inputs, he behaves as if the stimuli were less intense.

Drugs (stimulants) can also be employed to facilitate conditioning. One must be careful in this regard, since Pavlov found that animals which exhibited maladaptive behavior tended to show paradoxical drug effects (bromides and caffeine). Slater and Kastenbaum (1966) found that geriatric patients functioning on a lower behavioral level than other geriatric patients tended to exhibit such effects. Lawton (1968) recently stated that a drug response may change significantly when an individual reaches old age. As an example, he mentioned that barbituates may produce excitement and caffeine may help elderly persons relax.

Pavlov found that the strength of the conditioned reflex was highly related to the retention of the reflex. An excellent study by Hulicka and Weiss (1965) demonstrated that young and old human Ss equated for original learning show the same retention for material. Overlearning also increases retention. Pavlov found that if he continued acquisition trials to well beyond the criterion of learning (usually some asymptotic level), resistance to extinction increased.

High anxiety level which sometimes occurs when elderly Ss are confronted with learning tasks can cause a phenomenological withdrawal from the task and thereby hinder learning. Desensititization to learning tasks can be useful in eliminating the anxiety. This procedure will be explained when we deal with the third category.

3) Feelings of Rejection and Fear of Death

Negative statements elders make about themselves to themselves derive from a number of sources:

1) Their present poor performance compared with their younger adult days.
2) Their present poor performance compared with that of younger adults.
3) The reaction of younger adults to their poor performance and appearance.
4) The reaction of other elders to themselves.

In a recent study, it was found that not only did young adults show greater preference for other younger age groups and certain animals than they do for the elderly, but that the elderly Ss themselves showed those same preferences (Cautela, Kastenbaum, & Wincz, 1967). It appears that elders model after younger individuals in their perception of elders. Experiments in modeling using elderly Ss might prove of value in demonstrating a practical application of this information.

Treatment

If the performance of elders can be improved according to the guidelines established in the previous sections, there should be a concomitant reduction in the avoidance expressed by other persons.

In my own work I have found Behavior Therapy procedures, such as Relaxation, Desensitization, and Thought Stopping, effective in reducing fear of rejection and excessive preoccupation with or fear of death in the elderly.

Relaxation

The geriatric patient is taught relaxation according to a modified version of Jacobson's (1938) procedure. I have found that it usually takes longer for geriatric patients to relax than it does for younger clients (Cautela, 1967). Once the client has demonstrated his ability to relax well, he is instructed to relax whenever he feels that he is about to enter a tense or anxiety-provoking situation, such as a job interview, on his way to a new residence, etc. He is also taught to relax as soon as he experiences anxiety in a particular situation. If, for example, he becomes anxious while an instructor in a rug weaving class is explaining something to him he is to relax immediately. If the relaxation procedure is practiced by the client as presented above, then the following results should be achieved:

a) Decrease in avoidance responses, thereby allowing approach responses to increase.

b) Prevention of response (anxiety) generalization to new stimuli, i.e., the client will not develop new fears.

c) The client perceives that he now has more control over his behavior. This usually results in an increase of self-worth. As we are aware, this feeling is one which is usually lacking in the elderly.

Desensitization

Well-controlled studies such as those by Paul (1966), Lang (1964), and Davison (1965) show that the desensitization procedure is effective in reducing anxiety. After the client can relax well, a hierarchy is constructed according to the degree of anxiety elicited by different aspects of the fear-provoking stimulus. These stimuli are presented in imagination (the least anxiety-inducing item first) while the client is relaxed until the image (usually visual) no longer leads to an anxiety response. There is usually direct transfer from the office situation to real life. It is not necessary that the stimulus to which the client is desensitized be an observable concrete one such as a dog or high place. It can be such abstractions as rejection by others, fear of criticism, etc. After carefully questioning the client, a hierarchy is constructed concerning aspects of rejecting situations. Data such as the degree to which different individuals disturb him when they show rejecting behavior are obtained. For instance, he may feel more anxiety when rejected by younger adults or by his family than by people of his own age. Data concerning what the other individuals say and what they are rejecting in the client (e.g., his appearance, his forgetfulness, etc.) are also elicited. Then, by presenting graded scenes to the client while he is relaxed, he can be desensitized to occasions of rejection. A maladaptive fear of death can also be reduced by desensitization in a similar manner. The Desensitization technique can be applied to any situation or element which elicits anxiety.

Thought Stopping

In the Thought Stopping procedure the patient is taught to say "stop" whenever a disturbing thought occurs. Examples of such thought are "I am old and not much use to anyone"; "I wonder if I'll die a painful death." Although the procedure appears simple, it is quite effective in reducing and, in many cases, eliminating undesirable thought and impulses.

References

Cautela, J. R. The Pavlovian theory of old age: *Gerontologist*, 1966, **6** (No. 3, Pt. II), 27. (Abstract)

Cautela, J. R. Behavior therapy with the aged. Paper presented at the meeting of the Eastern Psychological Association, Boston, April, 1967.

Cautela, J. R., & Kastenbaum, R. A reinforcement survey schedule for use in therapy, training, and research. *Psychological Reports*, 1967, **20,** 1115-1130.

Cautela, J. R., Kastenbaum, R., & Wincz, J. The use of the reinforcement survey schedule and the fear survey schedule to discover possible reinforcing and aversive stimuli in a delinquent population. Paper present at the meeting of the Eastern Psychological Association, Boston, April, 1967.

Corsellis, J. A. N. Mental illness and the aging brain. *Maudsley Monograph* No. 9. London: Oxford University Press, 1962.

Davison, G. C. *The influence of systematic desensitization, relaxation, and graded exposure to imaginal aversive stimuli on the modification of phobic behavior.* Unpublished doctoral dissertation, Stanford University, 1965.

Doty, B. A. Effects of handling on learning of young and aged rats. *Journal of Gerontology,* 1968, **23,** 142-144.

Eisdorfer, C. Verbal learning and response time in the aged. *Journal of Genetic Psychology,* 1965, **107,** 15-22.

Epstein, L. J., & Simon, A. Organic brain syndrome in the elderly. *Geriatrics,* 1967, **22,** 145-150.

Gantt, W. H. The conditional reflex as an aid in the study of the psychiatric patient. In C. Franks (Ed.), *Conditioning techniques in clinical practice and research.* New York: Springer, 1964.

Gellerstedt, N. Zur Kenntnis der Hirnveranderungen bei der normalen Altersinvolution. *Uppsala läkareförenings förhandlingar,* 1933, **38,** 193-408.

Goldfarb A. I. Prevalence of psychiatric disorders in metropolitan old age and nursing homes. *Journal of the American Geriatrics Society,* 1962, **10,** 77-84.

Gray, J. A. (Ed.) *Pavlov's typology.* New York: Pergamon Press, 1964.

Hulicka, I. M., & Weiss, R. L. Age differences in retention as a function of learning. *Journal of Consulting Psychology,* 1965, **29,** 125-129.

Jacobson, E. *Progressive relaxation.* Chicago: University of Chicago Press, 1938.

Lang, P. J. Experimental studies of desensitization psychotherapy. In J. Wolpe, A. Salter, & L. Reyna (Eds.), *The conditioning therapies.* New York: Holt, Rinehart, & Winston, 1964.

Lawton, A. H. Characteristics of the geriatric person. *Gerontologist,* 1968, **8,** 120-123.

Paul, G. L. *Insight vs. desensitization in psychotherapy.* Stanford: Stanford University Press, 1966.

Pavlov, I. P. *Lectures on conditioned reflexes.* New York: International Publishers, 1928.

Pavlov, I. P. *Experimental psychology and other essays.* New York: Philosophical Library, 1957.

Rothchild, D. Pathologic changes in senile psychoses and their psycho-biologic significance. *American Journal of Psychiatry,* 1937, **93,** 757-788.

Simon, A. The geriatric mentally ill. *Gerontologist,* 1968, **8** (No. 1, Pt. II), 7-15.

Slater, P. E., & Kastenbaum, R. Paradoxical reactions to drugs: Some personality and ethical correlates. *Journal of the American Geriatrics Society,* 1966, **14,** 1016-1034.

Talland, G. A. Age and the immediate memory span. *Gerontologist,* 1967, **7,** 4-9.

Wolpe, J. *Psychotherapy by reciprocal inhibition.* Stanford: Stanford University Press, 1958.

TOWARD A PSYCHIATRY OF THE LIFE-CYCLE: IMPLICATIONS OF SOCIOPSYCHOLOGIC STUDIES OF THE AGING PROCESS FOR THE PSYCHOTHERAPEUTIC SITUATION

ROBERT N. BUTLER, M.D.

OLD people and children have become increasingly socially visible since the seventeenth century. Augmented survivorship, joined with certain socio-cultural conditions, has "unfolded" the life-cycle, making its stages or phases prominent. Rousseau, Victor Hugo, the Swedish sociologist Ellen Key, and the French historian Philippe Ariès are among those who have emphasized the social and historical evolution of the child in the last two centuries (Ariès, 1962). In this century, old people have grown conspicuous in number and social significance.

The social and psychologic sciences and the professions have not succeeded in keeping pace with these changes. Sociology remains primarily class-conscious (Gordon, 1949). Psychology has demonstrated great interest in child development in this century, but the majority of these studies do not go beyond early adulthood. The life-cycle as a whole, in all its phases, has not been a central preoccupation of the psychologic and social sciences. The mass media seem somewhat more conscious of the significance of age-grading in human affairs, of stages of life, and of inter-generational conflicts (Poppy, 1967; Demography, 1966; Twenty-five and Under, 1967). Medicine, including psychiatry, has been most fascinated by the younger, attractive, well-paying patients with acute and/or esoteric diseases.

I have no identification with "geriatric psychiatry" per se nor with a "young people's" psychiatry. I am interested in how people live their lives, how they change in the course of time, and how they die. I am particularly interested in the interior subjective experience of the life-cycle, of aging, of changes in the body image and the self-concept ("the changing self"), and of approaching death (Butler, 1960; 1963b; 1963c). I would like to see the development of a comprehensive body of knowledge concerning the life-cycle as a whole, its stages, its modes, and the complex interplay of individual life-cycles with socioeconomic, cultural, and historic conditions. I am interested in life-cycle-ology or life-cycle psychiatry.

The paper might have been entitled: "How the concepts of the life-cycle and of historic psychology should be considered in psychotherapy and in social organization." I wish to consider the influences of stage-characteristics, of certain features of middle and later life, upon psychotherapy with old people and upon potential social changes.

Evidence from many sources supports the conclusion that the immediate personal, social, and medical situation significantly influences the adaptation of the aged. Variations in personality and life history help account for the lack of uniform effects of personal, social, and medical variables, for example, the impact of widowhood, retirement, and increasing blindness. I assume that characteristics pertinent to stages in the life-cycle also contribute to adaptation. I assume that the degree of realization of these life-cycle stage-characteristics may be influenced by psychotherapy and by the sociocultural situation.

There are many aspects of psychiatric work with the elderly. I have dealt with some of these elsewhere, ranging from technique to countertransference to organic brain disorders in both inpatients and outpatients (Butler, 1960; 1963b; Butler, Dastur, and Perlin, 1965). Here I will concentrate upon psychotherapy with patients having predominantly psychologic problems and functional disorders of old age. I will use my psychotherapeutic work primarily as a source of data about later life rather than as a basis for discussing psychotherapeutic technique or results.

My work with old people, begun in 1955, has ranged from the healthy experimental subject (Birren et al., 1963; Butler, 1963a) to the private office patient to the patient in the more extreme situations of private and state hospitals and nursing homes (Butler, 1960; Butler et al., 1965). In the preparation of this paper I have reviewed my records from the comprehensive and intensive study of 17 hospitalized patients at Chestnut Lodge, 71 patients from private office practice, and 47 community-resident, healthy, aged volunteer research subjects. These samples have been characterized elsewhere (Butler, 1960; 1966; Birren et al., 1963).

GRIEF AND RESTITUTION

Of the many matters that could be discussed respecting psychotherapeutic experience with the aged, I shall begin with the proposition that a fundamental issue of psychotherapy with old people is the problem of death and loss. It is death that sets in motion all the basic questions that must be faced by both the therapist and the old person. What kind of life have I led? What am I to do now, in the face of death? I am referring to psychologic events and not to a moral drama, although for some persons, the latter defines the experience of old age, that is, the resolution of the problem of guilt.

All sociopsychologic studies pertain in some way to the central problem of the relations between the interior psychologic experience of approaching death and the social and cultural conditions that further shape and influence it. However, many sociopsychologic studies tend to approach this essential problem cautiously, dealing with limited or partial aspects of the problem, such as interaction and/or isolation, or morale and life satisfaction (Cumming and Henry, 1961; Neugarten, 1966; Neugarten, Havighurst, and Tobin, 1961; Kutner et al., 1956; Lowenthal, 1965). However, the factor of death has been directly studied by some (Glaser and Strauss, 1965).

In research work with older people and in practice, one sees the problem of death manifest in many different ways. One observes the defensive and adaptive maneuvers that older people undertake, including counterphobic behavior and denial (Birren et al., 1963). Counterphobic behavior may be revealed in the almost obscene efforts of some older people to be young, wearing inappropriate dress and make-up and undertaking a variety of activities unsuitable to their age. One sees old people who cannot bear to look at themselves in a mirror and whose drawings show signs of dissolution despite intact cognitive and psychologic functions (Butler, 1963c).

One finds older people preoccupied by recollections of the aging and death of their own parents and their own fears of possible replication of their parents' experience. On the other hand, some older people make unusual efforts to appear dignified and gracious in the face of illness and death. Through analysis one learns that insomnia may be a fight to stay awake rather than a fight to go to sleep, and thus reflects the fear of death. Fears of death may reach paranoid proportions marked by the belief that medicines are poison, and to the point of misinterpreting aging changes and disease states as the results of external agents (Butler, 1966). Thus, intimations of mortality may be revealed in projection. Fears of death are exploited by business charlatans who play upon the magic wishfulness of old people by quackery and fraud. Hypochondriasis not uncommonly (but not exclusively) expresses concern with death.

It is quite correct that many old people show no direct signs of fear of death. However, one must not conclude, therefore, that the problem of death does not exist for them. One may study the person at a particular stage of his adaptation to the reality of death. In our National Institute of Mental Health sample (Birren et al., 1963), for example, overt fear was present in 30 per cent and denial in 15 per cent. A realistic adjustment to, or the resolution of, the problem of death had occurred in 55 per cent of this healthy sample. Medical diseases, disadvantageous social circumstances, and so forth, may compound the problem. However, if one can imagine the most idealized

32

socioeconomic conditions, the most culturally-enriching circumstances, there would remain the essential question of man's resolution of the issues of his past life when confronted with death.

Case history:

Chief complaint: "I can't catch my breath." This is the case of an otherwise fortunate man who was always in a hurry and had eventually to stop to catch his breath.

A sixty-eight-year-old, highly intelligent and intellectual sociologist developed a severe cough upon his return from an extended and exciting journey abroad. An X-ray shadow increased the medical suspicion of a malignancy. Without prior discussion and preparation the patient was inadvertently but directly told this by a secretary arranging his admission for surgery. The operation revealed a lung abscess and the patient responded well physically both to the operative procedure and in the recovery period, with one exception: he could not catch his breath. His internist suggested an extended vacation and later tranquilizers, and gave reassurance. After some months the doctor strongly recommended psychotherapy as he realized the patient was becoming increasingly agitated and depressed without adequate medical explanation. The patient was extremely tense and restless. He appeared somewhat slovenly. His pants hung loose from his suspenders and his fly was partly open. In short, he gave an impression of organic mental disorder but he spoke clearly and well. Despite his obvious gloom, he managed some humor and clarity in giving his present and past history.

His situation was socially and personally favorable. He had a good relationship with a devoted wife. He had many good friends and professional colleagues. He was well regarded professionally. He was under no pressure to retire, and consultancies were open to him. He had a wide range of interests in addition to his professional field. His relationships with his brothers and sisters were good. With the exception of the chief complaint, his physical status was excellent. He believed his physician that there was no major organic disease, that is, he was not suffering from a fear that he was being misled. But despite all of this he was tense and depressed. Recurrent dreams included one in which "a paper was due" and another in which he was "behind in an exam." He had never taken out any life insurance. He had made no conscious admission to himself that he might age. He had made nothing of birthdays. He did not have a very clear concept of the natural evolution of the life-cycle. He did not have a sense of stages and development of middle and later life. He had an enormous capacity for work and had kept busy all his life as though unaware of the passage of time. He had never been bored. He had great capacity for self-discipline and was not given to marked expression of either grief or anger but only to a narrow spectrum of affects, including fearfulness and pleasure. He was a kind of Peter Pan and he and his wife eventually concluded in the course of his psychotherapeutic work that he, and in some measure she, had imagined themselves to remain in their twenties instead of in their late sixties. As he reviewed his life and the realities of aging and death, he became freer in his expression of more negative affects. His depression and tension improved and he had remained well in a follow-up of some six months. He was no longer short of breath.

The problem of death, then, is a central theme of late life, a primary characteristic of this stage of the life-cycle. The problem of death, of course, is divisible into partial deaths or losses or separations or irreversible changes or crises, depending upon how one wishes to describe them. Psychotherapeutic work with older people involves the management of these small deaths, these intimations of mortality. Put succinctly, the psychotherapy of old age is the psychotherapy of grief and of accommodation, restitution, and resolution. "Coming to terms with," "bearing witness," reconciliation, atonement, construction and reconstruction, integration, transcendence, creativity, realistic insight with modifications and substitutions, the introduction of meaning and of meaningful, useful, and contributory efforts: these are among the terms that are pertinent to therapy with older people.

However, one obviously cannot operate in the vacuum of an idealized socioeconomic and medical situation. One must be the physician first of all, treating the patient from the comprehensive viewpoint (Butler, 1963c). When the modifiable, the treatable, has been dealt with, then one is the psychotherapist of grief.

But also of ambiguity. Our society, and the persons immediately around the older person, tend to create situations of ambiguity in order to overcome their own anxiety and because of their wish to help the older person. Thus, in addition to the problem of grief, there is often the problem of ambiguity, of uncertainty, of transition, for example, not knowing whether and not having been told whether a disease exists or not, not being certain one's driver's license will be renewed. Ambiguity may be transmuted into a major stereotypic expectation. Families and society may expect dignified and gracious aging requiring the suppression and delay of grief. In summary, then, there are three concerns: How to live in the present with one's losses, how to account for one's past life, and how to meet death.

One major premise exists in this work and that is the assumption of human elasticity. To put it differently, one must consider the reality of forces toward inner change, toward intrapsychic alterations, making possible accommodation, restitution, and resolution. In this sense, the goal of psychotherapy is to define and seek possibilities. Psychotherapy, conditioned by our culture and conducted by therapists in turn conditioned by our culture, often occurs in an atmosphere of futility. Yet the possibilities for intrapsychic change may be greater in old age than at any other period in life (in the absence of severe organic brain disease). One motive for change is the proximity of death. The patient and the therapist must collaborate in assessing together assets as well as deficits.

Elsewhere I have presented summary tables of the changing internal and external conditions that affect the subjective experience, the behavior, and the adaptation of old people, based on studies at the National Institute of Mental Health, at Chestnut Lodge, and in private practice (Butler, 1966). A person may attain old age and die without any losses—personal losses, such as widowhood, as well as social and economic losses—but this is extremely unlikely. Kramer (1965), for instance, has indicated the importance of widowhood to the development of psychopathology and to psychiatric hospital admission in old age. There is a meshing of the social and the personal—it is conflictual retirement or conflictual widowhood that is important. Mysterious but still obscure aging-changes, in addition to physical disease, add their losses.

Personality profoundly shapes the experience of old age. Despite many writings to the contrary, however, the generalization that personality characteristics are accentuated or exaggerated with age is a poor one. In fact, certain personality features mellow or entirely disappear. Others prove insulating and protective, although they might formerly have been impairing, such as a schizoid disposition (Birren *et al.*, 1963).

I began by referring to the changing historic conception of the life-cycle. History is pertinent in two respects: first, with respect to the variation over time in the status and roles of old people; and, second, with respect to the way in which his own era influences the older person. Barbara Tuchman's *The Proud Tower* and Frederick Lewis Allen's *The Big Change* give one a sense of the impact of historic experience upon older people. Our work as psychotherapists, our understanding of the patient, is much enhanced by our effort to empathize with the historic era through which the older person has passed. Presently-living old people have experienced more profound and a greater number of social and technologic changes than probably any other generation.

History shows itself also in the language of old people. Certain euphemisms such as "delicate condition" or "limbs," are heard; "machines" may be used in place of cars and "marketing" may occur instead of shopping, and so forth. But we are concerned not only with such historic and cultural variations in language but with idiosyncratic psychodynamic translations in language that are relevant to age. For instance, an older person's seemingly unfounded fear of going blind may be translated as a subjective concern that he has been blind to significant experiences and feelings throughout his life.

We need a historic psychology or paleo-psychiatry pertinent to our considerations of the psychologic development of man over his life-cycle. The nineteenth century virtues of conscientiousness and ambitiousness have become represented in the twentieth century under the term compulsiveness, as a pejorative. Fletcherism, ptomaine poisoning, Lactobacillus bulgar, focal infections, laxatives, are some of the special features of the medical-cultural heritage to be found in the language of the elderly.

Historic and other variables may blend. For instance, relocation through urban renewal may adversely affect a particular individual, who may have a personal reaction to being removed from the familiar immediate structure. And it is not uncommon today to see a person in his sixties grieving over the death of his parents (whose long survival was the result of medical advances, a historical variable).

Table I suggests several features salient to survival, that is, anti-obsolescence. Heredity is beyond individual human control, but other variables are subject to varying degrees of individual and social influence—for example, chronic

TABLE I. FEATURES SALIENT TO SURVIVAL: ANTI-OBSOLESCENCE

Features	Positive Pole	Negative Pole
Biologic Survival 1. (Heredity; Disease; Accident)	Health	Illness
Energy 2. (Psycho-physical)	Activity Level*	Quiescence
Life-enhancing Attitude 3. (Berenson)	Vitality* (Liveliness)	Inertia (Early Senility)
Affirmation 4. (Adaptiveness)	Resourcefulness (Modifiability) (Complexity)	Resignation
Centrality 5. (Center of Forces)	Power (Usefulness)	Powerlessness (Uselessness)
Interpersonal Responsiveness 6.	Self-Revelation (Candor)	Reticence
Intimacy 7. (Mutuality)	Affiliation (Bonds)	Loneliness (Isolation)
Changeableness 8. (Wish to change identity) (Forces of Contra-Identity)	Sense of Possibility (Incompleteness)	Closure (Completeness)
Renewal Function 9.	Self-Education (Autodidacticism)	Obsolescence

* Activity and Vitality are not synonymous; quiescent vitality and inert activity are not uncommon.

cigarette smoking, accidents, and disease, not to mention suicide and war. There is an old adage—we do not die; we kill ourselves.

The features numbered 4-9 are of a psychosocial character and derive from the National Institute of Mental Health study (Butler, 1967) and from observations in the course of psychotherapy. In the table, the positive pole represents a possible goal of psychotherapy.

Much is made of the wish to maintain a sense of identity. Little attention has been paid to the wish to change identity, to preserve and exercise the sense of possibility and incompleteness against a sense of closure and completeness. This emphasis is not in contradiction to Erikson's concept of a maintenance of the sense of identity as critical to health. This concept implies process and not status.

36

There has been some disagreement in the literature concerning education as a significant force in maintaining the mental health of older people. Goldfarb and his associates (Pollack, Kahn, and Goldfarb, 1958), for example, found education to be important. On the other hand, in our NIMH sample, where the range of health and education was narrow, education did not carry any significant weight (Birren *et al.*, 1963). I suggest that the important variable may be not formal education per se as measured by the number of years or even by the quality of education, but rather the extent to which the individual becomes capable of a continuing self-education process.

PSYCHOLOGIC ISSUES IN LATER LIFE

Table II delineates some features observed to be salient in late life and to the resolution of the problem of death or the contraction of futurity. These

TABLE II. Features Salient to Late Life and the Resolution of the Problem of Death (the Contraction of Futurity)

Features and Issues	Positive Pole	Negative Pole
Legacy (Forwardness)	Continuity (Historicity) (Relation to "benign indifference to the universe") Succession; Organ Legacy	Discontinuity (Absence of Sense of Life-Cycle and Posterity)
Elder Function (Direct Transmission)	Counseling (Teaching; Sponsoring)	Withholding (Nothing to Offer)
Autobiographic Process	"Life Review"	Denial
Serenity	Sense of Value of Time	Time Panic Boredom
Attachment to Objects (Memorial; Orientation)	Familiarity	Unfamiliarity Wish for Permanence Collecting; Hoarding
Presentness (Immediacy)	Surprise (Sense of Wonder; Expectation)	Disillusionment (Cynicism)
Perspective	Acknowledgement (Innocence) (Authenticity)	Imposture (Pretense)
Identity*	Generativity	Self-Absorption (Stagnation)
Identity*	Integrity	Despair (Hopelessness)

* These dimensions are based on Eriksonian concepts of identity.

features are believed to contribute to the behavior of old people along with the immediate situation of losses described above and the past history of the individual. It is likely that these features interrelate with each other. Their relative importance varies from individual to individual, and they are not automatically fulfilled qualities; rather they reflect potentialities. It is undecided whether these features are to be regarded primarily as psychobiologic or as acquired psychosocial characteristics.

Mark Twain, bitter and despairing in his old age, said that the future does not worry about us, so why should we worry about the future? However, it would appear that the older person who does show concern about the future tends toward greater psychologic health. Here again, the positive pole represents a possible goal of psychotherapy. Legacy, for example, is not only a theoretic notion but also may be illustrated practically. A businessman finds it difficult to "let go" and retire, despite increasingly incapacitating physical and perhaps mental changes. He must be helped to acknowledge these changes and to collaborate in setting up appropriate succession within his firm. The alternative would be continued denial of his waning capacities and a willful, angry insistence upon his ability to run the firm himself—even if it means "running it into the ground." A sense of continuity following the successful development of a mechanism of succession is infinitely more free of anxiety and despair than is the feeling of discontinuity.

In passing, one may make an important clinical point. At times one will see an older person who suddenly has received a prescription from a doctor or a spouse to quit a job or to retire before methods of succession have been established or before new plans have been laid out by or for the individual. In such circumstances, it may be much wiser to introduce partial and gradual retirement or to take a leave of absence rather than to undertake a sudden and complete change.

Those older people who exercise what I have called the "elder function" also appear to experience less despair and anxiety. These persons participate directly in counseling, teaching, sponsoring, consulting—carrying out functions that only older people with their accumulated experience and knowledge can carry out. One also can make a point concerning technique. When the patient feels that the doctor is learning from him, there is considerable therapeutic benefit, providing this is not a contrived strategy.

The "autobiographic process" manifests itself in many ways throughout the life-cycle, at times reflecting predominantly self-analytic or introspective qualities, at other times suggesting a need for self-documentation. The daily journal or diary is distinctly different from the retrospective memoir. I have proposed elsewhere that with old age comes the inauguration of a process I have called the life review (Butler, 1963b), which is "prompted by the realization of approaching dissolution and death" and "characterized by the progressive return to consciousness of past experiences, and, particularly the resurgence of unresolved conflicts," which can be "surveyed and reintegrated," and if successfully reintegrated, can give "new significance and meaning to one's life" and "prepare one for death, mitigating one's fears." I have found this naturally occurring process to be useful and central in my psychotherapeutic work, and harness it to that end. Etigson and Tobin (1966) have pursued the life review concept and found that "in spite of remarkable thematic consistency in reminiscences, changes were found which were related to current life stress." They are further studying how the "qualities of the life review . . . covary with adaptation." Gorney, of the Committee on Human Development, University of Chicago, has found an increased and intense introspection in later life that appears to wane again after the early seventies (Personal Communication). The life review process may not be apparent unless one becomes involved in an intensive, inquiring, psychoanalytically-oriented relationship. Defensive and selective denial may be prevalent. One underlying question is that of King Lear: "Who is it that can tell me who I am?"

Man lives by the calendar, the more so as he ages. Old people tend to come early for their psychotherapeutic sessions and to be concerned about time and schedules. This may or may not have any bearing on the pre-existence of obsessional-compulsive behavior. At times one may see frank "time panics." Some older people report boredom or the experience of time being heavy upon their hands. These subjective states do not relate exclusively to clinical depression, but do express a connection with the use of one's time in the proximity of death. In the course of therapy it is striking when the individual begins to show both tranquility and an increasing sense of the value of time.

The attachment to objects that is seen with age has a memorial function and contributes to the maintenance of orientation. Such familiarity is not to be confused, however, with an undue and pathologic collecting mania or need to hoard. The latter symptom may be present at any point in the life-cycle although it is somewhat more frequent in old age and is connected with fears of ruin and of loss that, again psychodynamically, often relate to the fear of death. The presence of objects with which one is familiar is orienting, comforting, and pleasurable. Pets can be most important to old people.

An immediacy or sense of presentness is very important. Goethe, at eighty, said that he was still capable of being surprised. A sense of wonder and expectation counters the possibility of disillusionment and cynicism. Apparently related is the sense of perspective, of appropriate acknowledgement rather than pretense or imposture. This is an important clinical point. It can be unfortunate if the psychotherapist tends to invoke inappropriately the *deus ex machina* of "irrational guilt." It is to the benefit of the patient if he can acknowledge any specific acts hurtful to others whether by commission or omission. It can, of course, be easy for the patient to fall into global self-condemnation that may dilute the specific issue(s). This defense should be openly handled.

Erikson (1963) was among the first of the psychoanalysts to make an effort to delineate the life-cycle as a whole. With respect to the middle-aged, Erikson has emphasized generativity and integrity.

Middle age is the fulcrum or working center of the younger and older generations. Table III, like my other tables, is offered tentatively, as an effort to hypothesize issues of heightened significance in the latter half of the life-cycle. These formulations derive from reviewing the material of 40 office patients aged forty to sixty years.

While in old age the autobiographic process appears to manifest itself as the life review, in middle age it has the quality of stocktaking, in which a greater opportunity to consider possibilities, alternatives, and the organization

TABLE III. FEATURES SALIENT TO MIDDLE LIFE

Issues	Positive Pole	Negative Pole
Stock-Taking	Possibility; Alternatives Organization of Commitments	Closure; Fatalism
Fidelity	Commitment to Self, Others, Career	Hypocrisy Self-Deception
Growth-Death (To Grow is to Die) (Juvenescence and Rejuvenation Phantasies)	Naturality	Obscene or Phrenetic Efforts (e.g. to be youthful) Hostility and Envy toward Youth and Progeny; Longing
Credulity	Ego-Beliefs Profound Realistic Convictions	"The True Believer" Right (Past) or Left (Future) Radicalism (e.g. Eric Hoffer)
Simplification of Persons Conservation Time Settling-In Place	Centrality of Specification Relationships, Rootedness Places and Ideas	Diffusion Confusion
Communication Complexity (Cues)	Abbreviation: "Matters Understood" Continuity: "Picking up where left Off"	Repetitiveness Boredom Impatience
"Prime of Life"	Maturity-Process Productivity	"Winner-Loser"

of commitments occurs. The other possibilities are closure and fatalism on the one hand, or an over-expansiveness on the other.

Fidelity appears as a critical element in mid-life. Fidelity refers to the testing of personal, professional, and other commitments. In adolescence one is concerned about the hypocrisy of others; in middle age with one's own; and in old age with neither or both. The problem of hypocrisy on the one hand and of self-deception on the other are the negative alternatives to the test. To my mind, this problem of fidelity underlies and includes the narrower question of marital fidelity. The latter is frequent in middle age and its nature is insightfully described in Tolstoy's *Anna Karenina*. Indeed, Konstantine Levin, a principal character, struggled with social fidelity. Levin's situation occupies a large part of this book and is as important as Anna's affair.

Naturalness in the handling of the relation of growing and dying is another critical issue in middle life. The man may begin to envy his son's increasing sexuality; the middle-aged woman, or man, may make obscene or phrenetic efforts to be youthful. Hostility toward and envy of youth may come to a head. Some people with the "Peter Pan problem" detest aging because it means symbolically the murder of the parent, that is, for oneself to grow, the parent must die. Phantasies of rejuvenation and juvenescence may be more frequent than is recognized.

The evolution of deep convictions or ego beliefs rather than stereotyped and fanatic beliefs is another central problem in middle life. Eric Hoffer's class of "true believers," either to the right or to the left, is indicative of the negative alternatives. Other features concern the reduction of communication complexity, a point emphasized by Bernice L. Neugarten, and the further simplification of living. Finally, middle age is often viewed as the "prime of life." In its best sense, it is a period of maturity and productivity but it is also the period in which preoccupations with being a "winner" or "loser" can have a harsh and phrenetic edge.

One "stage" of life is "mobile." Contemporary idiom refers to the "teeny-bopper" who is "in," "with it." A "teeny-bopper" can be eleven or twelve, that is, a pubescent "going on twenty," or can be a middle-aged forty-year-old, "going on twenty." This point is made to remind us of the still far from decisive delineation of the issues and features of the life-cycle. How many of these "stages" are "mobile" because they are in part the consequences of social, cultural, and historical conditions remains a relevant question.

DISCUSSION

Before making a final summary statement, I will touch upon the range and limits of psychotherapy with older people, and suggest some sociopsychologic research that would be of great value to the psychotherapist.

No intensive psychotherapeutic units for aged patients existed when we established one at Chestnut Lodge in 1958 (Butler, 1960). Here, intensive psychotherapy was employed that was defined as individual, insight-oriented psychotherapy involving up to four or five sessions a week with patients in residence in a psychotherapeutically-oriented milieu. Also, my private office practice derives principally from a psychoanalytically-oriented position.

However, over the years, I have dealt with a wide range of older patients and have employed an equally wide range of approaches. The range of problems met and the development of various strategies and techniques in psychotherapy and in the general management of psychiatric problems of later life will be the subject of another paper.

However, psychotherapy and the psychiatric treatment of the aged is a "drop in the bucket," considering the major problems that confront people in old age. Psychiatry cannot possibly cope with the accumulated problems of an entire individual life time, despite the typically American belief in total cure, nor can psychiatry begin to play a significant role in overcoming the enormous social problems that older people face. Indeed, we must be careful that a Gresham's law does not evolve in community psychiatry wherein bad psychiatry drives out good psychiatry. We need all kinds of first aid efforts and measures in our work with older people in the community, but these are slight, indeed, and await more fundamental social, cultural, and economic changes. Poverty among the aged remains an enormous problem, for a prime example. Society requires remodeling, balancing the requirements of each stage of the life-cycle and extending beyond purely economic considerations. For instance, age discrimination in employment is tied to the problem of economic productivity. Our social system is economically rather than comprehensively and humanistically oriented. A humanistic social reorganization would be likely to include programs of continuing education throughout the life-cycle. A portfolio of possibilities should exist to meet the many exigencies of the stages of the life-cycle.

It is interesting to speculate upon the kinds of sociopsychologic research that would aid the psychotherapist in his work. Certainly, the social processes involved in succession, which we discussed earlier, would be very helpful. For instance, one wishes for further understanding of the most appropriate timing for the increasing delegation of authority and the final giving up of control to a successor. Consideration of mechanisms other than those of consultancies and appointments as chairmen of the board would be useful.

The problem of relocation, transplantation, or geographic mobility is an important one (Aleksandrowicz, 1961; Lieberman, 1961). It would be interesting to compare the effects of various living arrangements of the elderly according to their association with death ("the last stop," *etc.*). Other studies, pertaining to integration within the life-cycle, are indicated (Rosow, 1961).

The memorial function, orientation, is important to problems of housing and moving.

A major problem is the social usefulness of older people. Social psychologists could contribute immeasurably by studying voluntary agencies and determining how to identify factors conducive to and impeding the appropriate utilization of the various skills and "stage" characteristics of older people; this is the matter of the logistic matching of skills with social needs. Studies of the usefulness and the problems of older people in Vista and the Peace Corps would be pertinent. It is surprising how often one will see someone with a Ph.D., with intact intellectual functioning, licking stamps for a charitable agency. Recent interest in the Swedish legal development of the Ombudsman leads one to pause and wonder if certain qualified older citizens might not make excellent Ombudsmen (Gellhorn, 1966). The older person has the accumulated experience and the leisure and he is comparatively free from worldly competition.

Critics of studies of the outcome of psychotherapy repeatedly refer to the need for information concerning the natural course of disorders for purposes of control. We need, in fact, data on the natural courses of lives. Studies of lives, the examination of the differential durability of the emotions, the characteristics and processes of change (Group for the Advancement of Psychiatry, 1966) and irreversibility, are all necessary. Major stereotypes still exist regarding the early fixity and stability of character, the resistance to change, and the time required to change; these are interrelated but all pertain directly to the understanding of the life-cycle as a whole and of late life in particular.

FINAL NOTE

Solon, the Greek lawgiver, said that no man could consider his life happy until it was over. And Nietzche stated, "that which does not kill me makes me stronger." This is a sensitive aspect of the psychotherapeutic situation and most certainly of the situation of old age. An increasing awareness on the part of both the patient and the therapist of aspects of survival and of adaptation to it are important. Obviously, the therapist, too, must be prepared to survive the painful losses of his older patients.

The therapist must not in any way be destructive to the processes of illusion and denial needed by his patients. One must discuss the fact of death, the facts of loss, the problems of grief, but always in the context of possibilities, restitution, and resolution. The same principle applies in work with older people as applies in work with patients of all ages: one must work compassionately and carefully to get behind the defenses rather than to attack them overtly As Dr. Relding said, in Ibsen's *The Wild Duck,* "Rob the average man of his life-illusion, and you rob him of his happiness at the same stroke."

In this paper, I have drawn upon my psychotherapeutic and research studies of middle-aged and older persons to suggest certain features as characteristic of the stages of later life. The subjective experience, behavior, and adaptation of people at any age depend upon the degree of fulfillment of the stage-characteristics as well as upon the immediate situation and past history (including personality structure). With old age come increasing losses and the reality of death. Psychotherapeutic and social efforts must both emphasize the possibilities of the present and deal with grief. Because of the wide variation in personalities, individualization must be considered in any planned alterations of social institutions just as it is in psychotherapy. Life-stage features, on the other hand, being universal, offer the psychotherapist and society broad guidelines for useful intervention on behalf of the elderly. How would the social and personal situation of the elderly differ if such needs as those for continuity, familiarity, and usefulness were more effectively met in our culture?

References

ALEKSANDROWICZ, D. R. 1961. Fire and its aftermath on a geriatric ward. Bull. Menn. Clin., **25**:23-32.

ARIÈS, P. 1962. Centuries of Childhood. A Social History of Family Life. Trans. by R. Baldick. New York: Alfred A. Knopf.

BIRREN, J. E., BUTLER, R. N., GREENHOUSE, S. W., SOKOLOFF, L., and YARROW, M. 1963. Human Aging: A Biological and Behavioral Study. Public Health Service Publication Number 986. Washington, D. C.: Government Printing Office.

BUTLER, R. N. 1967. Aspects of survival and adaptation in human aging. Amer. J. Psychiat., **123**:1233-1243.

BUTLER, R. N. 1963a. The facade of chronological age: An interpretative summary. Amer. J. Psychiat., **119**:721-728.

BUTLER, R. N. 1960. Intensive psychotherapy for the hospitalized aged. Geriatrics, **15**:644-653.

BUTLER, R. N. 1963b. The life review: An interpretation of reminiscence in the aged. Psychiatry, **26**:65-76.

BUTLER, R. N. 1963c. Psychiatric evaluation of the aged. Geriatrics, **18**:220-232.

BUTLER, R. N. 1967. Research and clinical observations on the psychological reactions to physical changes with age. Mayo Clin. Proc. **42**:596-619.

BUTLER, R. N., DASTUR, D. K., and PERLIN, S. 1965. Relationships of senile manifestations and chronic brain syndromes to cerebral circulation and metabolism. J. Psychiat. Res., **3**:229-238.

CUMMING, E. and HENRY, W. E. 1961. Growing Old: The Process of Disengagement. New York: Basic Books.

DEMOGRAPHY. The Command Generation. 1966. Time, **88**:50-54 (July 29).

ERIKSON, E. H. 1963. Childhood and Society. New York: W. W. Norton, 2nd ed.

ETICSON, E. C. and TOBIN, S. S. 1966. Effects of stress on reminiscence in the aged. Paper presented at the American Psychological Association meeting, New York, New York, September.

GELLHORN, W. 1966: Ombudsmen and Others; Citizens' Protectors in 9 Countries. Cambridge: Harvard University Press.

GLASER, B. G. and STRAUSS, A. L. 1965. Awareness of Dying. Chicago: Aldine Publishing Co.

GORDON, M. M. 1949. Social class in American sociology. Amer. J. Sociol. **55**:262-268.

GROUP FOR THE ADVANCEMENT OF PSYCHIATRY. 1966. Psychiatric Research and the Assessment of Change. Report Number 63. New York: Group for the Advancement of Psychiatry.

KRAMER, M. 1965. Trends in the usage of psychiatric facilities by the aged and their implications for community mental health programs and related research. Mimeographed.

KUTNER, B. D., FANSHEL, A. M., and LANGNER, T. S. 1956. Five Hundred Over Sixty. New York: Russell Sage Foundation.

LIEBERMAN, M. A. 1961. The relationship of mortality rates to entrance to a home for the aged. Geriatrics, **16**:515-519.

LOWENTHAL, M. F. 1965. Antecedents of isolation and mental illness in old age. Arch. Gen. Psychiat., **12**:245-254.

NEUGARTEN, B. L. 1966. Adult personality: Toward a psychology of the life cycle. Paper presented at the American Psychological Association meeting, New York, New York, September.

NEUGARTEN, B. L., HAVIGHURST, R. J., and TOBIN, S. S. 1961. The measurement of life satisfaction. J. Gerontol., **16**:134-143.

POLLACK, M., KAHN, R. C., and GOLDFARB, A. I. 1958. Factors related to individual differences in perception in institutionalized aged subjects. J. Gerontol., **13**:192-197.

POPPY, J. 1967. The generation gap. Look, **31**:26-32 (February 21).

ROSOW, I. 1961. Retirement housing and social integration. The Gerontologist, **1**:85-91.

TWENTY-FIVE AND UNDER. The inheritor. 1967. Time, **89**:18-23 (January 6).

Situational factors contributing to mental illness in the elderly

JOHN ARSENIAN, PH.D.

Common, real, and ideological features of conflict, disappointment, and loss in the aging process are reviewed, classified, and particularized following a general theory of tension tolerance based on the assumption that every person has a psychological breaking point.

▶ This paper, which is focused on the elderly and aging, is a reformulation of a broader theoretical paper on situational factors contributing to mental illness in the United States.[1]

Most of the observations are commonplace—so familiar as to be truisms or cliches. It is the paradox of a familiar truth that its effectiveness is diminished partly because "everybody knows it" and partly because "it was ever thus." The

46

impetus to action is replaced by habituation or sigh of resignation.

It is cruel to summarize for the aging those situational features of living which may contribute to such alienation of mind and impairment of body that one is no longer of this world. The capacity to anticipate makes possible a calendar of cumulative blows which finally level a man.

At the same time it is a tribute to man's capacity to endure and transcend, for in spite of this gloomy summary, most people manage to live and die without becoming mentally or socially disordered.

Familiar basic assumptions

Behavior is a result of human and environmental forces.

Human forces encompass such concepts as wishes, needs, drives, resolves, anticipations, and fears—for instance, the desire for self-respect and social approval, the resolve to be self-supporting, and the fear of ill health.

Environmental forces include such patterning and regulating agencies as customs, social arrangements, social habits, and laws—for instance, respect for the elderly, maximal ages for employment, and compulsory retirement laws.

Human actions stem from needs which are initially biological, promoting survival, but later biosocial, having undergone social patterning.

Needs, tension, and "breaking point"

It is hypothesized that every need has attached or available an amount of tension such that, reaching a given level, it prompts action. Where tension is aroused and there is not appropriate action to reduce it (or where a deficit exists without satisfaction) tension can mount until a person reaches a breaking point. Hunger prompts food seeking; fatigue inclines one to rest. A prolonged absence of satisfaction may result in delusions. Social isolation inclines people to talk to themselves; protracted isolation may result in hearing voices.

It is hypothesized that every person has a "breaking point" or threshold for disorganization which is a product of heredity and personal life history experiences. This threshold for disorganization is influenced by critical events in living, their timing, and both cumulative and counteractive effects which move the "breaking" threshold up or down.

"Breakdowns"

Nervous breakdowns are assumed to be the result of an overloading of tension, felt as nervousness, strain, and worry to the point of being overburdened. Alternatively "breakdowns" may result from tension and deficit, or undersupply, experienced as boredom, frustration, isolation, starvation, or loneliness.

In the elderly, approach to overloading and possibly, if not counteracted, to breakdown is signaled and shown by varied signs of behavioral and personality disorganization: agitated activity, insomnia, stuporous depression, and internal stimulation of images and memories of past pleasures or present fears which seem to be coming from outside as visions or voices. There is also frequently overconcern about some body part or function which becomes the focus of disease. The progress of the "disease" depends upon one's restorative potential, one's inner resources, and the impact and support of the then present human and social environment.

Culture

Every human society chooses from many possible ways of regulating social conduct certain clustered ways which define its "culture" or habitual ways of perceiving, ordering, doing, thinking, and believing. For example, the distribution of prestige, respect, and deference in relation to age varies from culture to culture. In some cultures the aged are revered simply for their years, in others they lose respect as they lose their powers and utility.

Social life cycle

Birth, growth, reproduction, decline, and death define man's biological life cycle. Every culture has a social life cycle which more or less parallels the biological cycle. People are graded by age, and each age division carries with it expected habits, privileges, titles, and duties. Age is often the criterion for advancement, for the right of passage from one stage in the social life cycle to the next. Thus, ages are specified for employment, marriage, and retirement.

Frustrations

Barriers and restraints to the most direct modes of satisfying human needs are part of a culture. The culture dictates the time and place and mode of reducing the tension associated with biological and social needs. Thus, a hungry old man may not simply take food from a grocery store; he must have the currency for exchange or qualify for "relief" or "old age assistance" by establishing his entitlement.

Where a need is aroused and the person meets a barrier, it produces an increment in tension. Because the need is frustrated, the tension mounts, and to it is added an increment from the irritation and annoyance at the barrier and its associated detour. For example, a sick person appearing at some hospitals may not be admitted unless accompanied by relatives, or may not be treated until he has answered numerous questions which are sometimes irrelevant to his immediate need. On the other hand, the patient's anxious questions about his condition are often ignored or neglected.

Stress

The term "stress" is used to describe any regularly repeated or long-continued relation between person and environment such that tension is, becomes, or may become high. A condition of dependence in older persons who are educated and pride themselves on independence could promote tension. Where this is a consequence of institutional practices, it is a "built-in" stress. Compulsory retirement at a given age is probably the chief source of stress for all who value work or the image of themselves as contributing something of value.

Modal life cycle and tension load

Societies, cultures, and social classes are habituated to more or less similar artifacts, systems of relationships, and path-goal patterns.

A modal life cycle serially details the things one is expected to do or not do, and it defines the tensions which one is allowed to reduce or expected to bear. Tension loadings differ for different age groups and social class groupings. Probably it it easier for leisure class groups to age than it is for working class persons because, accustomed to leisure, they know how to fill the time agreeably. They face no abrupt change in space, place, or status, but continue to see and negotiate with familiars.

Transitional supports

Transitions from one stage or group to another sometimes associated with initiation rites or rites of passage are notable events in the modal life cycle and have lay recognition as "milestones."

The banquet to honor those who have served the company for twenty-five years, the last day of employment, the day one becomes a grandparent or 50, 60, 65 or 70, the twenty-fifth or fiftieth wedding anniversary—at these points the ceremony or rite marking the transition may be more or less stressful and the immediate situation as well as the long-range situation may involve either an elevation or lowering of tension.

It seems appropriate that major changes in the life situation be associated with a ceremony of recognition and a definition of the rights and privileges attached to the new station. Failing this, the self and others may not be clear about one's standing, rights, and duties, and such lack of definition prompts tension linked with feelings of confusion.

Major shifts in tension loading which are unanticipated or allowed as coming, but denied their psychological impact, may produce profound shock, depressive reactions, and even death, as instanced by the near simultaneity of death of long-married partners or the death of vigorous men shortly following retirement. As these major changes in position are common, some indeed, inevitable occurrences, it is fitting that society considers how to supply some transitional support.

Sources of tension

In general, the 3 major sources of increased tension may be categorized under the headings of loss, ideological stress, and conflict. They are here applied to the elderly. Each has some major varieties which will be itemized; some are briefly illustrated. Because illustration is sometimes superfluous since we all know these things, the presentation may dwell more on the less obvious and less significant. The reader is invited to provide a corrective weighting to the items discussed.

Loss

The longer one lives, the more losses one stands to sustain. Losses are clinically associated with depression, melancholy, longing for restoration, sometimes with agitated states, and sometimes with angry suicidal thoughts, as if one could get even with a cruel fate by a final act of self-assertion. Following are some types of loss:

1. *Catastrophic loss* increases tension by the sudden event of death or removal by separation of some loved or significant person or thing, creature, or situation which served as the mainspring, mainstay or reservoir of tension involvement and tension-reducing activity. In interdependent elderly mates, sometimes the death of one is a catastrophe to the survivor. Loss of home or a beloved pet may similarly have a shocklike effect.

2. *Chronic insufficiency* defines the class of situations in which the individual gets some gratification for needs but not enough, as in a substandard

52

diet or possibly in rooming home social contact. The individual may not be consciously aware of his deficit although it may affect his mood, irritability, and stress tolerance. The cumulative effect may render him queer or confused.

3. Some needs are more vital, more pivotal for survival than others. Unlike chronic insufficiency, which may produce no overt response, *central need frustration* may produce a violent response, an upsurge of despair, rage or jealousy that sometimes ends tragically. A lonely separated woman whose only remaining source of love was her affectionate dog literally lost her reason when, on returning home, she found her pet gone. She wandered inconsolable looking for her pet until she collapsed.

4. As contrasted with sudden catastrophic loss, *loss by attrition* is like growth in reverse, so gradual as to be unnoticeable except by technics of continuous observation. Examples of this are the loss of hair in the male or of youthful contours in women, the loss of one's feelings of mastery or vigor or, more subtly psychological, the loss of ideals about the self or about the ultimate value of things.

5. If a man can endure "just so much" at a given time in his life, *"the last straw,"* or the loss of endurance, refers to added insult, annoyance, threat, injury, frustration, or barrier to an expected consummation. This latest increment may trigger a massive response cumulatively discharging pent-up feelings or once and for always shifting the life balance from hope to surrender.

Areas of loss

The losses previously enumerated are classified by their type and source. Turning now to a crude cumulative index of the areas of loss, these will be listed. They range from the biological to the philosophical. Generally, with aging, people's competences and attributes are subject to attrition and diminished effectiveness unless systematic counteractive procedures are undertaken. So the extended concept of loss is meant to include the ideas of diminution and attrition.

Considering these many possible and sometimes inevitable losses, our grammar of words and actions seems to be lacking. The word "vacuum" seems fitting to cover the pain, ache, emptiness, loneliness, aloneness, apartness, sadness, melancholy, and self-pity. These are common reactions to the loss, but there may be nothing to fill the vacuum.

The cluster of psychologic responses attending losses are well known: depressive reactions, mourning, grief, resignation, and, on the adaptive side, denial, counteraction, and pious acceptance with hopeful expectation supported by religious faith in a life hereafter.

Losses can be cushioned somewhat by strong faith, philosophical maturity, and by more practical countermeasures in securing physical supplies such as food, shelter, support, comfort, security, and health. Also, anticipation of psychological losses can lead some toward planning to avoid conditions of being unloved, disrespected, or passed by as if one did not count.

Ideological stress

Ideological stress, as a major source of tension loading, seems to have less potential for discomfort and distress in the elderly than most other age groups. The term "ideological stress" is used to refer to explicit or implicit discrepancies in thinking, feeling, and valuing, to the extent that conflict and tension may rise. Bearing in mind that the United States is yet a short-lived conglomeration of peoples and traditions, the set of arrangements called the "American way of life" is not rationally chosen to cover or guide many contingencies of living, aging, working, seeking, choosing, and valuing. So in the culture there exist conflicts between theory and practice, between ideals and reality, aspirations, expectation, and actions.

Growing to maturity involves reaching some stability regarding these potentially and logically debatable issues. Most adults do not seem bothered by the inconsistencies and paradoxes. Is it because the elderly are wiser, or bored, or feel resigned, or only because the debates have themselves become so familiar as to reduce the residual tension inherent in the persisting contradictions? Or is it because some know better than to debate issues which are essentially insoluble by debate?

But if in argument the philosophical elderly have the advantage of no longer being bewildered and upset at implicit contradictions in value, say, opportunism as a means to a valued end, or nepotism or racial discrimination in a democracy, there are moments when their feelings are seriously wounded. There is the point where one can no longer readily mobilize feelings of resiliency and capability to counteract a threat exemplifying an ideological stress. For example, if verbally attacked by an authoritarian boss, a young man can disdainfully tell him to "go to hell." An older man, sensible of his responsibility to family and his retirement credits, may

55

Table 1   Loss (attrition) with progressive aging

1. **Biological losses**
   a. Global function
      health
      vigor, power
      motility
   b. Organismic parts and functions
      hair, teeth, contours, etc.
      fertility, potency
   c. Perceptual apparatus
      eyes, ears
   d. Organs surgically removed

2. **Psychological losses linked to biology**
   a. Memory
   b. Motoric skills linked with reaction time
   c. Virility, libido
   d. "Looks"

3. **Psychological losses centering on esteem**
   (These have as a core need for self and others'
      respect and anxiety about being neglected and
      by-passed)
   a. Self-esteem
   b. The regard of others (respect)
   c. Influence, power
   d. Prestige positions

4. **Personal losses**
   (These have at center a need for affection from
      those who care out of love, fondness, duty, re-
      spect, loyalty)
   a. Parents
   b. Mate
   c. Dependent children
   d. Brothers, sisters
   e. Extended kin
   f. Best friends

5. **Social losses**
   (These have as their core needs for recognition and
      approval)
   a. Friends
   b. The circle, "our set"
   c. The community of those who remember one's
      prime years
   d. Memberships
   e. Interdependent adults

6. **Losses of identity and utility**
   (These have as a core needs for security, stability
      and supplies)
   a. Position, job, employment
   b. Usefulness, productivity
   c. Familiar place, home
   d. Familiar place of employment
   e. Familiar surroundings: faces, places, objects
   f. Familiar routines

7. **Philosophical losses**
   (These have as a core needs for cognitive and con-
      native mastery)
   a. Purpose in living
   b. Joy of living
   c. Will to live

have to swallow his pride, love of freedom, and justice to retain an equity built up by years of hard work. The wound to his feelings of manliness is borne for a good reason, but his image of himself is not wholly comfortable.

In vital areas of the family, work, love, organizational belonging, leisure, and worship or faith, there are positions of stress with unstabilizing vacillation in public sentiment and official values which may or may not accord with private values. Tacitly the person's value system is expected to shift, yet integrity is founded on perseverance in one way— that is, on loyalty to a principle. For example, a self-supporting old age provided for by one's own savings and planning may still be the individual's value, but this may be undermined by the provisions of assistance and social security benefits to the aged. We sometimes hear of elderly people who starve rather than accept public assistance.

Table 2   Directional shift with aging

independence . . . . dependence		
usefulness . . . . uselessness		
helping . . . . helplessness		
potency . . . . impotence	inertia—	
competence . . . . incompetence	death	
belonging . . . . separation		
activity . . . . passivity		
mobility . . . . immobility		

Directional shift with aging

Considering the major problem areas of living, loving, working, belonging, and worshiping, the following continua express attitudinal positions which may shift for the elderly and may occasion some inner or external tension as they involve, possibly an alteration in self-image and others' regard, sometimes of major proportions. Sometimes minor shifts on one continuum may mean all the difference for a given person—for example, between caring to live and not caring any longer.

In considering table 2, reckon that aging by attrition and loss tends to shift the adult person from the left to the right and that individuals have varying resources and competences to counteract the general trend.

There are some additional philosophical considerations which invite tension because of discrepancies between theory and facts or ideals and reality. The will to live may shift toward a surrender to death, and hope may shift toward despair. Orientation to life here and now may shift to the sweet past or a wished-for afterlife.

The universal tragedy or melancholy of aging may be countered by vigorous and more or less effective efforts to disprove these states or quieter belief that "the best is yet to be."

Finally, the possibilities of confusion from ideological stress may be briefly suggested in the family, in areas of sex, and in status by referring to some stereotypes that suggest mixed views of what is normal or normative. There may develop tension to the extent that it remains unclear where a person stands, or feels he should stand.

Consider these contrasting alternatives:

head of family	— "has been"
wise old man	— "old fool"
vigorous (sexual) man	— "old goat"

Not only are some possibilities tension-loaded because they are incapacitating, depriving, and insulting, but the

58

lack of a tradition for suggesting what is the proper conduct or image may itself be productive of tension, and the possibility that the individual may resent and resist the stereotype, if there were one, could also create tension.

Conflict

It is self-evident that conflict produces tension. Incompatible goals, values, wishes, and so forth, are related to tension to the extent that choice is difficult and the factors involved are emotionally important to the individual. Several stock types of conflict have been described: (1) as between one or the other of two attractive situations; (2) as between one or the other of two unattractive situations; (3) as requiring one to endure and suffer the negative aspects of an otherwise attractive situation; and (4) as between two alternatives where each has something good and something bad about it. A few familiar conflicts faced by the aged will be cast in these molds, as shown in table 3.

Some recommendations

It is worth repeating that the most remarkable thing about aging is that, in spite of these manifold losses and sources of confusion and conflict, most elderly people manage adaptively and philosophically to live out their years.

Nevertheless, it seems possible to suggest some strategies for assisting people against the stressful vicissitudes of aging.

To counter the effects of loss, there is indicated a careful consideration of possibilities of finding and supplying substitutes, surrogates, and transitional supports. Whatever specific modes can be found or developed, these should be readily available and regularly and automatically instituted. While rehabilitative medicine is still on the threshold of developing artificial parts to replace those biologically worn feeble, already at hand are tonics, transfusions, and tranquilizers which can counteract some losses of function due to aging. Replenishment of physical and psychological supplies counteracts the trend toward depression.

Also, a series of cushions or buffers against predictable major losses could be instituted: spiritual, in the form of religion and philosophy, and social, in the form of congenial small groups who, from the experience of mutually facilitated recall of the "good old days," could find pleasure in each other's present company.

Ideological stress, whether from real conflict of values or from strains which are hidden or politically denied, should be clarified where possible. In this way, perhaps the discrepancy between the ideal and the real could be reduced and the hierarchy of values in our pluralistic society more clearly understood.

Some profit might come from clarification of the distribution of deference as it is linked with aging. Is a man to be esteemed for his years, or is this to be allocated on the basis of merit? What criteria confer merit? Are these to remain the same or change from the sixth to seventh to eighth and ninth decades of life? Are these not matters for general ideological clarification?

Regarding conflicts, where most can be reduced to the model of conflicts in paths or conflicts in goals, much stress can be avoided by social arrangements which insure that available paths are effective and that goals can be reached by so arranging life matters that a

Table 3   Familiar conflicts faced by the aging

1. Forced choice between valued alternatives (+ person +)

   To accept age gracefully, quietly   vs.   To counteract age vigorously
   To "step down" and give others a   To "stay in there" and show
   chance   others one is as good as ever

2. Forced choice between unpleasant alternatives (− person −)

   To live in pain   To die
   "I don't want to be a burden."   "I want to die."
   "I don't want a life-preserving   "I don't want to die."
   operation."
   "I don't want to live in a   "I can't live alone in
   nursing home."   my room."

3. One situation with positive and negative valence (person ±)

   Death
   "I'm ready any time."   and   "There's nothing in the
                                         world like breathing."

   Aging
   "Do I look old?"   "Ain't I a wonderful 91?"

   Sex
   "I was always afraid when we were intimate together on account of his double rupture."

   Living arrangements
   "I don't want anyone around telling   and   lonesomeness
   me what to do."
   "I'd like to live with the children,
   but they haven't enough room."

4. Forced choice between ambivalent alternatives (± person ±)

   To live in a state hospital where   To live at home where one
   life and medical needs are provided   has more freedom but less
   for, but one's pride is damaged and   immediate medical care in case
   freedom is limited   of emergency

succession of satisfying experiences and outcomes can be attained.

The particulars of what to do and how to do it are not within my competence, but their function can be set down. With the elderly, as indeed, with all other age groups, we must seek to provide approved satisfying outlets for such increments in biologic and psychologic tension as otherwise in an ever-growing percentage of our population lead to "breakdowns." Correlatively, where deficient revitalizing experience prompts tension from boredom, envy, apathy, and depression, we must rediscover duties, responsibilities, entitlements, privileges, and pleasures reserved for the elderly so that their—and our—protracted existence will become unlike boring, benign, or pathetic parasitism.

REFERENCE

1. ARSENIAN, JOHN: Situational factors contributing to mental illness in the United States: a theoretical summary. Mental Hygiene 45:194-206, 1961.

A SAMPLING OF ATTITUDES TOWARD AGING

A. D. ZAMPELLA, M.D.*

ABSTRACT: A questionnaire survey was made of 48 patients concerning their attitudes toward old age and retirement. The patients were in either a nursing home or a group medical practice in the Greater New York area; their ages ranged from 56 to 90 years. The factors investigated were: choice of retirement area, retirement attitudes, employment, recreation, religion, marriage, relationships with neighbors, family living arrangements, illness and incapacitation, Medicare, the past, the future, and death. The findings led to certain conclusions which may be helpful as guidelines in the care of the aged and in early essential planning for retirement.

In this study, the elderly person who was endowed with a feeling of mature, self-earned independence and physical well-being, who enjoyed adequate income and housing and was happily married, retained his self-esteem and integrity. He was less likely to become a burden on his family, friends or community, or to regress into illness that required early admission to an institution. His morale was high, even with a multiplicity of physical disorders. He retained the strong desire to maintain the identity of his personality within the mainstream of community and family life. On the other hand, *undue* identification with the aged and the process of aging, especially when complicated by unfortunate developments such as social, economic, emotional, personal and physical losses, evoked lifelong personality defenses in the elderly, even toward death with its increasing proximity.

The best approach to care of the elderly would seem to lie in preventive medicine, i.e., averting illness by a program of health care throughout the years. This program would stress natural processes, minimizing the pathological while maintaining the physiological.

Descriptions of aging are as varied and depreciative as they are numerous. Roget's Thesaurus describes age as oldness, elderliness, advanced age, ripe old age, senility, senescence, gray hairs, grand climacteric, declining years, decrepitude, superannuation, second childhood, dotage, vale of years, decline of life, "the sear and yellow leaf" (Shakespeare), ripe, mellow, declining, waning, past one's prime, hoary, venerable, ancient, patriarchal, timeworn, passé, antiquated, effete, stricken in years, having one foot in the grave, senior, superior (as in rank or standing), opposite of junior.

THE PROBLEM

There is little agreement in attitudes toward aging. Since the multitude of opinions expressed in the literature concerning the aged usually emphasize the pathological, it seemed pertinent to obtain some "grass roots" data which would include other aspects of aging. This was done by eliciting information directly from the elderly on matters such as choice of retirement area, retirement attitudes, employment, recreation, religion, marriage, neighbors, family, housing arrangements, illness, Medicare, the past, the present, the future, and death.

MATERIALS AND METHODS

A questionnaire survey was made of 48 patients in a group medical practice and in a nursing home in the Greater New York Metropolitan Area. Active in questioning the patients were a physician, a registered nurse, and a social worker. The patients were assured that there would be complete discretion about revealing their identity.

The ages of the respondents ranged from 56 to 96 years, and there were more than twice as many females as males. Most were active elderly people less than 75 years old.

Limitations of the survey. Most of those queried originated in a health service setting. This factor had to be considered because the presence of illness influenced answers in some categories. However, it would be difficult to find many elderly persons who had not consulted a doctor either occasionally or on a continuing basis. Characteristics such as marital and financial status affected the tone of the responses. Geographical factors influenced certain answers, since the subjects resided in a suburban section of Greater New York. Undoubtedly ego-protective factors colored some responses. Nevertheless, repetition of the questions in various contexts and degrees elicited valuable information.

The study was at best a sampling of attitudes, but it is a continuing one, with data being constantly added to this fund of knowledge concerning the elderly.

RESULTS

When asked how they happened to live in the area, prominent among the answers were: retirement, health, and the desire to be near "loved ones." However, they spoke of "closeness at a distance" in respect to their children and grandchildren, an understandable phenomenon in this day of modern rapid transportation.

Most of the subjects said they preferred to live in their present area. Some expressed a desire to live in a warmer climate such as Florida or California, and a lesser number indicated they would like to divide their time between a northern and a southern climate.

Most stated they were resigned or realistic about retiring or becoming elderly. A few of those stricken by infirmity during an active period of life were resentful about their present relative inactivity.

64

Retirement was equated largely with economic and physical dependency and curtailment of normal activity. They expressed it in various ways: "That beautiful salary I won't be getting"; "I lack sufficient money"; "My eyesight is failing"; "I am non-productive"; a retired sea captain stated "I miss the sea"; a former nurse to Admiral Dewey of Manila Bay fame said she "missed nursing"; others said "I can't do the things I used to do"; "I don't like to be dependent"; "It troubles me to be disabled, I can no longer be active." A few who were economically and physically independent said they were enjoying retirement.

The great majority had retired because of ill health, although mandatory retirement age was the reason advanced in some cases. Others stated that their husbands or their daughters "retired" them. The concept of *full* retirement seemed an odious one.

Almost none of this retired group was active in any form of gainful employment. Those not so engaged wished they could be gainfully employed.

Recreational activity was largely sedentary and was as follows, in order of preference: reading, gardening, television, sewing and crocheting, music, handicrafts, movies, visiting friends or relatives, games, art, writing, fishing, boating, community activities, and travel. Exercise was limited.

Most of those queried indicated that they would be willing to engage in a recreational program in a center outside their homes. Some went so far as to suggest the nature of the program, stating, "I would like to see silent movies and plays of *my* age," and "I enjoy an old fashioned song-fest of *our* songs." Recreation, creative work, or handiwork on a "take it or leave it" basis was considered most desirable.

Francis Bacon put it a little differently: "Age appears best in four things—old wood best to burn, old wine to drink, old friends to trust, and old authors to read."

Almost all indicated that they were free to come and go in the community as they pleased, to choose their own friends and company, to manage their own finances, to select their own clothes, to observe any desired religious duties, to write letters and receive mail without censorship, to have ready access to a telephone, to retain some of their personal belongings, to have visitors frequently, to have privacy when desired, to take vacations or weekend trips, and to move from their homes if they found them unsatisfactory.

Almost all were adherents of a formal religion but the number was about evenly divided between those who attended services regularly and those who did not. Religious convictions persisted in spite of a falling off of formal observances.

Most were still married (some for the second time), a lesser number were widowed, and a few were divorced or had never married. Those who lived with spouses were in better contact and expressed more contentment.

Living arrangements varied from living with spouses, friends or relatives in an individual home to living alone or in a nursing home.

The majority considered it desirable to live in their own individual homes equipped for light housekeeping and with ample easily-graded garden space, in a community close to shopping centers, beauty parlors, barber shops, recreational services, part-time employment, transportation, churches, medical, hospital and convalescent facilities, visited by their own doctor. Included were services to lessen physical strain, e.g., outside maintenance and repairs, landscaping, care of grounds, snow removal, police patrol, waste disposal, and local transportation.

In the event of incapacitation, the majority indicated they would resort to nursing home accommodations; a few stated their spouse or relatives would care for them; and some stated they "just didn't know what they would do."

Responses were elicited concerning preoccupation with the past, the future, and death. Most disclaimed any concern about the past, although a few expressed frustration at not having attained goals. Wilmot spoke of this discontent when he said: "Then Old Age and Experience, hand in hand, lead time to death, and make him understand, after a search so painful and so long, that all his life he has been in the wrong."

Many expressed little concern with the future but many were worried about health and finances. The subject of death was discussed willingly. Fear of death was denied by most—almost as if it were being blocked from consciousness—and admitted by a very few who were more infirm, but with death not imminent.

In the words of Sophocles: "No man loves life like his that's growing old" and Euripides observes "Old Men's Prayers for death are *lying* prayers, in which they abuse old age and long extent of life. But when death draws near, *not one* is willing to die, and age no longer is a burden to them."

About as many considered themselves physically fit as those who thought otherwise, the latter group rating their infirmity as mild to moderate in severity.

Almost all had subscribed or intended to subscribe to Medicare.

A majority were collecting Social Security payments, and others were collecting pensions or some form of disability insurance. A smaller number were still self-sustaining from employment.

DISCUSSION

Much has been said concerning the subject of aging, but there is little of a definitive nature other than the opinions of observers rather than of participants in the process.

Many views are timeworn and repetitious and have been ill-conditioned by our modern-day industrial society. This society fosters a *chronological* rather than a *biological* retirement age, placing a premium on youth, subordinating the older person, fostering in him a spirit of dependence, and even forcing compulsory retirement and limiting his earnings under Social Security.

The increase in the life span in the past half century, from age 47 to almost 70, has been the average rather than the maximum. Pertinent is the observation of Victor Hugo that "40 is the old age of youth; 50, the youth of old age."

Paradoxically, attitudes of youth toward society and the elderly are carried over into later life, and become directed toward themselves when old age sets in. After all, who are the old but the older young? Disraeli said, "Youth is a blunder; manhood a struggle; old age a regret."

Cicero observed in his classic essay on old age, "First, that it withdraws us from active employment; second, that it enfeebles the body; third, that it deprives us

66

of nearly all physical pleasures; fourth, that it is the next step to death." Speaking of death, he reminded us that the old have achieved what the young can only hope for; "The one *wishes* to live long;_the other *has* lived long."

In our study, the relatively well adjusted and independent old people were chiefly those who enjoyed relative freedom from worries concerning housing, finances, gainful employment, health, availability of medical assistance when needed, and the fear of the *indignity* of classification as "senile." In this context, senility becomes not an inevitable biological phenomenon but a *cultural* artifact and a *social* ill.

Dr. Alfred Worcester, in his beautifully written compassionate monograph entitled, "The Care of the Aged, the Dying, and the Dead," speaks of Carlyle's description of his mother when nearly 80 years old: "It is beautiful to see how, in the gradual decay of all other strength, the strength of her heart and affections still survives—as it were, fresher than ever—the *soul* of life refuses to grow old with the *body* of life." "Evidently she was kindly cared for; and, as certainly, many of the distressing changes of character, too often met with in the aged, are the direct results of insufficient or improper care."

More than 2,000 years ago Plato quoted the reply of the aged Cephalus to the question, "Is life harder towards the end, or what report do you give of it?" . . . "Old age has a great sense of calm and freedom; when the passions relax their hold, then . . . . We are freed not of one mad master only, but of many . . . . He who is of a calm and happy nature will hardly feel the pressure of age; but to him who is of an *opposite* disposition, youth and age are equally a burden."

Death Anxiety

DEATH ANXIETY SCALE MEANS, STANDARD DEVIATIONS, AND EMBEDDING

DONALD I. TEMPLER   AND   CAROL F. RUFF

Summary.—A table of means and standard deviations on the Death Anxiety Scale for 23 categories of *S*s was presented. Embedding of the Scale's items apparently had little or no effect upon scores.

Although no actual norms have been established for the Death Anxiety Scale (DAS), a considerable amount of relevant data has been collected both during and subsequent to its construction and validation (Templer, 1969, 1970). Table 1 presents the means and standard deviations for 23 categories of *S*s from 7 different studies involving over 3600 adults and adolescents. Scale scores range from 0 to 15; means of normal *S*s tend to be roughly from 4.5 to 7.0; the standard deviations a little over 3.0. Psychiatric patients obtain higher scores than normals. Females consistently have higher DAS scores than males. In the project involving over 2500 *S*s from 19 to 85 yr. of age, there was no relationship between age and DAS scores (Templer, Ruff, & Franks, 1971).

In the construction and validation of the DAS, the items were embedded in the last 200 items of the MMPI. In a study relating DAS score to GSR elicited by death-related words, the DAS items were embedded in the 156 MMPI items that constitute Byrne's Repression-Sensitization Scale (Templer, in press b). However, in the other studies the DAS items were not embedded (Templer & Dotson, 1970; Templer, Ruff, & Franks, 1971[1]). The advantage of not embedding the DAS items is the saving of administration time.

In order to determine if the embedding of the items has an effect upon DAS score, the DAS was administered to 158 students at Hopkinsville (Kentucky) Community College. The items were embedded for 78 *S*s, 30 males and 48 females; and not embedded for 80 *S*s, 32 males and 48 females. The embedded items were placed in the last 200 items of the MMPI. For the non-embedded DAS, items were placed before the 200 MMPI items so that both groups would complete questionnaires in approximately equal time and thereby obtain the impression that they were working on identical material. The embedded and non-embedded DAS items were given to every other *S*.

The DAS means are 7.08 and 7.30 for the embedded and non-embedded administrations respectively ($t = .45$, ns). The standard deviations are 3.36 and 2.75 for the embedded and non-embedded administrations respectively, and the variances are 11.29 and 7.58 ($F = 1.49$, $p < .05$).

Since there did not appear to be any readily apparent explanation for the significant difference in variance, replication was done to rule out a Type I error. The DAS was administered in a similar fashion to 186 different students

TABLE 1
DAS MEANS AND STANDARD DEVIATIONS IN VARIOUS STUDIES

Ss	M	SD
134 Lincoln University undergraduate Negroes*	· 6.35	3.28
124 Lincoln University undergraduate whites*	6.16	3.21
Templer (1969, 1970)		
77 Murray University undergraduates	5.13	3.10
32 Heterogeneous psychiatric patients	6.78	2.97
21 High death anxiety psychiatric patients	11.62	1.96
21 Controls for high death anxiety psychiatric patients	6.77	2.74
Templer and Dotson (1970)		
104 Male Western Kentucky University undergraduates	6.07	3.12
109 Female Western Kentucky University undergraduates	6.66	3.07
Templer, Ruff, and Franks (1971)		
123 Male apartment house residents	4.85	2.88
160 Female apartment house residents	6.11	3.31
299 Adolescent males	5.72	3.07
444 Adolescent females	6.84	3.21
569 Fathers of adolescents	5.74	3.32
702 Mothers of adolescents	6.43	3.22
78 Male heterogeneous psychiatric patients	6.50	3.55
59 Female heterogeneous psychiatric patients	7.15	3.72
13 Male psychiatric aides	5.08	2.25
112 Female psychiatric aides	6.33	3.24
Templer [in press (b)]		
49 Heterogeneous psychiatric patients	7.13	3.45
Templer [in press (a)]		
46 Retired males	4.15	3.29
29 Retired females	4.41	3.43
Templer (unpublished study)†		
217 Bloomfield (N. J.) College males	6.69	2.72
167 Bloomfield (N. J.) College females	7.84	2.99

*Pandey & Templer. †D. I. Templer. Death anxiety: extraversion, neuroticism and smoking. (Unpublished paper)

at Hopkinsville Community College. The DAS mean for the 93 Ss with the DAS items embedded is 6.70; that for the 93 Ss with the items not embedded is 6.95 ($t = .50$, ns). The standard deviations are 3.43 and 3.29 for the embedded and non-embedded administrations respectively, and the variances are 11.76 and 10.79 ($F = 1.09$, ns). A reasonable conclusion is that the embedding of DAS items has little or no effect upon scores.

REFERENCES

TEMPLER, D. I. Death Anxiety Scale. *Proceedings of the 77th Annual Convention of the American Psychological Association*, 1969, 4, 737-738.
TEMPLER, D. I. The construction and validation of a Death Anxiety Scale. *Journal of General Psychology*, 1970, 82, 165-177.
TEMPLER, D. I. Death anxiety as related to depression and health of retired persons. *Journal of Gerontology*, in press. (a)
TEMPLER, D. I. The relationship between verbalized and non-verbalized death anxiety. *Journal of Genetic Psychology*, in press. (b)
TEMPLER, D. I., & DOTSON, E. Religious correlates of death anxiety. *Psychological Reports*, 1970, 26, 895-897.
TEMPLER, D. I., RUFF, C. F., & FRANKS, C. M. Death anxiety: age, sex and parental resemblance in diverse populations. *Developmental Psychology*, 1971, 4, 108.

DEATH ANXIETY: EXTRAVERSION, NEUROTICISM, AND CIGARETTE SMOKING

Donald I. Templer, Ph.D.

There were significant positive correlations between the Death Anxiety Scale (DAS) and the Neuroticism Scale of the Eysenck Personality Inventory but not with the Extraversion Scale of this inventory. The mean DAS score of cigarette smokers was neither significantly different from that of non-smokers nor from that of ex-smokers. However, within the cigarette smoking group, there was a significant negative correlation ($r = -.25$) between DAS score and number of cigarettes smoked per day.

The purpose of this research was to determine (1) the correlation of the Death Anxiety Scale (DAS) with the Extraversion and Neuroticism Scales of the Eysenck Personality Inventory and (2) the relationship of DAS score to cigarette smoking.

The reliability and construct validity of the DAS have been determined by a diversity of procedures, and its correlations with the Minnesota Multiphasic Personality Inventory have been reported with both college students and psychiatric patients (Templer, 1969, 1970, in press). Subsequent research has explored the relationship of the DAS to religious variables (Templer & Dotson, 1970), age, sex, and family resemblance (Templer, Ruff, & Franks, 1971), galvanic skin response to death related words (Templer, 1971a), health variables in elderly persons (Templer, 1971b), and race. (Pandey & Templer, in press).

The Eysenck Personality Inventory Neuroticism and Extraversion Scales assess Eysenck's two major orthogonal dimensions of personality (Eysenck, 1947, 1957). Neuroticism refers to the continuum of emotionality. Introverts are more persistent, methodical, and conscientious, and condition more readily than extraverts. Extraverts are more outgoing, impulsive, and apt to transgress the laws of society. Eysenck maintains that both neuroticism and extraversion are constitutionally determined. Introverted individuals who are high in neuroticism are called "dysthymics" by Eysenck and are prone to anxiety, depression, and obsessive-compulsive symptomotology. The extraverted neurotics have hysterical or psychopathic manifestations.

Smoking behavior and the Eysenck Personality Inventory were included in the same death anxiety study because of the demonstrated positive association between extraversion and cigarette smoking (Eysenck, 1965). If, in the present research, the DAS had been related to both the Extraversion Scale and smoking behavior, the relationship of the DAS to smoking with the influence of the Extraversion Scale statistically removed would have been determined.

METHOD

Subjects were 384 undergraduates, 217 males and 167 females, at Bloomfield College, Bloomfield, New Jersey. They were administered the DAS, the Eysenck Personality

TABLE 1

Questions about cigarette smoking.		
1. Are you now a cigarette smoker?	Yes ___	No ___
2. If the answer to question 1 is yes, how many cigarettes do you smoke in an average day?	_____	
3. If the answer to question 1 is no, have you ever been a cigarette smoker?	Yes ___	No ___

Inventory, and the questions contained in Table 1. The DAS was not embedded since a recent study indicated that embedding has little or no effect upon DAS score (Templer & Ruff, 1971).

Because females tend to score higher on DAS and Neuroticism and lower on Extraversion (Templer, Ruff, and Franks, 1971; Eysenck, 1958; Eysenck, 1960), the DAS correlations with Extraversion and Neuroticism were calculated for males and females separately as well as combined. The DAS relationships to smoking behavior were not analyzed separately for the sexes because of the nonsignificant difference in the proportion of male (83 out of 217) and female (52 out of 167) cigarette smokers (χ^2 = 2.08).

RESULTS

Table 2 presents the DAS, Extraversion, and Neuroticism means and standard deviations. The product-moment correlation coefficients between DAS and Extraversion are not statistically significant for the male (r = .03), female (r = −.07), and combined (r = .00) groups. The correlations between DAS and Neuroticism are significant at the .001 level for the male (r = .36), female (r = .31), and combined (r = .36) groups.

The DAS mean of the 135 cigarette smokers and the 279 students who do not smoke were both 7.19. The 78 former cigarette smokers mean of 7.47 was also not significantly different from the 135 cigarette smokers mean of 7.19 (t = .71). However, for the cigarette smokers the product-moment correlation coefficient between DAS score and number of cigarettes smoked was −.25 ($p < .01$).

DISCUSSION

The significant correlations between DAS and Neuroticism is congruent with previous research that consistently shows a positive association of the DAS with measures of general anxiety or maladjustment—the Welsh Anxiety Scale, Welsh Anxiety Index, Manifest Anxiety Scale, Cornell Medical Index, and Byrne's Repression-Sensitization Scale (Templer, 1969, 1970, 1971a, 1971b).

Although the correlation between DAS and Extraversion scores is zero, further analysis was carried out to investigate the possibility that introverted and extraverted subjects who are high in neuroticism might differ. It seems plausible that the introverted neurotic or "dysthymic" could have higher death anxiety than the extraverted neurotic or "hysteric" because of the former's greater propensity to ruminate about past occurrences and future events.

The DAS score of those subjects (hysterics) who were over a standard deviation from the mean on both the Neuroticism and Extraversion Scales were compared to the DAS scores of subjects (dysthymics) who were over a standard deviation from the mean on the

TABLE 2
DAS, Extraversion and Neuroticism Means and Standard Deviations

	N	DAS Mean (SD)	Extraversion Mean (SD)	Neuroticism Mean (SD)
Male	217	6.69 (2.72)	13.88 (3.63)	13.28 (4.01)
Female	167	7.84 (2.99)	14.31 (3.28)	14.74 (4.05)
Combined	384	7.19 (2.89)	14.07 (3.48)	13.91 (4.09)

Neuroticism Scale and below the mean more than a standard deviation on the Extraversion Scale. The 10 "hysterics" obtained a DAS mean of 9.30; the 23 "dysthymics" obtained a DAS mean of 8.25 ($t = 1.33$, ns). The standard deviations are 1.64 and 2.85 for the "hysterics" and "dysthymics" respectively, and the variances are 2.68 and 8.11 ($F = 3.03$, $p < .05$). The hypothesis of higher death anxiety of "dysthymics" was certainly not supported. There seems no readily apparent explanation for the difference in variance.

The findings with respect to smoking appear paradoxical. The DAS mean of cigarette smokers is neither statistically different from that of the total non-cigarette smoker group nor from that of the subjects within this group who previously smoked. Yet, within the cigarette smoker group there is a significant negative correlation between DAS score and amount of smoking.

The explanation here advanced for the seemingly paradoxical findings in regard to smoking is admittedly speculative. Perhaps, death anxiety does not affect whether one starts or stops smoking because it is outweighed by such other variables as extraversion or social pressure. However, death anxiety may limit the amount of cigarette smoking in persons who already have this habit.

A similar phenomenon probably results from the use of "scare" tactics to promote highway safety. Such procedures probably don't cause people to give up driving. They are more likely to motivate the people who drive to do so more slowly.

The smoking-DAS finding may serve as a model for a more general perspective upon self-destructive behavior such as drug abuse, alcoholism, excessive eating, and a criminal mode of life. Death anxiety may exert some control upon amount of self-destructive behavior, but it is ineffective in eradicating it.

The inability of death anxiety to completely eliminate self-destructive behavior probably can be understood both in terms of the motivational strength of the behavior under consideration and of the defense mechanism against death anxiety. A considerable amount of clinical literature states or implies that most people extensively employ denial and repression in coping with the matter of death (Templer, 1971a). Consistent with this viewpoint is the lack of a significant positive correlation between DAS score and number of physical symptoms and disorders endorsed on the Cornell Medical Index (Templer, 1971b). In fact, when the effect of psychiatric disturbance was statistically removed, there was actually a significant negative correlation between DAS score and score on the somatic section of the Cornell Medical Index. Also consistent with extensive employment of denial and repression in dealing with death is the absence of any relationship between DAS score and age in a project involving over 2,500 subjects from teens throughout the eighties (Templer, Ruff, & Franks, 1971). Apparently, nearness to death or its probability within a given period of time is not ordinarily an important determinant of death anxiety—at least not in people who are presumably not terminally ill. It is fortunate that most people are not continually obsessed with and tormented by the prospect of their death. However, the denial of this inevitable fact of life could result in the over-utilization of defense mechanisms.

REFERENCES

Eysenck, H. J. *Dimensions of personality.* London: Routledge & Kegan Paul, 1947.

Eysenck, H. J. *The dynamics of anxiety and hysteria.* London: Routledge & Kegan Paul, 1957.

Eysenck, H. J. A short questionnaire for the measurement of two dimensions of personality. *Journal of Applied Psychology*, 1958, 42, 14-17.

Eysenck, H. J. *Smoking, health and personality.* New York: Basic Books, 1965.

Eysenck, S. B. G. Social class, sex and response to a five-part personality inventory. *Educational and Psychological Measurement*, 1960, 20, 47-54.

Pandey, R. E. and Templer, D. I. The death anxiety of Negro and White college students, in press, OMEGA.

Templer, D. I. Death Anxiety Scale. *Proceedings of the 77th Annual Convention of the American Psychological Association*, 1969, 4, 737-738.

Templer, D. I. The construction and validation of a Death Anxiety Scale. *Journal of General Psychology*, 1970, 82, 165-177.

Templer, D. I. The relationship between verbalized and non-verbalized death anxiety. *Journal of Genetic Psychology*, 1971a, 119, 211-214.

Templer, D. I. Death anxiety as related to depression and health of retired persons. *Journal of Gerontology*, 1971b, 26, 521-523.

Templer, D. I., & Dotson, E. Religious correlates of death anxiety. *Psychological Reports*, 1970, 26, 895-897.

Templer, D. I., & Ruff, C. F. Death Anxiety Scale means, standard deviations, and embedding. *Psychological Reports*, 1971, 29, 173-174.

Templer, D. I., Ruff, C. F., & Franks, C. M. Death anxiety: Age, sex, and parental resemblance in diverse populations. *Developmental Psychology*, 1971, 4, 108.

THE RELATIONSHIP BETWEEN VERBALIZED AND NONVERBALIZED DEATH ANXIETY [1]

Donald I. Templer

A. Introduction

The purpose of this study was to determine the relationship between verbalized and nonverbalized death anxiety. The former was measured by the Death Anxiety Scale (DAS) of Templer (15), the latter was determined by galvanic skin response (GSR) to death related words. These two measures and their discrepancy were related to the repression-sensitization dimension of personality.

It has been previously demonstrated that GSRs are obtained to death related words (1, 2, 10). Alexander et al. (2) noted an inconsistency between their experimentally obtained reactions and the literature which indicated scant fear of death in the subjective reports of normals, and have inferred the presence of unconscious death anxiety. Thus, there is some evidence that GSR might tap a level of death anxiety different from that which one is aware of and willing to express on a paper and pencil instrument.

The exploration of a relationship between these two death anxiety measures appeared important in view of the large amount of clinical literature that states or implies that death anxiety is an almost universal human experience, and that the defense mechanisms of denial and repression account for people dealing with death anxiety in different ways and with different degrees of effectiveness (1, 2, 3, 6, 7, 8, 9, 11, 13).

In a review by Stern and Plapp (14), it was concluded that "subjects who report less disturbance or anxiety display heightened autonomic reactivity." The greater reporting of disturbance and lesser autonomic reactivity was ascribed to the sensitizers. The psychometric instrument used in such research was the Repression-Sensitization (R-S) Scale of Byrne (4, 5). This purports to measure the continuum of repressing or denying threat to ruminating upon

[1] The author is grateful to John Stern and Harry Kotses for their helpful suggestions.

it. It therefore seems reasonable that discrepancy between reported and auto-nomically reflected death anxiety would be related to the repression-sensitization dimension.

B. Method

Ss were 49 heterogeneous adult psychiatric patients in Malcolm Bliss Mental Health Center, St. Louis. They were administered the DAS and the R-S Scale before the experimental procedure. The 15 DAS items were ran-domly embedded in the 156 items of the R-S Scale. Such embedding appeared appropriate for the DAS items, since the R-S items are from the Minnesota Multiphasic Personality Inventory (MMPI), and the DAS items were embedded in the last 200 items of the MMPI during its reliability and validity determination.

A Beckman Type R dynograph with a Meeco GSR coupler was used. Silver disc electrodes were attached to the second and fourth finger of the left hand with corn pads and Beckman paste. After the electrodes were attached to the finger S was given the following instructions: "Shortly after I leave the room you will hear a number of words. Please listen carefully to these words."

Thirty words were presented to the Ss at 30-second intervals. Ten of the words were death related words, 10 were high in other affective content, and 10 relatively neutral in content. Three of the death related words were "funeral," "death," and "burial." Alexander et al. (2) found these words produced greater magnitude GSRs than banal words. The other seven death related words were "suicide," "murder," "casket," "cancer," "cemetery," "eter-nity," and "corpse." The relatively neutral words, taken from the Word As-sociation Test of Rapaport et al. (12), were "hat," lamp," "book," "paper," "trunk," "spring," "rug," "chair," "horse," and "water." The 10 affective words, designated as traumatic by Rapaport et al. were "love," "father," "breast," "fire," "intercourse," "mother," "fight," "drink," "suck," and "dirt."

A word from each of the three categories was grouped together for 10 con-secutive sets. The order of the words within a set was randomly determined. The specific word from each category was also randomly determined. This arrangement permitted a comparison of GSR magnitude to words within a set without consideration of base levels, in addition to controlling for habitua-tion. A decrease in skin resistance 300 ohms or greater with a latency from .5 to 5 seconds was regarded as a response. In the case of multiple responses, the first was scored. Each subjects death-GSR (DGSR) score was the proportion of word sets that the GSR to the death word exceeded that to the neutral word.

C. Results and Discussion

The product moment correlation coefficient between DAS and DGSR was .30 ($p < .05$). As a check upon the assumption that GSR to death related words was an affective reaction at least somewhat specific to the concept of death rather than a response given to any affective concept, the proportion of word sets that the GSR to the other affective word exceeds that to the neutral word was also correlated with DAS score. This correlation was .00. In support of the assumption that the words designated as affective actually were such in this study, for 27 Ss the proportion of word sets that the GSR to the affective word exceeded that to the neutral word was over .50; for 12 Ss the proportion was less than .50 ($\chi^2 = 5.7$, $p < .05$). For 32 Ss the proportion of word sets that the GSR to the death related word exceeded that to the neutral word was over .50; for seven Ss the death related word was less than .50 ($\chi^2 = 16.0$, $p < .01$).

R-S correlated .51 ($p < .01$) with DAS and .02 with DGSR. For the determination of the extent that discrepancy between the two death anxiety measures correlated with R-S, each Ss z score for DGSR was subtracted from his DAS Z score. This measure correlated .38 ($p < .01$) with R-S.

It was concluded that the two measures of death anxiety are significantly, although modestly, related. Discrepancy between the two measures is correlated with repression-sensitization. However, there appears insufficient basis to maintain that autonomically detected death anxiety is a measure of repressed death anxiety. A more accurate statement would be that it is independent of repression-sensitization. This is in contrast to the DAS which is rather highly correlated with repression-sensitization.

D. Summary

The relationship between the Death Anxiety Scale and GSR to death related words was investigated. The former is a paper and pencil self-report instrument; the latter has been employed by previous investigators as a measure of unverbalized death anxiety. A modest but significant positive correlation was found between the two death anxiety measures. Both the discrepancy between these two measures and the Death Anxiety Scale were positively correlated with the R-S Scale. R-S was not significantly correlated with GSR to death related words.

REFERENCES

1. ALEXANDER, I. E., & ADLERSTEIN, A. M. Affective responses to the concept of death in a population of children and early adolescents. *J. Genet. Psychol.,* 1958, **13**, 167-177.

2. ALEXANDER, I. E., COLLEY, R. S., & ADLERSTEIN, A. M. Is death a matter of indifference? *J. of Psychol.,* 1957, **43**, 277-283.

3. BLUESTONE, H., & McGAHEE, C. Reaction to extreme stress: Impending death by execution. *Amer. J. Psychia.,* 1962, **119**(5), 393-396.

4. BYRNE, D. The repression-sensitization scale: Rational, reliability, and validity. *J. Personal.,* 1961, **29**, 334-349.

5. ────. Repression-sensitization as a dimension of personality. In B. A. Maher (Ed.), *Progress in Experimental Personality Research.* New York: Academic Press, 1964. Pp. 169-220.

6. CHRIST, A. E. Attitudes toward death among a group of acute geriatric patients. *J. Geront.,* 1961, **16**, 56-59.

7. COREY, L. G. An analogue of resistance to death awareness. *J. Geront.,* 1961, **16**, 59-60.

8. FEIFEL, H. Older persons look at death. *Geriatrics,* 1956, **61**, 127-130.

9. LIFTON, R. J. Psychological effects of the atomic bomb in Hiroshima: The theme of death. In G. H. Grosser, H. Wechsler, & M. Greenblat (Eds.), *The Threat of Impending Disaster: Contributions to a Psychology of Stress.* MIT Press, 1965. Pp. 152-193.

10. MEISNER, W. W. Affective response to psychoanalytic death symbols. *J. Abn. & Soc. Psychol.,* 1958, **56**, 295-299.

11. McCULLY, R. S. Fantasy productions of children with a progressively crippling and fatal disease. *J. Genet. Psychol.,* 1963, **101**, 203-216.

12. RAPAPORT, D., GILL, M. A. & SCHAFER, R. Diagnostic Psychological Testing. New York: Internat. Univ. Press, 1968.

13. RHUDICK, P. J., & DIBNER, A. S. Age, personality, and health correlates of death concerns in normal aged individuals. *J. Geront.,* 1961, **16**, 44-49.

14. STERN, J. A., & PLAPP, J. M. Psychophysiology and Clinical Psychology. In C. D. Spielberger (Ed.), *Current Topics in Clinical and Community Psychology.* New York: Academic Press, in press.

15. TEMPLER, D. I. The construction and validation of a death anxiety scale. *J. Gen. Psychol.,* 1970, **82**, 165-177.

Carrier Clinic Foundation
Belle Mead, New Jersey 08502

THE CONSTRUCTION AND VALIDATION
OF A DEATH ANXIETY SCALE [1]

DONALD I. TEMPLER

A. INTRODUCTION

Three methods of assessment have been employed in research on the topic of death anxiety: (*a*) interviews, (*b*) projective techniques, (*c*) questionnaires. With the exception of one questionnaire (2), neither the reliability nor the validity of any instrument or procedure reported in the literature has been determined.

Although a number of the interview procedures have been loosely structured (7, 14, 20, 33), other investigations have employed a specific set of questions (3, 8, 9, 18, 21, 33, 34). These interviews have ranged from the lengthy 32 questions of Bromberg and Schilder (3) to the simply worded and straightforward two questions of Jeffers *et al.* (21). The latter investigators asked, "Are you afraid to die?" and "Do you believe in life after death?" Although some of the articles have been concerned primarily with the clinical impressions, most of the investigations have at least employed frequency counts in their analysis of data.

Some researchers have employed conventional projective instruments. Rhudick and Dibner (30) administered 12 TAT cards in the usual manner. They defined death concern as the introduction of death into a story, and rated each story with death concern from one to three points depending upon the usual frequency of a death theme for that card as determined by a pilot study. Shrut (36) administered the TAT and a Sentence Completion Test to a group of elderly people. He reported that clinical impressions were utilized, and offered no description of criteria or quantification.

McCully (26) asked children to make up stories. Mauer (25) required high school students to write essays on "what comes to mind when I think

[1] This research is based upon a Doctoral dissertation submitted to the Department of Psychology, University of Kentucky, in partial requirements for the Ph.D. degree. The author wishes to express his gratitude to the members of his dissertation committee: Jesse G. Harris, Jr., Chairman, Juris I. Berzins, Albert J. Lott, Frank A. Pattie, and E. Grant Youmans.

of death." Faunce and Fuller (17) administered incomplete sentences with death involved stems to college students. Corey (10) utilized a procedure in which a picture of a reclining figure was presented to subjects who were supposed to specify whether the figure was "sleeping" or "dead."

Most questionnaires and checklists have been rather brief (15, 16, 32, 38). Some questionnaires were fairly extensive (23, 27, 37). Means (27) had college women rate the extent to which several hundred objects and ideas evoked fear in them. Only a small percentage of the items pertained to death.

Boyar's Fear of Death Scale or FODS (2) seems more adequate than other instruments thus far reported in the literature. Boyar obtained an initial pool of items on the basis of individual interviews. He then had judges rate the adequacy of his items. Next, the items were embedded in filler items. The split-half reliability was determined, and item-item and item-test correlations were computed. To determine the validity of the FODS, subjects were administered the Scale before and after a movie intended to increase death anxiety. Since the Fear of Death Scale scores for this experimental group increased to a significantly greater extent than did those of the control group shown a relatively innocuous movie, Boyar concluded that the validity of his Scale was established. Boyar was apparently not concerned with the development of construct validity (12) by a diversity of procedures.

B. THE DEATH ANXIETY SCALE: CONSTRUCTION AND VALIDATION

1. *Rationale and Selection of Items*

The Death Anxiety Scale (DAS) was developed by a procedure that was somewhat different from that of the Fear of Death Scale (FODS) by Boyar. The DAS items reflect a wider range of life experiences than the FODS items which cover primarily the act of dying, the finality of death, and corpses and their burial.

Forty items were devised on a rational basis. Twenty-three of these were keyed "true" and 17 were keyed "false."

Seven judges then rated the face validity of these items. The judges were a clinical psychologist, two graduate students in clinical psychology, and four chaplains in a state mental hospital. The direction of the question intended by the author to indicate greater death anxiety was specified, and the judges were instructed to rate each item from one to five on this basis: 1) Irrelevant to death anxiety, 2) Slightly associated with death anxiety, 3) Moderately associated with death anxiety, 4) Considerably associated with death anxiety, 5) Very greatly associated with death anxiety.

The average rating for each item was calculated. Nine items received an average rating of below 3.0 and were discarded. The 31 items that received an average rating of 3.0 or higher were embedded in 200 filler items—the last 200 items of the Minnesota Multiphasic Personality Inventory (MMPI), none of which are scored on the nine primary clinical scales. The reasons for the selection of the MMPI items will be described later.

2. Item Analyses

To determine internal consistency, item-total score point biserial correlation coefficients for three independent groups of subjects were utilized. The groups were (a) 45 college students in a sophomore undergraduate psychology class at the University of Kentucky; (b) 50 college students from age 25 to 57 in a number of different classes in several different colleges in Kentucky and Tennessee; (c) 46 students in an introductory psychology class at Western Kentucky University.

It was decided to retain those items that had point biserial coefficients significant at the .10 level in two out of three analyses. Table 1 contains the 15 retained items. The probability of a truly zero correlation being significant at the .10 level in two out of three analyses is .028.

TABLE 1
THE 15 DAS ITEMS

Key	Content
T	I am very much afraid to die.
F	The thought of death seldom enters my mind.
F	It doesn't make me nervous when people talk about death.
T	I dread to think about having to have an operation.
F	I am not at all afraid to die.
F	I am not particularly afraid of getting cancer.
F	The thought of death never bothers me.
T	I am often distressed by the way time flies so very rapidly.
T	I fear dying a painful death.
T	The subject of life after death troubles me greatly.
T	I am really scared of having a heart attack.
T	I often think about how short life really is.
T	I shudder when I hear people talking about a World War III.
T	The sight of a dead body is horrifying to me.
F	I feel that the future holds nothing for me to fear.

Phi coefficients were computed as a means of determining relative independence of items. Since none of the coefficients of correlation between retained items exceeded .65, it can be inferred that there is not excessive interitem redundancy.

3. Reliability

Thirty-one of the 37 Hopkinsville Community College subjects who participated in the agreement response set research, described below, completed the DAS a second time, three weeks after the first administration. The product-moment correlation coefficient of .83 between these two sets of scores demonstrates acceptable test-retest reliability. A coefficient of .76 (Kuder-Richardson Formula 20) demonstrates reasonable internal consistency with these 31 subjects.

4. Response Sets

Nine of the 15 items that comprise the DAS are keyed "true" and six are keyed "false." To determine whether or not the DAS is appreciably related to agreement response set, it was correlated with the 15 items that Couch and Keniston (11) considered their best short scale measure of agreeing response tendency. The subjects employed were 37 students at Hopkinsville (Kentucky) Community College. Nineteen of the subjects were in an introductory psychology class and 18 were in a class of freshman English. The product-moment correlation coefficient was .23, which was not significant at the .05 level. It appears that the agreement response set accounts for little of the variance of the DAS.

The DAS and the Marlowe-Crowne Social Desirability Scale (13) were administered to 46 introductory psychology students at Western Kentucky University. The Social Desirability Scale, the content of which is independent of psychopathology, is an instrument that measures the tendency to respond in a socially desirable direction. The product-moment correlation coefficient between the two scales was not significant ($r = .03$). It would appear that the response set of social desirability is not appreciably related to the death anxiety variable.

5. Validation Procedures

In an effort to establish the construct validity of the DAS, two separate projects were undertaken. In the first, the subjects were psychiatric patients in a state mental hospital. In the second, the subjects were college students.

a. DAS scores of high death anxiety patients and controls. In this project, the DAS scores of 21 presumable high death anxiety psychiatric patients were compared with those of control patients. The patients were drawn from Western State Hospital, a state supported mental hospital in Hopkinsville, Kentucky. The names of patients who had spontaneously verbalized fear of, or preoccupation with, death were obtained by three methods: (*a*) referrals by hospital chaplains who had been told of death anxiety in counseling sessions, (*b*) a list of names obtained from the Director of Nursing by consulting with her professional nursing staff, (*c*) patients' records.

The control subjects were matched for diagnosis, sex, and approximate age. Table 2 lists the DAS scores and other pertinent information about each patient used in the study. The 21 high death anxiety subjects had a DAS mean of 11.62. The control group obtained a mean of 6.77. A *t* of 5.79 was significant at the .01 level (two-tailed test). Therefore, it can be concluded that psychiatric patients who spontaneously verbalize death anxiety concern have higher DAS scores than other psychiatric patients.

b. The DAS score correlates of college students.

(1). Description of method and procedure. The DAS, Boyar's FODS, a sequential word association task, and the MMPI were administered to 77 advanced undergraduates at Murry State University. After the subjects completed the first 366 items of the MMPI, they were given a 15-minute break. In the second part of the session, they were given the sequential word association task, the DAS (the 15 items of which are embedded in the last 200 items of the MMPI), and the FODS. The rationale and pilot work for these procedures will be described below.

Boyar's FODS was employed as one means of determining the validity of the DAS. As has been already pointed out, the construct validity of Boyar's FODS has not been thoroughly determined. Nevertheless, it is probably the most adequate death anxiety instrument previously developed.

A sequential word association task was utilized as another validation procedure. Osipow and Grooms (28) found an increase in the number of idiosyncratic words and a decrease in the number of popular responses across the link of chains on a sequential word association test. It was reasoned that the projective determination of the associations increases as the association chain progresses and that, therefore, the sequential word association task may be of clinical value. In the task used in the present study, the subjects were required to write down 10 associations to the word death and to four other words. The four buffer words were included to render the nature of the research less obvious to subjects.

The following directions were given to the subjects:

> This is an experiment that has to do with words. I am trying to find out what other words come into a person's mind when he hears various words. I am going to say some words, and I want you to write down the first 10 words that come into your mind. For example, if I were to say "dog," the first 10 words that might come into a person's mind could be

TABLE 2
Das Score of High Death Anxiety Patients and Controls

	High death anxiety patients					Control patients			
Patients	Sex	Age	Diagnosis	DAS score	Patients	Sex	Age	Diagnosis	DAS score
1-A	M	24	P	12	1-B	M	21	P	6
2-A	M	21	S	14	2-B	M	24	S	12
3-A	M	25	S	6	3-B	M	21	S	3
4-A	M	62	P	11	4-B	M	60	P	9
5-A	M	66	MD-D	14	5-B	M	64	IPR	10
6-A	M	49	S	9	6-B	M	41	S	10
7-A	F	27	P	15	7-B	F	21	P	4
8-A	F	25	N	11	8-B	F	37	N	5
9-A	F	45	N	11	9-B	F	45	N	7
10-A	F	41	S	12	10-B	F	36	S	6
11-A	F	49	S	9	11-B	F	46	S	4
12-A	F	36	S	9	12-B	F	33	S	8
13-A	F	56	MD-D	15	13-B	F	55	MD-D	10
14-A	F	35	N	13	14-B	F	31	N	4
15-A	F	24	N	13	15-B	F	30	N	8
16-A	F	74	S	13	16-B	F	72	S	6
17-A	F	35	N	14	17-B	F	37	N	7
18-A	M	32	P	10	18-B	M	38	P	6
19-A	M	23	S	11	19-B	M	21	S	2
20-A	F	24	S	8	20-B	F	28	S	8
21-A	F	41	S	14	21-B	F	41	S	7

Note: S = Schizophrenia, P = Personality disorder, IPR = Involutional psychotic reaction, N = Neurosis, MD-D = Manic depressive-depressed type.

house, puppy, cat, food, bone, bite, mad, collie, beagle, and leash. [Pause.] The first word is "love.". . . [After the completion of each sequence, the next word was introduced by phrases as follows.] The next word is "hate." . . . The next word is "paper.". . . The next word is "life.". . . The next word is "death."

The pilot study utilizing this procedure was carried out with 40 students in an introductory psychology class at Western Kentucky University. These subjects were also administered the DAS. After preliminary examination of these data, it was noted that the subjects who obtained high DAS scores tended to give words that described emotions. A product-moment correlation coefficient of .41 ($p < .01$) between DAS score and number of words the investigator considered descriptive of emotions was obtained. To cross-validate this procedure, the word association task and the DAS were administered to 48 students in another undergraduate psychology class at Western Kentucky University. Ten judges, three clinical psychologists, and seven graduate students in clinical psychology were provided with a list of all associations given and with the directions to "Please check all words you consider directly descriptive of 'emotions' (e.g., fear, hate, lonely, sad)." The following 27 words were judged as describing emotions by six or more of the judges: *Anxiety, bereavement, cry, crying, dread, emptiness, fear, fears, feeling, grief, hate, heartbroken, hope, hurt, loneliness, lonely, love, misery, mourn, mourning, sad, sadness, sorrow, tears, unhappiness, unhappy, worry.*

The correlation coefficient between subjects' DAS scores and number of their words judged as describing emotions by six or more of the 10 judges was .31, which is significant at the .05 level.

Thus, a positive relationship between number of emotional words and DAS score has been established. It is plausible that the appearance of affective words is a sign of death anxiety. Rapaport (29) maintained that affective responses in a word association test represent an association disturbance. Also, research has demonstrated that sensitizers are prone to give more emotional responses to various types of projective materials than repressors (5, 24), and that the sensitization-repression dimension correlates very highly with anxiety (22). In the validity portion of the present research, only those words that were judged descriptive of emotions in the pilot study were counted.

The MMPI was employed for two reasons, the first of which is that the MMPI contains three well-known measures of anxiety, the Manifest Anxiety Scale (1, 39), the Welsh Anxiety Scale (40), and the Welsh Anxiety Index (41). If the DAS correlates as highly with each of these scales as they intercorrelate with each other, then it could be argued that the DAS measures anxiety in general rather than death anxiety in particular. The scale would then not have what Campbell (6) termed discriminant validity. On the other hand, modest positive correlations with scales of general anxiety were predicted, since such has been the case with other specific scales of anxiety: e.g., Sarason's Test Anxiety Scale (31).

Anxiety is a vague and multidimensional concept, and one operational definition of the term will not here be attempted. Instead, it may be stated that the DAS is being correlated with whatever each of the three scales employed measures. Each of the anxiety instruments, based upon a separate rationale, has supporting evidence for the validity of the scale. The Taylor Manifest Anxiety Scale was devised by judgmental means. The Welsh Anxiety Scale was based upon factor analysis of the MMPI. The Welsh Anxiety Index has a rational basis. It is computed by using MMPI clinical scale scores.

The second reason for the utiliztation of the MMPI was that it was considered worthwhile to determine the relationship of the DAS to personality variables, particularly as measured by the MMPI scales. A large percentage of the literature upon death anxiety concerns discusses, or at least mentions, personality variables. The only empirical studies that have related death anxiety to personality variables have used the MMPI and have reported conflicting results (2, 30, 38).

TABLE 3
CORRELATIONS OF DAS WITH OTHER VARIABLES FOR COLLEGE STUDENTS ($N = 76$)

Variable	Correlation with DAS
FODS ($N = 70$)	.74**
L	.05
F	.13
K	—.43**
Hs	—.04
D	.03
Hy	—.01
Pd	—.24*
Mf	—.14
Pa	—.09
Pt	.04
Sc	—.08
Ma	.12
Si	.25*
Welsh Anxiety Scale	.39**
Welsh Anxiety Index	.18
Manifest Anxiety Scale	.36**
Emotional words ($N = 77$)	.25*

* Significant at .05 level.
** Significant at .01 level.

(2). Results and discussion. Product-moment correlation coefficients between the DAS and the other variables for college students are presented in Table 3. Correlations with the FODS, number of emotional words, anxiety scales, and conventional MMPI scales will be discussed in that order.

A noteworthy finding is the high correlation coefficient of .74 between the DAS and FODS. Table 4 contains the correlations of the FODS with the other variables. It is apparent that these correlations parallel very closely those for the DAS. Although it was anticipated that the DAS would be more independent of the FODS in view of the different rationale and item content, the high relationship found provides mutual evidence for the validity of both scales.

TABLE 4
CORRELATION WITH FODS ($N = 69$)

Variable	Correlation with FODS
DAS ($N = 70$)	.74**
L	—.06
F	.10
K	—.33**
Hs	.11
D	.20
Hy	—.03
Pd	—.27*
Mf	—.09
Pa	—.06
Pt	.19
Sc	.01
Ma	.00
Si	.25*
Welsh Anxiety Scale	.36**
Welsh Anxiety Index	.25*
Manifest Anxiety Scale	.41**
Emotional words	.20

* Significant at .05 level.
** Significant at .01 level.

However, the uniqueness of the DAS as a measure of death anxiety has not been established. At the inception of the present research the FODS appeared to the author to have limitations. The content of the items was narrow, and the fact that only one procedure was employed to assess validity would seem inadequate for a study with a new scale in a relatively unexplored area, such as death anxiety. Nevertheless, the high correlation between the DAS and the FODS provides little basis for arguing the superiority of one instrument over the other, either in terms of construction and content, or in terms of established validity.

The correlation of .25 between the DAS and number of emotional word associations is significant at the .05 level. The fact that a projective technique which seems to tap death anxiety correlates significantly with the DAS is another indication that the DAS does measure death anxiety.

The coefficients of correlation of the DAS with the Manifest Anxiety Scale and the Welsh Anxiety Scale were .39 and .36, respectively. These values were significant at the .05 level. The DAS correlation coefficient with the Welsh Anxiety Index is not significant at the .05 level. It can be said that death anxiety correlates positively with general anxiety, although not as highly as the intercorrelations which are found among these scales of general anxiety. These correlations are presented in Table 5.

TABLE 5
INTERCORRELATIONS OF GENERAL SCALES OF ANXIETY

Variable	Welsh Anxiety Index	Manifest Anxiety Scale
Welsh Anxiety Scale	.69	.78
Welsh Anxiety Index		.60

The DAS correlated significantly with only three of the conventional MMPI scales. The rather low correlations with the MMPI variables do not support the impressions of a number of clinicians who maintain that death anxiety is associated with certain syndromes of psychopathology (3, 4, 19, 35). However, the results of the study do not necessarily contradict the viewpoints of these writers, since the population here studied was a presumably normal one that probably contains few individuals as abnormal as the patients referred to in the clinical literature.

In order to determine whether the low correlations obtained were a function of a relative absence of severe psychopathology in the college population utilized, it was decided to administer the DAS and the MMPI, with the DAS items embedded in the last 200 items of the MMPI, to patients from a definitely abnormal population. These were 32 patients in the admission wards of Western State Hospital who had a diagnosis of psychosis, neurosis, or personality disorder, and who were able to complete the questionnaires. Table 6 contains the correlations between the DAS and the MMPI variables for the psychiatric population.

With the exception of the positive correlations of the DAS with the scales of general anxiety, the correlations are quite different from those obtained with a normal population. With the psychiatric patients the DAS correlated

TABLE 6
CORRELATION WITH DAS FOR PSYCHIATRIC PATIENTS

MMPI Scale	Correlation with DAS
L	—.27
F	.41*
K	—.10
Hs	.17
D	.47**
Hy	.34
Pd	.35*
Mf	.31
Pa	.39*
Pt	.49**
Sc	.56**
Ma	.16
Si	.02
Welsh Anxiety Scale	.44*
Welsh Anxiety Index	.36*
Taylor Manifest Anxiety Scale	.48**

* Significant at .05 level.
** Significant at .01 level.

positively with a number of scales that purport to measure different types of psychopathology.

The highest correlations were .56 for Sc, .49 for Pt, and .47 for D. This is consistent with the clinical literature. It has been stated that schizophrenics, obsessive-compulsives, and depressed persons have a high level of death anxiety.

C. SUMMARY

The study involved the construction and validation of a Death Anxiety Scale (DAS). Thirty-one items were selected by a judgmental rating procedure from an initial pool of 40 items. Point biserial correlations were then computed, and the 15 items with significant item-total score correlations constituted the final DAS. Internal consistency and test-retest reliability were determined. The response sets of social desirability and agreement response tendency did not correlate significantly with DAS scores. The validity of the DAS was investigated by two separate procedures: (*a*) presumable high death anxiety psychiatric patients were found to have significantly higher DAS scores than control patients; (*b*) DAS scores correlated significantly with Boyar's FODS scale, another death anxiety questionnaire, and with a sequential word association task. DAS correlations with MMPI variables were obtained and discussed.

REFERENCES

1. BENDIG, A. W. The development of the short form of the Manifest Anxiety Scale. *J. Consult. Psychol., 1956,* 20, 384.

2. BOYAR, J. I. The construction and partial validation of a scale for the measurement of the fear of death. Unpublished Doctoral dissertation, University of Rochester, Rochester, New York, 1964.

3. BROMBERG, W., & SCHILDER, P. Death and dying. *Psychoanal. Rev.,* 1933, 20, 133-185.

4. ————. The attitude of psychoneurotics toward death. *Psychoanal. Rev.,* 1936, 23, 1-25.

5. BYRNE, D. Repression-sensitization as a dimension of personality. In B. A. Maher (Ed.), *Progress in Experimental Personality Research.* New York: Academic Press, 1964. Pp. 169-220.

6. CAMPBELL, D. T., & FISKE, D. W. Convergent and discriminant validation by the multitrait-multimethod matrix. *Psychol. Bull.,* 1959, 59, 81-105.

7. CAPRIO, F. S. A study of some psychological reactions during prepubescence to the idea of death. *Psychiat. Quart.,* 1950, 24, 495-505.

8. CHANDLER, A. R. Attitudes of superior groups toward retirement and old age. *J. Geront.,* 1950, 5, 254-261.

9. CHRIST, A. E. Attitudes toward death among a group of acute geriatric patients. *J. Geront.,* 1961, 16, 56-59.

10. COREY, L. G. An analogue of resistance to death awareness. *J. Geront.,* 1961, 16, 59-60.

11. COUCH, A., & KENISTON, K. Yeasayers and Neasayers: Agreeing response set as a personality variable. *J. Abn. & Soc. Psychol.,* 1960, 60, 151-174.

12. CRONBACH, L. J., & MEEHL, P. E. Construct validity in psychological tests. *Psychol. Bull.,* 1955, 52, 281-302.

13. CROWNE, D. P., & MARLOWE, D. A new scale of social desirability independent of psychopathology. *J. Consult. Psychol.,* 1960, 24, 349-354.

14. CUMMING, E., & HENRY, W. E. Growing Old: The Process of Disengagement. New York: Basic Books, 1961.

15. DICKSTEIN, L. S., & BLATT, S. J. Death concern, futurity, and anticipation. *J. Consult. Psychol.,* 1966, 30, 11-17.

16. DIGGORY, J. C., & ROTHMAN, D. Z. Values destroyed by death. *J. Abn. & Soc. Psychol.,* 1961, 63, 205-210.

17. FAUNCE, W. A., & FULTON, R. L. The sociology of death: A neglected area of research. *Soc. Forces,* 1958, 36, 205-209.

18. FEIFEL, H. Attitudes of mentally ill patients toward death. *J. Nerv. & Ment. Dis.,* 1955, 122, 375-380.

19. FREUD, S. Notes upon a case of obsessional neurosis. In *The Standard Edition of the Complete Psychological Works of Sigmund Freud (vol. 10).* London, England: Hogarth Press, 1909.

20. HACKETT, T. P., & WEISSMAN, A. D. Reactions to the imminence of death In G. H. Gross, H. Wechsler, & M. Greenblat (Ed.), *The Threat of Impending Disaster: Contribution to a Psychology of Stress.* Cambridge, Mass.: MIT Press, 1965.

21. JEFFERS, F. C., NICHOLS, C. R., & EISDORFER, C. Attitudes of older persons toward death. A preliminary review. *J. Geront.,* 1961, 16, 53-56.

22. JOY, V. L. Repression-sensitization and interpersonal behavior. Paper read at American Psychological Association, Philadelphia, Pennsylvania, August, 1963.

23. KALISH, R. A. Some variables in death attitudes. *J. Soc. Psychol.*, 1963, **59**, 137-145.

24. LEFCOURT, H. M. Repression-sensitization: A measure of the evaluation of emotional expression. *J. Consult. Psychol.*, 1966, **30**, 444-449.

25. MAUER, A. Adolescent attitudes toward death. *J. Genet. Psychol.*, 1964, **195**, 75-90.

26. McCULLY, R. S. Fantasy productions of children with a progressively crippling and fatal disease. *J. Genet. Psychol.*, 1963, **102**, 203-216.

27. MEANS, M. H. Fears of 1000 college students. *J. Abn. & Soc. Psychol.*, 1936, **31**, 291-311.

28. OSIPOW, S. H., & GROOMS, R. R. Norms for chain of word associations. *Psychol. Rep.*, 1965, **16**, 796.

29. RAPAPORT, D. Diagnostic Psychological Testing (vol. 2). Chicago, Ill.: Yearbook Publishers, 1946.

30. RHUDICK, P. J., & DIBNER, A. S. Age, personality, and health correlates of death concerns in normal aged individuals. *J. Geront.*, 1961, **16**, 44-49.

31. SARASON, S. B. Interrelationships among individual differences variables, behavior in psychotherapy and verbal conditioning. *J. Abn. & Soc. Psychol.*, 1948, **56**, 339-355.

32. SARNOFF, I., & CORWIN, S. E. Castration anxiety and the fear of death. *J. Personal.*, 1958, **27**, 375-385.

33. SCHILDER, P. The attitudes of murderers toward death. *J. Abn. & Soc. Psychol.*, 1936, **31**, 348-363.

34. SCOTT, C. A. Old age and death. *Amer. J. Psychol.*, 1896, **8**, 67-122.

35. SEARLES, H. F. Schizophrenia and the inevitability of death. *Psychiat. Quart.*, 1961, **36**, 631-665.

36. SHRUT, S. D. Attitudes toward old age and death. *Ment. Hyg.*, 1958, **42**, 259-266.

37. STACEY, C. L., & MARKIN, K. The attitude of college students and penitentiary inmates toward death and a future life. *Psychiat. Quart. Suppl.*, 1952, **26**, 27-32.

38. SWENSON, W. M. Attitudes toward death in an aged population. *J. Geront.*, 1961, **16**, 49-52.

39. TAYLOR, J. A. The relationship of anxiety to the conditioned eyelid response. *J. Exper. Psychol.*, 1951, **41**, 81-92.

40. WELSH, G. S. Factor dimensions A & R. In G. S. Welsh & E. G. Dahlstrom (Eds.), *Basic Readings in the MMPI in Psychology and Medicine*. Minneapolis, Minn.: Univ. Minnesota Press, 1956. Pp. 265-281.

41. WELSH, G. S. An anxiety index and an internalization ratio for the MMPI. In G. S. Welsh & W. D. Dahlstrom (Eds.), *Basic Readings in the MMPI in Psychology and Medicine*. Minneapolis, Minn.: Univ. Minnesota Press, 1956. Pp. 298-307.

THE CONFRONTATION WITH DEATH

E. de WIND

In considering the human reactions to the
atrocious experiences in the German concentration camps, and to other recent forms of man-
made disaster, we must take into account not
only the nature of the stress inflicted on the
victims but also the duration of the trauma they
had to endure. In the camps, those who were not
immediately sent to the gas-chamber—and
especially those few who survived throughout—
lived in constant confrontation with death over
a period of months or even years.

When we consider the fate of concentration
camp victims, we must keep clearly in mind that
we are dealing with a very heterogeneous group
of people, and that, in addition, it is unrealistic
to treat the camp itself as a unit. In Auschwitz
only a small minority of those who were put to
work had any possibility of holding out. Most
prisoners were made to do such heavy work on
so little food that they soon became exhausted
and were selected for the gas-chamber. But even
among those who, accidentally, were living under
relatively favourable conditions, there were
essential differences in their chances of survival.
These differences can be discerned only on very
close scrutiny, and perhaps only by one who
knows that world from personal experience.

Yet while recognizing how intricate was the world of the camp, there did exist a number of conditions to which all the prisoners were subject. Everybody suffered physical exhaustion and constant, continuous humiliation. The indefiniteness of the imprisonment, the end of which no one could foresee, was an extremely heavy stress for every one of the prisoners. Beyond all these, I consider being daily confronted with death as psychologically extremely traumatic. This confrontation was most striking in the extermination camps. While in camps like Buchenwald and Dachau many prisoners died each day, death was, so to say, a side effect. In Auschwitz, and above all in Treblinka, death was the very purpose of the almost perfect destructive apparatus devised by the persecutors.

In order to examine the psychological implications of the confrontation with death, let us take first the experience of a mountaineer suddenly confronted with death by a fall. His experience provides the most clearly defined example of a severe trauma, although it is one that usually lasts only a few seconds. The reactions have been described by Pfister in a paper, " Shock Thinking and Shock Phantasies in Extreme Danger of Death " (1930). In this paper he describes how, when mountaineers fall in the mountains, after the first few seconds of the fall their fear disappears and threads of all kinds of thoughts arise that show no logical connexion with the actual happening. Memories of youth may appear, having a certain analogy with the present danger but in which the person has been saved. This obviously is connected with comforting memories, with the illusion: "Just as I was saved then I shall be saved now."

One of Pfister's patients relates that during his fall he had a feeling of sitting in a dog-cart. He was saved by falling onto a thick layer of snow, and afterwards he could not understand what that dog-cart had meant. He asked his mother, and learned that as a 2-year-old child he had been dragged by a big dog for a distance of over a mile; everyone had been surprised that he had survived. Here we can clearly see the consolatory function of such threads of thought.

As with the mountaineers, we see that most

of the ex-prisoners can remember nothing of their very first days in the camp. The memory is lost. During that time, secondary-process thinking is switched off and the more sophisticated ego-functions, such as reality-testing, are suppressed, since to experience the whole reality at once would be overwhelming and would cause chaos. In the camp, too, enormous quantities of affect have to be controlled, yet one must remain capable of reacting more or less adequately.

Sometimes the process of regression goes too far. Then there remains only what might be called a rudimentary psycho-motoric ego. If this state prevails, the end will soon follow. The most necessary reactions, every kind of warning and adaptive activity, have been lost. I saw strong young men succumb in a few days to a state of total apathy. A Dutch doctor was accidentally kicked in the heel. He got a slight inflammation, put himself to bed, and after four days he died, without showing any clear symptoms of illness. This may be called a form of suicide. With others it took longer and physical exhaustion was manifested along with a state of mental apathy.

Whereas the trauma of the mountaineers was short, the prisoners, insofar as they survived the initial selection for the gas-chamber, had to cope with reality for an indefinite length of time. Then, often after a period of deepest regression, a progressive development took place—a re-organization of the personality, in which there occurred a re-cathexis of those fragments of the surrounding world that could be useful for survival. Such an adaptation can be compared to the way in which a young child discovers the external world in the first development of the reality principle. There too, there is as yet no experience of the world's totality and continuity. Only the here-and-now exists: yesterday and tomorrow are equal, and both are without reality.

If a prisoner eats his daily bread-ration all at once, although it would be wiser to divide it over twenty-four hours, he has, of course, a rational explanation for this. He says: " Next minute the bread may be stolen." One could also say that his hunger cannot be stilled. But a closer analysis shows us that these are only rationalizations. In his reality no " tomorrow " exists. Of course the prisoner knows that there is a " later-on ", that there exists another world on the other side of the barbed wire, but this does not interest him much. " Later on " and " the other world " are no longer cathected. To sum up, we can say that the prisoner lives to an extreme degree in his immediate place and time. The world is fragmented and primary process functioning plays an important role in his mode of thinking. The relation between actual happenings and the world outside the camp has become vague. But in this same way the end, the gas-chamber, could be a reality and yet be experienced as not having any relation to the here-and-now.

To cope with reality, the prisoner had to build up a system of defence mechanisms on the weakened and archaically functioning ego. There exists an extensive literature on this topic. In this context I only want to express my disagreement with Bettelheim's opinion about identification with the aggressor being the main type of defence. An active attitude like playing the role of an SS man oneself would sooner or later have aroused new aggression in the guard, and this might then mean the end of the prisoner. However, there were undoubtedly certain minor traits in the SS men which the prisoners imitated, consciously or unconsciously. These lent a sort of protective colouring to the prisoner. I am referring here to the imitation of passive attitudes rather than to an identification with the cruelty and ego-ideals of the SS man.

One instance of such imitation was by a doctor, who had to report the number of sick persons each morning to the SS inspector. He told me that from the very beginning he would click his heels sharply when making his report. Thanks to this, the SS man always seemed to be satisfied and no difficulties ever occurred. Also, those who could make their beds perfectly and who could react quickly to military commands did not draw attention to themselves, since they were behaving exactly according to the same rules of obedience as were demanded of the SS men.

As I said earlier, I believe the continuous confrontation with death to have been of the utmost importance in the complex of psychically traumatizing events. Although the prisoner lived always in the here-and-now, death was also always present. This was an actuality that could never be fully isolated or split off from the immediate awareness. An attitude towards death had therefore to be developed that made the thought of dying bearable. Psychologically seen, it is very doubtful whether anyone can imagine death as absolute nothingness. Indubitably, the prisoners in the camp could not do so. What did death mean to them? For some it meant the ultimate security, a return to the mother's womb. I once heard a remarkable instance of a patient who tried to commit suicide by jumping between blocks of ice in winter. When the analyst later asked what he had expected to find, the patient answered that it would have been so nice and warm there.

Another aspect of death is that of joining the Father. At the feet of the God of Vengeance, the prisoner will look down upon his former tormentors and see how they finally become the victims of revenge. Undoubtedly, analogies exist between the concentration camp prisoner's concept of death and that of old men or incurable patients, described by Eissler in *The Psychiatrist and the Dying Patient* (1955), and by Norton in " Treatment of a Dying Patient" (1963). There is an old people's home in the country in Holland that has the encouraging name of " Throughway ". The old people sit in front of their houses, quietly smoking their pipes, without bothering about their destination. This must be a state of mind similar to that of the prisoner who was allowed on Sunday to sit in the sun in front of his barrack for half an hour.

One of the ways in which the prisoners coped with the ever-present imminence of death was by treating it with macabre humour. Over the gate at Auschwitz stood the motto: " Arbeit macht frei ". The prisoners completed it: " Arbeit macht frei, Krematorium drei " (Labour makes free, crematorium three) On a drawing made by an Israeli artist, when he was in camp as an 11-year-old, you see a chimney smoking and in the smoke the picture of a man burning.

In the joke as well as in the drawing the latent content is the belief that although the body has been burned the soul is freed and lives on.

It is obvious that the prisoner whose mental apparatus has undergone these changes would show serious defects of adjustment on returning to normal society, and that a re-adaptation would have to take place. I cannot here deal with the complex of social and psychological factors upon which the success of this re-adaptation depended. I wish only to make some remarks about the specific difficulties and the possibilities of therapy.

Each time the prisoner managed to protect himself with the help of passive and masochistic attitudes, he undoubtedly experienced some narcissistic gratification. Personalities with a certain degree of flexibility in this direction did far better than those of more rigid character structure, who were unable to deal with their aggression. But on returning to normal society, the ex-prisoner was unable to rid himself of the fear caused by the image of his own death, with which he had been confronted. Too often, he was—or still is—inclined automatically to associate " future " and " death ". For this reason, he has restricted himself once again to a state of social isolation, to a here-and-now.

One of the most typical of the after-effects from which the ex-prisoner suffers is the tendency to react to difficulties in his life immediately with painful fantasies and anxiety dreams about the camp. The latent content of these might be: " I was able to manage the difficulties then; I can manage them as well now." These dreams, just as do the mountaineers' threads of thought, thus have a consolatory function comparable to that of examination dreams.

The avoidance of the image of his own death gives rise to a persistent syndrome in the ex-prisoner. The therapist who deprives the ex-prisoner of his defence mechanism leaves him alone with his weakened ego and subject to severe, free-floating anxiety. The situation in the treatment of such patients is comparable to that in the analysis of borderline schizophrenics: the therapist, on breaking down the " as-if " self, often has to offer himself as an auxiliary ego. A

98

comparable parameter technique turned out to be helpful in the analysis of severely traumatized ex-prisoners. But to these patients, the analyst could offer something else: namely, the patient's own self as it must have been before imprisonment, before what has been called " the break in the life-line ".

In the beginning of their analysis, ex-prisoners tend to minimize their camp experiences, attaching the emotions aroused by those experiences to the here-and-now or to the events and persons of their life before imprisonment. One patient always described his mother as a most demanding and cruel woman, ascribing to her the traits of an SS man. The analyst instructed him to find out from those who had known her what his mother had really been like. By constantly confronting the patient with the results of this inquiry, he was able to re-establish the original representation of the mother and thus to undo the retro-projection. Only after the patient's ego had been strengthened in this way, could the experiences of the camp be recollected, together with tremendous outbursts of aggression.

The ability to deal with aggression is of the utmost importance for the ex-prisoner. Suppressed aggression gives rise either to psychosomatic illness or to chronic depression; externalized aggression leads to what Hoppe calls " hate addiction ". Today, for many of the ex-prisoners, the most serious problem is that they so often direct their aggression onto their children. thus fulfilling the Biblical saying that the sins of the fathers shall be visited upon the children unto the third and fourth generation. Many of those who escaped the Nazi terror are now ageing people, too old to start analysis or ever to be totally free of the after-pains of their suffering. But by helping them to deal with their aggression, the therapist may be doing important preventive work in the interest of those to whom the future belongs.

In a paper entitled " Death and the Mid-Life Crisis ", Jaques (1965) argues that depression in middle-aged people is a normal phenomenon, occurring when they realize that they themselves will also have to die. Medical evaluators estimating the work-disability of former prisoners are often inclined to compare the late sequelae of persecution to such normal phenomena, or to describe them as "involutional depression". While the survivor-syndrome may sometimes be evoked or reinforced by the thought of ageing, the survivor, in contrast to other people, has never been without the image of death; he cannot rid himself of it and therefore can no longer face the future. He falls back upon the defence mechanisms described, because for him death has become too obtrusive a reality. This may explain the persistence of the late or lasting after-effects of the confrontation with death in the concentration camp.

REFERENCES

EISSLER, K. (1955). *The Psychiatrist and the Dying Patient*. (New York: Int. Univ. Press.)

JAQUES, E. (1965). "Death and the mid-life crisis." *Int. J. Psycho-Anal.*, **46.**

NORTON, J. (1963). "Treatment of a dying patient." *Psychoanal Study Child.*, **18.**

PFISTER, O. (1930). "Schockdenken und Schockphantasien bei höchster Todesgefahr." *Int. Z. Psychoanal.*, **16.**

USE OF THE
DEATH ANXIETY SCALE IN
AN INTER-RACIAL SETTING

R. E. Pandey, Ph.D. and
Donald I. Templer, Ph.D.

ABSTRACT—The purpose of this study was to assess possible differences between black and white college students on Templer's Death Anxiety Scale (DAS) and to determine whether the DAS adequately measures death anxiety in black populations. Ss were 258 undergraduates from Lincoln University, 124 whites (66 males; 58 females) and 134 blacks (72 males; 62 females). No mean differences between race and sex categories were found to be significant. Therefore, the assumption is supported that blacks and whites share similar attitudes toward death.

The purpose of the present study was to assess possible differences between black and white college students on the Death Anxiety Scale (DAS). Although one other project (Kalish and Reynolds, on-going research) has also compared death attitudes of blacks and whites, no study to our knowledge has been done with equivalent comparability of the two ethnic groups in terms of age, social class, and education.

DEVELOPMENT OF DEATH ANXIETY SCALE

The DAS (Templer, 1969, 1970, in press a) is a 15 item true-false instrument, the reliability and construct validity of which have been assessed by a variety of procedures (Templer, 1970). The original 40 items were devised upon a rational basis and were intended to reflect a wide range of life experiences. Twenty-five of the original items were eliminated by judgmental means and by an item analysis. The 15 remaining items that constitute the DAS were found to have adequate reliability, to be not significantly associated with response sets, and to have moderate correlations with scales of general anxiety. In support of the validity of the DAS, psychiatric patients who spontaneously verbalized death anxiety in counseling sessions were found to have higher scores than patients matched for age, sex, and diagnosis. Also, the DAS correlated rather highly with the Fear of Death Scale, the product of an unpublished doctoral dissertation of Boyar (1964). The correlations with the Minnesota Multiphasic Personality Inventory both with college students and with psychiatric patients were determined.

Subsequent research has demonstrated that females consistently have higher DAS scores than males (Templer, Ruff, and Franks, 1971). In that project, involving over 2,500 subjects from the teens through the eighties, there was no relationship between age and DAS score. The DAS scores of adolescents resembled those of their parents, with the correlations with the same-sexed parent being significantly higher for both the male and female adolescents. DAS score was found not to be significantly related to religious affiliation, belief, or intensity of devotion with college students (Templer and Dotson, 1970).

In a study with elderly persons (Templer, in press b), DAS was positively correlated with the Minnesota Multiphasic Personality Inventory Depression Scale, and with the psychiatric and total scores of the Cornell Medical Index. However, DAS was not significantly related to the somatic section of the Cornell Medical Index. Moreover, when the effect of psychiatric score was statistically removed, there was actually a significant negative correlation between DAS score and the Cornell Medical Index somatic section.

In a study relating the DAS to the Eysenck Personality Inventory and to smoking behavior (Templer, 1972), DAS score was found to be significantly correlated with Eysenck's Neuroticism Scale, but not with his Extraversion Scale. DAS scores of cigarette smokers, nonsmokers, and ex-smokers did not differ. However, within the cigarette smoker group, there was a significant negative correlation between DAS score and number of cigarettes smoked per day. DAS score significantly correlated with GSR to death-related words (Templer, in press c). Bryne's Repression Sensitization Scale was fairly highly correlated with the DAS, but independent of the GSR measure of death anxiety. The Repression Sensitization Scale was significantly related to discrepancy between the DAS and GSR, which were respectively conceptualized as verbalized and unverbalized measures of death anxiety.

In all of the above described research with the DAS, a negligible number of blacks were included. Therefore, it could not be certain (1) that the DAS adequately assesses death anxiety in black populations; and (2) that the generalizations about death anxiety derived from whites can be extended to blacks.

It seemed possible that some of the DAS items have a greater degree of application for persons from the white culture. It is conceivable that blacks could have different attitudes toward death because of the realities of their subculture, e.g., the shorter life expectancy and the greater probability of dying by violent means. Endless speculation based upon the stereotype-laden folklore of the Anglo-American culture is possible. It could be argued, for example, that the greater "superstition" supposedly present in blacks would favor their having greater anxiety in an area permeated with mystery and ignorance such as death. On the other hand, stereotype-based arguments could also point to opposite predictions, e.g., that blacks are "carefree," do not worry much about the future, and should, therefore, have less apprehension about death. It is obvious that speculation, especially that based upon racist folklore, is no substitute for research.

METHOD

Subjects were students from Lincoln University, Jefferson City, Missouri. This is a four-year integrated college where the enrollment is approximately half white and half black, totalling 2,500 students. The school offers master's degrees in a few subjects, such as education and counseling. White students generally come from Jefferson City or nearby communities, whereas most of the black population is from St. Louis and Kansas City. However, a sizable portion of the black students come from the various southern states. Because this state-supported school does not have any admission requirements beyond the high school diploma, most students score below

102

the 50th percentile of the SCAT which is administered to freshmen at the beginning of each semester.

Of the 258 undergraduates studied, 66 of the 124 whites were male and 58 were female. Of the 134 blacks, 72 were male and 62 were female. All subjects were administered the DAS. They were also asked to indicate the occupation of their fathers. This was in order to employ the Duncan Index (1961) to determine socio-economic status so that this variable could be controlled if it were significantly related to death anxiety. A total of 174 of the subjects listed a paternal occupation that was contained in the Duncan classification.

RESULTS

The 134 blacks obtained a DAS mean of 6.36 and a standard deviation of 3.28; the 124 whites obtained a mean of 6.16 and a standard deviation of 3.21 ($t=0.49$, ns). The 72 black males and 66 white males had DAS means of 6.31 and 5.91 respectively ($t=0.70$, ns). The 62 black and 58 white females obtained DAS means of 6.42 and 6.45, respectively ($t=0.05$, ns). The mean differences between the sexes were significant neither for the blacks ($t=0.20$) nor the whites ($t=0.93$). The product-moment correlation coefficient between DAS score and the Duncan Index was not significant ($r=0.01$).

DISCUSSION

The similarity of black and white DAS means and standard deviations suggests both that the DAS does adequately measure death anxiety in blacks and that the death anxiety of blacks and whites is not very different. Further support for this contention is the higher DAS mean for females both with the black and white subjects. This sex differential has been well documented in a number of studies with white subjects (Templer, Ruff, and Franks, 1971; Templer and Ruff, 1971). However, the difference between black male and female DAS means is less than has ever been obtained with whites.

The absence of any demonstrated racial differences in death anxiety can be viewed as another instance of the behavior and attitudes of blacks and whites being less disparate than stereotyped and ignorance-based assumptions would lead one to predict. Blacks were brought to the United States from widely scattered African tribes, and so their cultural beliefs and attitudes were not as unified as were those of immigrants of other ethnic groups. This lack of unification made black attitudes and values susceptible to assimilation of the concepts and values of the dominant white culture. Perhaps this is why blacks and whites today share a common core of attitudes toward death.

The present findings of black and white DAS similarity and of the near zero correlation of DAS with a measure of socio-economic status possibly have implications for death anxiety theory beyond those of racial differences. They suggest that subculture, in general, is not a variable that accounts for a great amount of death anxiety variance. This should not be completely unexpected when the diversity of personality, psychopathology, and child-rearing practices within any subculture of our society is considered. Closer attention in death anxiety research should probably be focused upon units smaller than that of a subculture. For example, Templer, Ruff, and Franks (1971) found fairly high DAS resemblances among family members, with the highest product-moment correlation coefficient of 0.59 being between husband and wife. It would appear that intimate interpersonal relationships are a greater determinant of degree of death anxiety than identification with one's subculture, at least, when such is based upon race in our society.

REFERENCES

Boyar, J. I. The construction and partial validation of a scale for the measurement of the fear of death. Ph.D. dissertation, University of Rochester, Rochester, New York, 1964.

Duncan, O. D. A Socio-economic Index for all occupations. In A. J. Reiss, (ed.), *Occupations and social status.* New York: Free Press of Glencoe, 1961.

Templer, D. I. Death Anxiety Scale. *Proceedings of the 77th annual convention of the American Psychological Association,* 1969, *4,* 737-738.

Templer, D. I. The construction and validation of a Death Anxiety Scale. *Journal of General Psychology,* 1970, *82,* 165-177.

Templer, D. I. Death anxiety: Extraversion, neuroticism, and cigarette smoking. *Omega,* 1972, *3,* 53-56.

Templer, D. I. Relatively non-technical description of the Death Anxiety Scale. *The Archives of the Foundation of Thanatology,* in press (a).

Templer, D. I. Death anxiety as related to depression and health of retired persons. *Journal of Gerontology,* in press (b).

Templer, D. I. The relationship between verbalized and non-verbalized death anxiety. *Journal of Genetic Psychology,* in press (c).

Templer, D. I., and Dotson, E. Religious correlates of death anxiety. *Psychological Reports,* 1970, *26,* 895-897.

Templer, D. I., and Ruff, C. F. Death Anxiety Scale means, standard deviations, and embedding. *Psychological Reports,* 1971, *29,* 173-174.

Templer, D. I., Ruff, C. F., and Franks, C. M. Death anxiety: age, sex and parental resemblance in diverse populations. *Developmental Psychology,* 1971, *4,* 108.

Relatively Non-Technical Description of the Death Anxiety Scale

Donald I. Templer, Ph.D.

The Death Anxiety Scale (DAS) has already been described in the psychological literature[4, 5] and is introduced herein to scholars of thanatology from diverse scientific and humanistic backgrounds.

The DAS was constructed to fill a need. Specifically, much of the research upon fear of death has been methodologically weak because of the absence of a measuring device with thoroughly determined reliability and validity.

In the initial phase of the research, 40 true-false items were devised upon a rational basis. It was the intention of the author that these items reflect a wide range of life experiences which could be permeated with death anxiety. Nine of these items were eliminated by the combined judgment of four psychiatric chaplains and three clinical psychologists. The 31 remaining items were subjected to a statistical analysis for the determination of internal consistency—that is, to assure that each retained item would be correlated highly enough with the total scale. Table 1 displays the 15 retained items that constitute the DAS.

Next, it was determined that the DAS does have adequate reliability. That is, there was reasonable stability in DAS scores of subjects who were administered the DAS a second time after a two week interval. Further research demonstrated that the DAS was not overly susceptible to any bias from subjects who are prone to give predominantly socially acceptable answers or have a decided preference for answering items either true or false.

The validity of the DAS was established by several procedures. First of all, 16 patients in a state mental hospital who had spontaneously verbalized fears of death to various professional persons were found to have higher DAS scores, to a statistically significant extent, than 16 control patients who were matched for age, sex and psychiatric diagnosis.

Additional validity assessment was carried out with college students. It was found that the DAS correlated substantially with the Fear of

Death Scale, a product of the unpublished doctoral dissertation of another psychologist.[1] The fact that this correlation was higher than the correlation of the DAS with scales of general anxiety permitted the inference that the DAS specifically measures death anxiety rather than only anxiety in general. Yet, the DAS does correlate significantly with three scales of general anxiety. There was also a significant correlation of the DAS with a number of word associations of emotional content to the word "death" on a word association test.

As part of the original construction and validation project, the correlations of the DAS with the Minnesota Multiphasic Personality Inventory (MMPI) were determined for both college students and psychiatric patients. For the college students, the correlations were fairly low, and this is probably attributable to the relative absence of psychopathology in the college student population. The significant correlations that were obtained suggest that the college student who is more prone to death anxiety is a sensitive and reflective individual who responds to frustration with anxiety rather than acting out his impulses. With the psychiatric patients, the DAS-MMPI correlations were considerably higher. The three highest correlations were with the Schizophrenia, Psychasthenia (obsessive-compulsive) and Depression Scales. This is consistent with the clinical literature that describes patients with these three corresponding syndromes as having high death anxiety.

Although the DAS is a recently developed instrument, a considerable amount of subsequent research with it has been carried out. In one study, the DAS correlated significantly with galvanic skin response (GSR) to death related words.[6] GSR is a decrease in electrical skin resistance caused by emotion or a novel stimulus. The DAS purports to measure the sort of death anxiety that one is aware of and willing to acknowledge, whereas GSR was assumed to be more likely to tap unverbalized or unconscious death anxiety. Consistent with this assumption is the fact that in this study the Repression-sensitization Scale[2] was unrelated to GSR but correlated highly and positively with the DAS. That is, the "sensitizer," who ruminates about death rather than denying its threat, is inclined to higher DAS scores than the "repressor."

Females consistently have higher DAS scores than males.[9] However, black and white college students do not differ significantly in DAS score.[3] Also, religious variables did not significantly relate to DAS score of college students.[8]

In a project involving over 2500 subjects from 19 to 85 years of age, there was no relationship between age and DAS score.[9] This was viewed as consistent with the results of another study in which degree of depression and psychiatric disturbance correlated positively with the DAS, but physical pathology did not.[7] The logical conclusion based upon both of these studies is that probability of or proximity to death is ordinarily not a crucial determination of death anxiety. Personality adjustment and presence or absence of a feeling of well-being are more important variables. It seems reasonable to assume that high death anxiety states can often be viewed in terms of a breakdown in the defense mechanisms that protect us from a total confrontation with that inevitable part of our existence that probably nobody can completely accept.

REFERENCES

1. Boyar, J. I.: The construction and partial validation of a scale for the measurement of the fear of death. Unpublished Doctoral dissertation, University of Rochester, Rochester, New York, 1964.

2. Byrne, D.: Repression—sensitization as a dimension of personality. In B. A. Maher (Ed.), *Progress in Experimental Personality Research.* New York, Academic Press, 1964, pp. 169-220.

3. Pandey, R. E. and Templer, D. I.: The death anxiety of negro and white college students. In preparation.

4. Templer, D. I.: Death Anxiety Scale. *Proceedings of the 77th Annual Convention of the American Psychological Association* 4: 737-738, 1969.

5. Templer, D. I.: The construction and validation of a Death Anxiety Scale. *Journal of General Psychology* 82: 165-177, 1970.

6. Templer, D. I.: The relationship between verbalized and non-verbalized Death anxiety. *Journal of Genetic Psychology* (in press).

7. Templer, D. I.: Death anxiety as related to depression and health of retired persons. In preparation.

8. Templer, D. I. and Dotson, E.: Religious correlates of death anxiety. *Psychological Reports* 26: 895-897, 1970.

9. Templer, D. I., Ruff, C. F. and Franks, C. M.: Death anxiety: age, sex and parental resemblance in diverse populations. *Developmental Psychology,* in press.

TABLE 1

THE 15 DAS ITEMS

Key	Content
T	I am very much afraid to die.
F	The thought of death seldom enters my mind.
F	It doesn't make me nervous when people talk about death.
T	I dread to think about having to have an operation.
F	I am not at all afraid to die.
F	I am not particularly afraid of getting cancer.
F	The thought of death never bothers me.
T	I am often distressed by the way time flies so very rapidly.
T	I fear dying a painful death.
T	The subject of life after death troubles me greatly.
T	I am really scared of having a heart attack.
T	I often think about how short life really is.
T	I shudder when I hear people talking about a World War III.
T	The sight of a dead body is horrifying to me.
F	I feel that the future holds nothing for me to fear.

DEATH ANXIETY IN RELIGIOUSLY VERY INVOLVED PERSONS

DONALD I. TEMPLER[1]

Summary.—Those religiously involved persons who have stronger religious convictions and attachment, attend religious functions more frequently, are certain of a life after death, and interpret the Bible literally have lower death anxiety.

In a previous study (Templer & Dotson, 1970), there were no significant relationships between eight religious variables and scores on the 15-item true-false Death Anxiety Scale (DAS) of Templer (1970). However, the authors cautioned against any absolute generalization about a lack of relationship between death, anxiety and religion. It was suggested that the absence of any significant relationship in that research could be attributed to Ss being college students for whom religion has little importance.

In the present research Ss were presumably very religiously involved. They had participated in one of two interdenominational, predominantly Protestant, evangelical retreats in the Midwest and the South in 1969. The DAS and the same religious inventory used in the earlier research were sent to all 390 participants of the retreats and 267 of them anonymously returned the questionnaires.

The mean DAS score was 3.40; the SD was 2.77. The Ms and SDs were 3.67 and 2.52 for the 106 males, and 4.21 and 2.91 for the 161 females ($t = 1.57$, ns). Table 1 presents the mean DAS score as a function of answer checked for each of the religious inventory questions. Table 1 also contains the F ratios for each of the eight religious inventory items. The analysis of variance is significant for five of these items.

It is apparent that the religiously involved persons, who are "more religious" in the traditional sense, have lower DAS scores. Those Ss who have a strong attachment to their religious belief system, attend religious functions more frequently, are certain of a life after death, believe the Bible should be interpreted literally, and judge the strength of their convictions to be strong compared to those of others apparently have lower death anxiety. Consistent with these findings is the fact that the DAS means, both for males and for females, were lower than in any research in which the DAS was employed (Templer & Ruff, 1971).

The present findings contrast with no significant relationship between the DAS and the same religious variables for an earlier sample of college students. They support the contention of Templer and Dotson that the absence of any relationship between the DAS score and religious variables with the 1970 study could be attributed to the lack of importance of religion in the lives of most college students. However, firm statements about casual relationships cannot be made. It is possible that it is the nature of traditional Christian beliefs that lead to a low level of death anxiety. Another possibility is Alexander and Adlerstein's (1958) contention that degree of certainty is more crucial than the content of one's belief. Perhaps, the staunch atheist would have lower death anxiety than a person who is uncertain about the existence of a supernatural. A third possibility is that the combination of a strong religious faith and low death anxiety is a function of personality characteristics, the nature of which remains to be determined.

---

[1]The author expresses his gratitude to Chaplain Earl Jabay of the New Jersey Neuro-Psychiatric Institute for his assistance in obtaining Ss.

TABLE 1
MEAN DAS SCORE AS A FUNCTION OF RELIGIOUS INVENTORY

Question	Answer Checked	N	M	F
1. What is your religious belief system?	Catholic	7	3.57	
	Jewish			
	Protestant	276	3.99	
	Non-believer	2	8.00	
	Other	11	3.82	1.47
2. How strong is your attachment to the belief system checked above?	Strong	105	3.73	
	Moderate	67	4.70	
	Weak	5	4.80	14.47†
3. How frequently do you attend an organized service or church group of some sort?	At least 1/wk.	228	3.86	
	At least 1/mo.	25	5.32	
	Several times/yr.	9	2.77	
	Rarely or never	4	6.00	3.45*
4. Are you presently of the same religious affiliation in which you were brought up as a child?	Yes	168	3.89	
	No	95	4.25	1.05
5. Do you believe in a life after death?	Yes	240	3.78	
	No	4	6.75	
	Uncertain	23	5.83	8.19†
6. Is the most important aspect of religion the fact that it offers the possibility of a life after death?	Yes	64	4.08	
	No	196	4.01	.03
7. Do you believe that the Bible should be interpreted literally?	Yes	93	3.20	
	No	158	4.48	13.11†
8. How is the strength of your religious conviction when compared to those of others?	Strong	218	3.71	
	About same	37	5.05	
	Weak	7	7.57	10.47†

$*p = .05, †p = .01.$

REFERENCES

ALEXANDER, I. E., & ADLERSTEIN, A. M. Affective responses to the concept of death in a population of children and early adolescents. *Journal of Genetic Psychology,* 1958, 13, 167-177.

TEMPLER, D. I. The construction and validation of a Death Anxiety Scale. *Journal of General Psychology,* 1970, 82, 165-177.

TEMPLER, D. I., & DOTSON, E. Religious correlates of death anxiety. *Psychological Reports,* 1970, 26, 895-897.

TEMPLER, D. I., & RUFF, C. F. Death Anxiety Scale means, standard deviations, and embedding. *Psychological Reports,* 1971, 29, 173-174.

RELIGIOUS CORRELATES OF DEATH ANXIETY

DONALD I. TEMPLER   AND   ELSIE DOTSON

Summary.—No significant relationships between Death Anxiety Scale score of 213 college students and several variables of religious affiliation, belief, and activity were obtained. The apparent absence of any such relationship was explained in terms of religion having a quite limited effect upon the attitudes and behavior of most college students in our society.

The purpose of this research was to determine the relationship between death anxiety and religious affiliation, belief, and activity. The results of previously reported studies are quite conflicting (Martin & Wrightsman, 1964). Some researchers have found a positive relationship between death anxiety and intensity of religious devotion (Feifel, 1959; Faunce & Fulton, 1958; Stouffer, 1949), and some have reported a negative relationship (Jeffers, Nichols & Eisdorfer, 1961; Alexander & Adlerstein, 1958; Swenson, 1961).

A likely explanation for this ambiguity in the literature is lack of an adequate method for measuring fear of death. In no study previously reported has the reliability or validity of the instrument for assessing death anxiety been determined. In the present study, the 15-item Death Anxiety Scale (DAS) was employed. The reliability and validity of this scale were determined by a diversity of procedures (Templer, 1969, 1970).

METHOD

*S*s were 213 students in junior and senior level psychology classes at Western Kentucky University. They completed the DAS along with the questions in Table 1. The instructions on the religious inventory were "Please put a check mark in the blank beside the statement which is most descriptive of you."

Although most of the questions about religious beliefs center around content, Items 2, 5, and 8 were designed to tap firmness of belief as well. Alexander and Adlerstein (1958) argued that degree of certainty rather than the nature of one's conviction is a more crucial variable with respect to death anxiety. They maintained that the person who has a strong religious faith and the person who denies the existence of a hereafter should experience less concern about death than the person who is very uncertain.

RESULTS

The 213 *S*s obtained a mean of 6.37 DAS items in the death anxiety direction. The standard deviation was 3.10. Table 1 presents the mean DAS scores as a function of answer checked for each of the religious inventory questions. The analyses of variance were not significant for any of the items. Also, the mean DAS score for the 109 females of 6.66 was not significantly greater than the mean of 6.07 obtained by the 104 males.

111

TABLE 1

MEAN DAS SCORE AS A FUNCTION OF RELIGIOUS INVENTORY

Question	Answer Checked	N	M	F
1. What is your religious belief system?	Catholic	22	5.73	
	Jewish	1	10.00	
	Protestant	180	6.25	
	Non-believer	2	7.00	
	Other	8	9.88	1.70
2. How strong is your attachment to the belief system checked above?	Strong	84	6.24	
	Moderate	110	6.41	
	Weak	19	6.53	.15
3. How frequently do you attend an organized service or church group of some sort?	At least once a week	104	6.38	
	At least once a month	47	6.28	
	Several times a year	37	6.46	
	Rarely or never	25	6.36	.02
4. Are you presently of the same religious affiliation in which you were brought up as a child?	Yes	175	6.49	
	No	38	5.76	1.51
5. Do you believe in a life after death?	Yes	166	6.25	
	No	6	5.67	
	Uncertain	41	7.05	1.46
6. Is the most important aspect of religion the fact that it offers the possibility of a life after death?	Yes	98	6.61	
	No	113	6.15	1.17
7. Do you believe that the Bible should be interpreted literally?	Yes	81	6.81	
	No	128	6.12	2.55
8. How is the strength of your religious conviction when compared to those of others?	Strong	74	6.29	
	About the same	114	6.39	
	Weak	21	6.00	.15

The absence of any significant relationship between DAS score and religious variables is inconsistent with the impressions of many persons in the mental health and religious professions. "Common sense" suggests that one's religious beliefs are among the most important determinants of the meaning and feeling that one attaches toward death. It seems surprising that, on the average, persons who differ with respect to such things as belief in an afterlife, fundamentalism, strength of conviction, and participation in church activities, have about the same level of death anxiety.

Since only one Jew and two non-believers were included, this research did not have sufficient power to permit generalizations about the death anxiety in these two groups. However, Catholics and Protestants apparently differ little in mean DAS score. This also could be considered surprising in view of the greater emphasis upon the rewards and punishment in an afterlife of Catholicism than contemporary Protestantism.

There appear to be two explanations for the lack of relationship between death anxiety and religious variables. One is a "balancing" interpretation that would argue, for example, that the non-believer, who does not have a hell to fear, also does not have a heaven to anticipate, so that his over-all level of death anxiety is the same as the believer. A weakness in this argument is that it would be unlikely that the opposing factors would exert approximately equal force in all of the eight religious inventory items for which no significant differences were found.

A more parsimonious explanation would be that religion is not an important determinant of death anxiety level, at least in most relatively normal populations. Religious and philosophical values do not form the cornerstone of life for most people in our society. Rather, it is one facet of life which tends to be compartmentalized from other aspects of living. Religious belief does not have a tremendous impact upon the sex life, social life, work, or recreation of the average person, and it probably in like manner does not have a tremendous impact upon feelings concerning death.

This is not to deny that in isolated instances a specific religious belief system can interact with dimensions of personality and psychopathology to affect the degree or nature of death anxiety. Variables of personality and psychopathology have been found to correlate fairly highly with DAS score in a psychiatric population (Templer, 1969, 1970). These correlations are consistent with impressions reported in the clinical literature of patients with certain psychiatric abnormalities, notably depressives, obsessive-compulsives and schizophrenics having high death anxiety. And both clergymen and mental health personnel are familiar with cases of death anxiety permeated with mental content of a specific religion, e.g., the obsessive-compulsive Catholic who ruminates about the punishment for his sins in hell or purgatory.

Nevertheless, the conclusion based upon the findings here presented is that, at least for many college students in our society, religious variables do not appear to be highly related to death anxiety.

REFERENCES

ALEXANDER, I. E., & ADLERSTEIN, A. M. Affective responses to the concept of death in a population of children and early adolescents. *Journal of Genetic Psychology*, 1958, 13, 167-177.

FAUNCE, W. A., & FULTON, R. L. The sociology of death: a neglected area of research. *Social Forces*, 1958, 36, 205-209.

FEIFEL, H. *The meaning of death.* New York: McGraw-Hill, 1959.

JEFFERS, F. C., NICHOLS, C. R., & EISDORFER, C. Attitudes of older persons toward death: a preliminary review. *Journal of Gerontology*, 1961, 16, 53-56.

MARTIN, D., & WRIGHTSMAN, L. S. Religion and fears about death: a critical review of research. *Religious Education*, 1964, 59, 174-176.

STOUFFER, S. A. *The American soldier: combat and its aftermath.* Princeton: Princeton Univer. Press, 1949.

SWENSON, W. M. Attitudes toward death in an aged population. *Journal of Gerontology*, 1961, 49-52.

TEMPLER, D. I. Death anxiety scale. *Proceedings of the 77th Annual Convention of the American Psychological Association*, 1969, 4, 737-738.

TEMPLER, D. I. The construction and validation of a Death Anxiety Scale. *Journal of General Psychology*, 1970, 82, 165-177.

Death Anxiety as Related to Depression and Health of Retired Persons

Donald I. Templer, PhD

THE purposes of this research were to determine (a) the correlation between depression and death anxiety in a population of elderly and late middle-aged individuals, and (b) the relationship between death anxiety and health in this population.

The Death Anxiety Scale (DAS) has been found to correlate significantly with both general and specific measures of maladjustment in different populations (Templer, 1969, 1970, 1971). The present study focused upon its relationship to depression, as measured by the Depression (D) Scale of the Minnesota Multiphasic Personality Inventory (MMPI), because depression is a condition that is especially prevalent in middle-aged and elderly persons. A substantial amount of literature demonstrates that depression increases with age (Aaronson, 1958; Calden & Hokanson, 1959; Canter & Day, 1962; Grinker, Miller, Sabshin, Nunn, & Nunnally, 1961; Hardyck, 1964; Kornetsky, 1963; Swenson, 1961). In previous research, the product moment correlation coefficient between the DAS and the MMPI-D Scale was statis-

The author wishes to express his gratitude to his father, Irvin L. Templer, for his assistance in obtaining Ss.

tically significant ($r=.47$) with psychiatric patients; the correlation with college undergraduates was a non-significant .03 (Templer, 1969, 1970).

The determination of the relationship between death anxiety and health was considered important because of the increase in health problems that tend to develop with advancing age. Predictions about the relationship between health and death anxiety were not made because of insufficient theoretical or empirical bases for such at the current stage of death anxiety research.

METHOD

The instrument employed for the global health assessment was the Cornell Medical Index (CMI), a 195-item symptom and history checklist that is divided into two general sections, somatic and psychiatric. Scoring consists of simply counting the total number of items checked (Brodman, Erdmann, Lorge, & Wolff, 1949; Brodman, Erdmann, & Wolff, 1956). Fear of death was assessed by the Death Anxiety Scale, the reliability and validity of which have been determined by a diversity of procedures (Templer, 1969, 1970).

The DAS, the D Scale, and the CMI were sent to 250 persons whose names were randomly obtained from a list of retired employees of the Western Union Telegraph Company; 75 persons anonymously completed and returned these questionnaires. The Ss ranged in age from 51 to 92 years, with 66 of the 75 Ss being from 60 to 79 years. The mean age was 69.7; the standard deviation 6.89; 46 Ss were male and 29 were female. The median and mode years of education were both 12. The differences between the 75 respondents and the 175 people who did not respond are a matter of conjecture. However, it is plausible that the latter group contained a greater proportion of individuals who were physically or mentally debilitated.

RESULTS

Table 1 presents the means and standard

deviations for the three instruments employed. The product-moment correlation coefficient between DAS score and the D Scale is .28 ($p < 0.01$). The correlations between DAS and CMI somatic, psychiatric, and total scores are .18 (ns), .54 ($p < 0.01$), and .34 ($p < 0.01$), respectively.

Table 1. Means and Standard Deviations of Death Anxiety Scale, MMPI Depression Scale, and Cornell Medical Index Scores.

	Mean	SD
Death Anxiety Scale score	4.25	3.32
MMPI Depression Scale score	20.16	6.29
Cornell Medical Index-somatic score	14.00	9.57
Cornell Medical Index-psychiatric score	3.93	5.58
Cornell Medical Index-total score	17.93	13.69

DISCUSSION

The positive correlation between death anxiety and depression was as predicted. An examination of the scatter plot reveals that all 8 Ss who had a D score of 28 or above had a DAS score above the mean, and 5 of these Ss had a DAS score over a standard deviation above the mean. It is tentatively suggested that high death anxiety is commonly part of a depressive syndrome in elderly persons. However, the prediction of depression on the basis of high death anxiety is possibly a less dependable inference than the inverse relationship. It appears reasonable that, at least in some cases, the high death anxiety of elderly persons may be viewed as primarily a concomitant of depression. In such instances, the death anxiety may be alleviated when the depression is treated symptomatically by such proved modalities as electroshock therapy and antidepressant drugs. In other cases, high death anxiety may be more effectively treated by direct removal through behavior therapy techniques, such as desensitization as suggested by Templer, Ruff, and Franks (1971).

The significant correlations between the DAS and the psychiatric and total scores of the CMI were expected, since previous research has demonstrated that both the DAS and the CMI correlate substantially with indicators of

116

general anxiety or maladjustment (Brown & Fry, 1962; Desroches, Kaiman, & Ballard, 1967; Desroches & Larsen, 1963; Matarazzo, Matarazzo, & Saslow, 1961; Templer, 1969). In the present research, the correlation coefficient between the somatic and psychiatric sections of the CMI is .62. However, the correlation coefficient between the DAS and the somatic section, when the influence of the CMI psychiatric score upon these measures was statistically removed, is $-.23$ ($p < 0.05$). This suggests a negative relationship between actual degree of somatic pathology and death anxiety level when psychiatric disturbance is taken into account.

The absence of any demonstrated positive relationship between death anxiety and somatic pathology could be viewed as consistent with the findings of Templer et al. (1971), who reported no relationship between age and DAS score in a project involving over 2500 Ss from 19 to 85 years of age from several different populations. Apparently, decline of somatic integrity is ordinarily not a crucial determinant of death anxiety level. This is congruent with the clinical literature that states or implies that the mechanisms of repression and denial are extensively used by most people in their coping with death anxiety (Templer, 1971). It is concluded that death anxiety is usually related more to degree of personality adjustment and subjective state of well-being than to reality-based factors; and it seems reasonable that high death anxiety states can often be understood in terms of a breakdown of defense mechanisms. Most attempts to treat high death anxiety in older people should probably involve the shoring up of existing defense mechanisms rather than depth exploration of psychodynamics.

REFERENCES

Aaronson, B. S. Age and sex influences on MMPI profile peak distributions in an abnormal population. *Journal of Consulting Psychology*, 1958, **22**, 203-206.

Brodman, K., Erdmann, A. J., Jr., Lorge, I., & Wolff, H. G. The Cornell Medical Index: an adjunct to medical interview. *Journal of the American Medical Association*, 1949, **140**, 530-534.

Brodman, K., Erdmann, A. J., Jr., & Wolff, H. G. *Manual for the Cornell Medical Index Health Questionnaire.* New York: Cornell University Medical College, 1956.

Brown, A. C., & Fry, J. The Cornell Medical Index Health Questionnaire in the identification of neurotic patients in general practice. *Journal of Psychosomatic Research,* 1962, **6,** 185-190.

Calden, G., & Hokanson, J. E. The influence of age on MMPI responses. *Journal of Clinical Psychology,* 1959, **15,** 194-195.

Canter, A., & Day, C. W. The influence of age and health status on MMPI scores of a normal population, *Journal of Clinical Psychology,* 1962, **18,** 71-73.

Desrochès, H. F., Kaiman, B. D., & Ballard, T. Factors influencing reporting of physical symptoms by the aged patient. *Geriatrics,* 1967, **22,** 169-175.

Desroches, H. F., & Larsen, F. R. The Cornell Medical Index as a screening device in a VA population. *Journal of Clinical Psychology,* 1963, **19,** 416-420.

Grinker, R. R., Miller, J., Sabshin, M., Nunn, R., & Nunnally, J. *The phenomena of depressions.* New York: Harper & Brothers 1961.

Hardyck, C. D. Sex differences in personality changes with age. *Journal of Gerontology,* 1964, **19,** 78-82.

Kornetsky, C. H. Minnesota Multiphasic Personality Inventory: Results obtained from a population of aged men. In J. E. Birren, R. N. Butler, S. W. Greenhouse, L. Sokoloff, & Merian R. Yarrow (Eds.), *Human aging: A biological and behavioral study.* Bethesda, Md: US Dept. of Health, Education, & Welfare, NIMH, 1963.

Metarazzo, R. G., Matarazzo, J. D., & Saslow, G. The relationship between medical and psychiatric symptoms. *Journal of Abnormal and Social Psychology,* 1961, **62,** 55-61.

Swenson, W. M. Structured personality testing in the aged: An MMPI study of the gerontic populations. *Journal of Clinical Psychology,* 1961, **17,** 302-304.

Templer, D. I. Death Anxiety Scale. *Proceedings of the 77th Annual Convention of the American Psychological Association,* 1969, **4,** 737-738.

Templer, D. I. The construction and validation of a Death Anxiety Scale. *Journal of General Psychology,* 1970, **82,** 165-177.

Templer, D. I. The relationship between verbalized and nonverbalized death anxiety. *Journal of Genetic Psychology,* 1971. (in press)

Templer, D. I., Ruff, Carol F., & Franks, C. M. Death anxiety: Age, sex, and parental resemblance in diverse populations. *Developmental Psychology,* 1971, **4,** 108.

118

THE RELATIONSHIP BETWEEN SUBJECTIVE LIFE EXPECTANCY, DEATH ANXIETY AND GENERAL ANXIETY

PAUL J. HANDAL

PROBLEM

Although research in the area of death anxiety is relatively limited, a number of studies have investigated the relationship between attitudes toward death, personality organization, and various demographic variables. However, the results of these studies have generated contradictory hypotheses and yielded inconclusive findings.

For example, Katsenbaum[7] investigated attitudes toward death in male and female adolescents. Although 15% of his Ss expressed concern about death, Katsenbaum concluded that most adolescents live in the present, reject death, and disconnect it from the rest of their lives. Similarly, Middleton[8] investigated death concern and, although his results showed that 13% of his Ss had a strong fear of death, it was concluded that college students were unconcerned about death.

Findings contrary to these were reported by Alexander, Colby and Alderstein[1] who reported that death was an affect-laden concept for college students equal to concern about sex and school. Similar findings were presented by Dickstein and Blatt[3] who reported that death concern is related to a foreshortened time perspective.

One difficulty in attempting to relate these contradictory findings is that these studies utilize diverse methods of measurement which may assess different components of attitudes toward death as well as different levels of awareness. In addition, Lester[5], in a recent review of the literature, voiced the criticism that the scales used as measures for death anxiety frequently fail to report validity information for the scale employed.

The present study primarily investigated some psychological correlates of death anxiety, thereby contributing to the determination of the construct validity of the death anxiety scale used. The study focused upon the relationship between death anxiety and the Ss' expressed expectations of their own life spans, that is Subjective Life Expectancy (SLE), which is viewed as a highly critical indicator of a complex attitude toward an emotionally charged topic[4] and not as a composite based upon demographic variables.[10]

METHOD

The Ss were 66 male and 50 female graduate students at a northeastern university. The males had an age range of 20 to 64, mean age 29.0 years, SD 9.15; for females, the age range was 22 to 49, mean age 33.4 years, SD 8.28.

A questionnaire was administered to the Ss requesting information about their projected life span, their estimate of the life expectancy for their own sex, and that of the opposite sex, age, occurrence of one or more deaths of family members (mother, father, spouse, or siblings), or in close friends, frequency with which death had been discussed in the family, and frequency of church attendance. In order to determine unrealistically high and low subjective life expectancy groups, all subjective life expectancy estimates were ranked from highest to lowest (independently for each sex), and the highest and lowest 20% comprised the unrealistically high and unrealistically low subjective life expectancy groups, respectively.

_____
This study was supported by PHS grant #MH-10486-02.

---

¹All projected life expectancies were required in the form of specific ages, not age ranges.

Thereafter, the same Ss also completed the Zuckerman [12] Affective Adjective Check List of Anxiety (short form) with the instructions reading, "Check the words which describe how you feel *now—today*." The final scale administered was a modified version of the Livingston and Zimet [6] Death Anxiety Scale. In its original construction, Couch and Keniston's [2] Response Set (tendency to agree or disagree) was controlled for an equal number of formally and colloquially toned statements dealing with reactions to, and attitudes toward, situations concerned with death were presented. However, the original scale had been designed for use with medical students and, as such, could not be administered to the general population due to the inappropriateness of several items. Tolor [9] revised this scale for administration to a less specific population. The revised form consists of 20 items in the form of statements to which there are six possible responses ranging from "strongly agree" to "strongly disagree".

Some examples of the questions are: (1) When I see a funeral procession, I never particularly wonder who the dead person is. (2) We are kidding ourselves if we think cancer is not a hopeless disease. (3) Death hardly concerns me. (4) Dying people don't make me uneasy. Responses are scored on a six-point scale yielding a minimum score of 20 and a maximum score of 120. Test-retest reliability with a three month interval was found to be .85.

Results and Discussion

Male Ss report their projected life span to be 72.86, SD 9.01 years; for female Ss, it is 72.12, SD 13.89 years. The difference between the sexes is not significant.

Based on U. S. Bureau of the Census [11] data, the life expectancy for a Caucasian male child born in 1962 is 67.6 years; for a white female child born in the same year it is 74.4 years. For males, the mean subjective life expectancy exceeds the actuarial data to a significant degree ($p < .01$), whereas there is no significant difference for females between their mean subjective life expectancy and the actuarial data.

The mean death anxiety score (DA) for male Ss is 66.14, SD 10.87; for female Ss it is 66.94, SD 10.11, indicating that there is no significant difference between the sexes.

Female Ss were classified as unrealistically high SLE, realistic SLE, or unrealistically low SLE on the basis of their SLE estimates and an analysis of variance was computed on the death anxiety scores. The results yielded an F of 5.31 (df 2/49, $p < .01$). Application of Duncan's Multiple Range Test indicated that: (1) Those Ss who have an unrealistically low subjective life expectancy obtain significantly ($F = 4.10$, df 40, $p < .01$) higher death anxiety scores (75.30) than Ss who have an unrealistically high subjective life expectancy (62.25). (2) Those Ss who have unrealistically low subjective life expectancies obtain a significantly (4.10, df 16, $p < .05$) higher death anxiety score than Ss whose subjective life expectancy is realistic (65.34). (3) When Ss whose subjective life expectancies are unrealistically high or low are combined and compared, by means of a t test, with Ss whose subjective life expectancy is realistic, there is no significant difference between their mean death anxiety scores. (4) Those Ss whose subjective life expectancies are unrealistically high obtain a lower death anxiety score (62.25) when compared with Ss whose subjective life expectancy is realistic (65.34). Although this difference is not significant, its direction is in conformity with the hypothesis.

Table 1 presents a Pearson product moment correlation of $-.37$ ($p < .01$) between subjective life expectancy and death anxiety for female Ss. After general anxiety is partialed out, the resulting partial correlation between death anxiety and subjective life expectancy is $-.32$ ($p < .05$). The same analyses were computed for male Ss, but no significant differences were found.

Table 1 presents the intercorrelations for male and female Ss on four dimensions. For females, a significant negative correlation is shown between subjective life expectancy and death anxiety on the one hand, while the correlation between

TABLE 1. INTERCORRELATIONS BETWEEN SUBJECTIVE LIFE EXPECTANCY (SLE), GENERAL ANXIETY (GA), DEATH ANXIETY SCALE (DAS), AND AGE FOR MALES AND FEMALES

	Age	SLE	GA
Males (DF = 64)			
SLE	−.11		
GA	.25*	−.17	
DAS	.16	−.02	.33**
df = 64			
Females (df = 48)			
SLE	−.10		
GA	−.11	−.26	
DAS	.19	−.37**	.33*
df = 48			

*$p < .05$; **$p < .01$.

subjective life expectancy and general anxiety approaches significance. Note that neither relationship is found among males. However, both male and female Ss show a significant positive correlation between general anxiety and death anxiety. It should be noted that the only significant correlation found for age was that between age and general anxiety for males only.

In considering the results for female Ss, it appears that a significant negative relationship exists between SLE and death anxiety.

However, when considering the results obtained with male Ss, several factors should be considered to explain the lack of relationship between SLE and death anxiety. It appears that SLE has different meanings for men and women. For women, SLE appears to be a critical indicator of attitudes toward death, whereas for men, it appears to be a manifestation of a defensive attitude toward death. This is based upon the fact that women, as a whole, estimate their SLE more realistically, whereas men, as a group, constantly overestimate their SLE to a significant degree in relation to the actuarial data. In addition, when men estimate the life expectancy of the male sex, rather than their own life span, their estimate does not differ significantly from the actuarial data (Mean estimate = 68.00, SD 8.04; actuarial data = 67.6 years). It should be noted that females can also accurately estimate the life span for their own sex. (Mean estimate = 70.67, SD 12.98; actuarial data = 74.4 years). Finally, the correlations shown in Table 1 raise additional doubt concerning the wisdom of regarding SLE as having equal import for men and women, since SLE is the only variable with which death anxiety is not similarly correlated for men and women.

Information relevant to the validity of the Death Anxiety Scale employed in the present study is presented by the correlations between general anxiety and death anxiety for both men and women. In both cases, the correlations are low although significant ($p < .05$). Thus the two measures seem to have only relatively little common variance and seem to tap different aspects of anxiety.

SUMMARY

This study investigated the relationship between subjective life expectancy (SLE), death anxiety, and general anxiety. A significant negative relationship was found between SLE and death anxiety for female but not for male Ss. Discussion centered upon the possibility that SLE does not have equal import for both men and women and evidence was reported which indicated that male Ss are relatively more defensive about death than are female Ss.

121

References

1. ALEXANDER, I., COLBY, R., and ALDERSTEIN, A. Is death a matter of indifference? *J. Psychol.*, 1957, *43*, 277-283.
2. COUCH, A. and KENISTON, K. Yeasayers and naysayers: Agreement response set as a personality variable. *J. abn. soc. Psychol.*, 1960, *60*, 151-174.
3. DICKSTEIN, L. S. and BLATT, S. J. Death concern, futurity and anticipation. *J. consult. Psychol.*, 1966, *30*, 11-17.
4. FARBEROW, N. L. (Ed.) *Taboo Topics.* New York: Atherton Press, 1963.
5. LESTER, D. Experimental and correlational studies of the fear of death. *Psychol. Bull.*, 1967, *67*, 27-36.
6. LIVINGSTON, P. B. and ZIMET, C. N. Death anxiety, authoritarianism and choice of specialty in medical students. *J. nerv. ment. Dis.*, 1965, *140*, 222-230.
7. KATSENBAUM, R. Time and death in adolescence. In H. Feifel (Ed.). *The Meaning of Death.* New York: McGraw-Hill, 1959.
8. MIDDLETON, W. Some reactions toward death among college students. *J. abn. soc. Psychol.*, 1936, *31*, 165-173.
9. TOLOR, A. Unpublished Data, 1966.
10. TOLOR, A. and MURPHY, V. M. Some psychological correlates of subjective life expectancy. *J. clin. Psychol.*, 1967, *23*, 21-24.
11. U. S. BUREAU OF THE CENSUS. *Statistical Abstracts of the United States.* (85th Ed.) Washington: U. S. Bureau of the Census, 1964.
12. ZUCKERMAN, M. The development of an affective adjective check list for the measurement of anxiety. *J. consult. Psychol.*, 1960, *24*, 457-462.

RELATION BETWEEN INSIGHT, REPRESSION-SENSITIZATION, INTERNAL-EXTERNAL CONTROL, AND DEATH ANXIETY

ALEXANDER TOLOR   AND   MARVIN REZNIKOFF

In a sample of 79 male college students, 3 of 4 hypotheses specifying the relationships between repression-sensitization, an expectancy of internal or external control of reinforcement, insight, and overt death anxiety were confirmed. The measures employed were the Byrne Repression-Sensitization scale, Rotter's I-E scale, the Tolor-Reznikoff Insight Test, and a Death Anxiety scale. It was found that: (a) the expectation of internal control of reinforcement is significantly and positively related to insight; (b) Ss with sensitization tendencies have significantly greater overt death anxiety than Ss with repressing defenses; and (c) Ss with external expectancies have significantly greater overt death anxiety than Ss with internal expectancies. There was no support for the prediction that sensitizers would be more insightful than repressors.

This study explored interrelationships among four scales tapping various elements in an individual's defense system. These measures are the Byrne (1961) Repression-Sensitization (R-S) scale; the Rotter (1966) scale measuring generalized expectancies for internal or external control; the Tolor-Reznikoff (1960) Test of Insight; and a Death Anxiety scale based on the work of Livingston and Zimet (1965).

In their conceptualization of insight as an important personality variable, Tolor and Reznikoff (1960) focused on individual differences in the ability to comprehend causative factors underlying or determining feelings, attitudes, and behaviors. Insight was regarded as lending itself to measurement on a continuum and also as involving an understanding of others and of the self. Within this definition, the amount of freedom achieved from self-deceptive reactions assumed a position of preeminence and served as the basis for the development of a new method of measuring insight. The approach revolves around an assessment of the individual's facility in penetrating the defensive maneuvers depicted in a number of hypothetical situations. Data on the validity of the Tolor-Reznikoff Insight Test are presented in the original study (1960) as well as in the studies by Tolor (1961), Schulberg (1962), and Lenarz and Vestre (1964).

The dimension of repression-sensitization refers to the continuum of a reaction tendency in the face of potentially threatening stimuli. The repressive extreme is characterized by avoidance, denial, and repression defenses, whereas the sensitizing extreme involves a mode of adaptation through alertness and approaching (intellectualizing and obsessional) behaviors. The underlying rationale, method of construction, and utility of the Repression-Sensitization (R-S) scale may be found in Byrne (1961), Byrne, Barry, and Nelson (1963), and Byrne, Golightly, and Sheffield (1965). On the basis of the underlying rationale of the R-S scale, it seems reasonable to assume that the repression-sensitization mode of adaptation bears a relationship to the concept of insight, as operationally defined by Tolor and Reznikoff (1960).

A third personality variable that seems to

be conceptually related to the previous two is the generalized expectancy or belief in internal or external control of reinforcement. Rotter (1966) differentiates between the degree to which an individual expects that reward or reinforcement will follow from, or be contingent upon, his own behavior or attributes, and the degree to which he believes or expects that it is contingent upon forces which are independent of his own actions and which are outside of himself. Rotter presents data on the development, reliability, and validity of a paper-and-pencil test measuring individual differences in this generalized expectancy (I-E scale). Theoretically one might assume that a tendency to believe that one's own behavior, skills, or internal dispositions determine rewards would be related to greater insight than a belief in external control of reinforcement.

Since the concept of death and the process of dying represent in our society phenomena that are potentially threatening to many individuals, the degree of overt anxiety experienced in this area may be regarded as one indication of a characteristic response to extremely threatening stimuli. Sensitization should therefore be related to a heightened degree of overt death anxiety as compared to repression. Similarly, since the person with an external orientation believes that factors beyond his control determine his failures, external expectancies should be more associated with overt death anxiety than the belief in internal control of reinforcement.

No specific predictions are made about the relationships between the expectation of external or internal control and the repression-sensitization dimension, or between overt death anxiety and the degree of insight.

In summary, then, the major hypotheses pertaining to repression-sensitization, insight, expectancy of internal-external control, and overt death anxiety are as follows: (a) Subjects who sensitize tend to be more insightful than those who repress; (b) Subjects who expect internal controls tend to be more insightful than those who anticipate external controls; (c) Subjects who sensitize tend to experience more overt death anxiety than those who repress; and (d) Subjects who believe in external controls tend to have more overt death anxiety than those who feel less subject to environmental forces.

METHOD

Subjects and Procedure

The Ss were 79 students enrolled in the introductory psychology course at Fairfield University, a men's liberal arts college. In age they ranged from 18 to 22 yr.

Each S was seen in two sessions with a 1-wk. interval between testing sessions. On the first occasion the following procedures were administered in the stated order: the Insight Test, the I-E scale, and the Death Anxiety scale. The following week, Ss were given the R-S scale. In addition, the students' records contained the Verbal Section score on the College Entrance Examination Board, Scholastic Aptitude Test (SAT) which was used as an estimate of intellectual status.

Instruments

The Tolor-Reznikoff Test of Insight (1960) consists of 27 hypothetical situations depicting common defense mechanisms. The S is required to select from among four possible explanations the ones which reveal the most and the least insight. The final score is based on the number of choices made in agreement with a previously determined consensus of experts. The higher the score the greater the amount of insight implied. This method of measurement was found to be valid in relation to such criteria as insight ratings of neuropsychiatric patients by psychologists and psychiatrists; patient versus non-patient status (Tolor & Reznikoff, 1960); Edwards Personal Preference Schedule (EPPS) needs (Tolor, 1961); and specialized training in the dynamic influences on human behavior (Lenarz & Vestre, 1964). The test-retest reliability coefficient, following a 1-wk. interval, was .86 in the Tolor and Reznikoff (1960) study.

The I-E scale (Rotter, 1966) is a 29-item forced-choice test measuring Ss' generalized expectations about how reinforcement is controlled, that is, whether by internal or external means. The I-E scale is scored in terms of the total number of external choices made so that high scores indicate an expectancy of external control and low scores indicate an expectancy of internal control of reinforcement. Six filler items are included which are in-

126

tended to make the purpose of the test more ambiguous. Responses are not highly influenced by a social desirability set and sex differences are minimal. Rotter (1966) cites a large number of investigations in support of the I-E scale's discriminant and construct validity. Test-retest correlations of .60 and .78 are reported by Rotter (1966) on studies with 1-mo. intervals.

The 20-item Death Anxiety scale is based on Livingston and Zimet's (1965) 24-item questionnaire to which Ss respond on a 6-point scale to indicate degree of agreement or disagreement. The original form was intended for use by medical students and therefore needed to be modified for application to other groups. The statements are balanced for response set (high and low death-anxiety items appear in an equal number of positive and negative statements) and for formal and colloquial expression. The test-retest reliability of the modified Death Anxiety scale employed in this study, based on a Pearson product-moment correlation, was .85 for a 3-mo. interval. Responses are scored on a 6-point scale with 1 point signifying strong disagreement and 6 points indicating strong agreement. The assignment of points is reversed for low-death-anxiety statements so that low scores indicate low death anxiety and high scores reflect high death anxiety.

The R-S scale is composed of selected Minnesota Multiphasic Personality Inventory (MMPI) items that measure a characteristic repression or sensitization response to threatening stimuli. The revised

TABLE 1

INTERCORRELATIONS FOR INSIGHT, SCHOLASTIC
APTITUDE TEST (VERBAL SECTION),
I-E SCALE, DEATH ANXIETY,
AND R-S SCALE

	In-sight	SAT	I-E scale	Death Anxiety	R-S scale
Insight		.455***	−.257*	.066	−.072
SAT			−.111	−.067	−.056
I-E scale				.232*	.334**
Death Anxiety					.508***
R-S scale					

Note.—$df = 77$.
* $p < .05$.
** $p < .01$.
*** $p < .001$.

R-S scale (Byrne et al., 1963), employed in the present study, consists of 127 scorable items having acceptable internal and test-retest reliabilities. For example, Byrne (1961) reports a test-retest reliability of .88 after a 6-wk. interval. The R-S scale is scored in such a way that low scores indicate repression and high scores point to sensitization. There are no significant sex differences on this scale. A number of studies (e.g., Altrocchi, Parsons, &

Dickoff, 1960; Joy, 1963; Ullmann, 1962) have found that R-S scores relate meaningfully to other personality dimensions consistent with the expectations for sensitizers and repressors.

RESULTS AND DISCUSSION

Table 1 presents the matrix of product-moment intercorrelations for the variables investigated. In view of the significant relationship between intelligence, as inferred from the Verbal Section of the SAT, and insight, partial correlations were also computed and are reported in Table 2.

The results confirm three of the four hypotheses, namely: (a) Ss' expectation of internal control of reinforcement is significantly related to insight; (b) sensitizing tendencies and overt death anxiety are significantly related; and (c) a belief in external controls is

TABLE 2

INTERCORRELATIONS AFTER THE EFFECTS OF
INTELLIGENCE HAD BEEN PARTIALED OUT

	Insight	I-E scale	Death Anxiety	R-S scale
Insight		−.235*	.108	−.052
I-E scale			.240*	.331**
Death Anxiety				.504***
R-S scale				

Note.—$df = 76$.
* $p < .05$.
** $p < .01$.
*** $p < .001$.

significantly related to overt death anxiety. It was also found that Ss' expectation of external control is significantly related to sensitization, and the expectation of internal control is associated with repression. The prediction that Ss who sensitize would also be more insightful than those who repress found no support in the data.

While none of the significant correlations is very high, with the possible exception of the relationship between R-S scores and death anxiety, they tend also to provide indirect support for the validity of the respective instruments involved. For example, in regard to the Tolor-Reznikoff Test of Insight, it is obvious that a considerable amount of variance is accounted for by intellectual factors. Nevertheless, the finding of a significant relationship between insight, as measured by this method, and internal expectations of control, even when the effects of intelligence are partialed out, contributes to the test's construct validity. It is noteworthy that none of the other measures employed is significantly affected by intelligence.

In view of the fact that all four scales have demonstrated satisfactory reliabilities, the relatively low intercorrelations cannot be attributed to errors of measurement. Correcting these intercorrelations for attenuation, as indicated in Table 3, does not increase them to any great extent. While some of these correlation coefficients are significant, the relatively low predictive validities which these results represent indicate that future research, replicating these procedures with additional samples, certainly would be desirable.

One might speculate on the reason for the failure to obtain the predicted relation between sensitization and insight. One possible

TABLE 3

INTERCORRELATIONS CORRECTED FOR ATTENUATION

	Insight	I-E scale	Death Anxiety	R-S scale
Insight		$-.305^*$	.126	$-.060$
I-E scale			$.316^*$	$.424^{**}$
Death Anxiety				$.586^{**}$
R-S scale				

Note.—$df = 76$.
$^* p < .01$.
$^{**} p < .001$.

explanation is that both the sensitizer as well as the repressor lack the necessary objectivity required for an adequate understanding of the self and of others. The assumption that both extremes on the sensitization-repression continuum may reflect poorer levels of adjustment than the midrange would lead to an expectation of a curvilinear relationship between R-S scale scores and indexes of psychological adjustment. However, a number of studies (Byrne, 1961; Byrne et al., 1965; Joy, 1963) have consistently found that sensitizers are the most maladjusted, that repressors are the best adjusted, and that neutrals fall in an intermediate position in adjustment. It would appear, therefore, that the relatively poor adjustment of the sensitizer might mitigate against his developing a high degree of insight, especially since it had previously been demonstrated (Tolor & Reznikoff, 1960) that insight is positively related to adjustment.

As for the finding that an external attitude is related to sensitization and an internal attitude to repression, it is noteworthy that a study by Efran (1963) disclosed that the tendency to repress failure is significantly related to scores toward the internal end of the continuum. Rotter (1966) interpreted these results as suggesting that the S who embraces an external attitude has less need to repress his failures than the more internally oriented S, since the former already accepts external factors as the responsible agents for his failures.

The finding that high death anxiety is associated with sensitization defenses is consistent with previous investigations. For example, Byrne and Sheffield (1965) found sensitizers to be more anxious than repressors in a sex arousal situation; Lomont (1965) obtained a significant correlation between R-S and the IPAT anxiety inventory; and Ullmann and McReynolds (1963) found sensitizers to be more anxious based on observers' ratings and the Welsh Anxiety Scale.

The close correspondence between the presently obtained relationship between death anxiety and sensitization, on the one hand, and various other measures of anxiety used in previous studies and sensitization, on the other hand, suggests the possibility that the newly constructed Death Anxiety scale measures general rather than specific anxiety. However, a recent study by Handal [1] reports only low, although significant ($r = .33$), correlations between the Death Anxiety scale and general anxiety, employing the Affect Adjective Check List (AACL) developed by Zuckerman (1960). Thus, the two measures have relatively little common variance and seem to tap some different aspects of anxiety.

Another possibility to be considered is that the pattern of intercorrelations reported is attributable to one or more response sets. The possibility that a response bias is contributing substantially to the common variance was carefully examined but rejected because of the following: (a) the correlation of the I-E measure with Marlowe-Crowne social desirability is low so that the median correlation reported by Rotter (1966) for several college samples is only $-.22$; (b) Livingston and Zimet (1965) in their construction of the Death Anxiety scale made efforts to control for response set; (c) on the Tolor-Reznikoff Insight Test (1960) it was demonstrated that there was no significant relationship between degree of pathology (neurotics versus psychotics) and degree of insight. Moreover, the items are so constructed that some of the most socially desirable alternatives are indeed scored as least insightful; and (d) Byrne (1961) found no support for the possibility that a tendency to respond deviantly is related to R-S scale performance. Despite the preponderance of evidence suggesting that a response bias was not operating to any major degree, future research might direct itself to this problem more specifically.

[1] P. Handal. Relationship between Death Anxiety, Subjective Life Expectancy, and General Anxiety. Unpublished manuscript, 1966.

REFERENCES

ALTROCCHI, J., PARSONS, O. A., & DICKOFF, H. Changes in self-ideal discrepancy in repressors and sensitizers. *Journal of Abnormal and Social Psychology*, 1960, **61**, 67–72.

BYRNE, D. The Repression-Sensitization scale: Rationale, reliability, and validity. *Journal of Personality*, 1961, **29**, 334–349.

BYRNE, D., BARRY, J., & NELSON, D. Relation of the revised Repression-Sensitization scale to measures of self-description. *Psychological Reports*, 1963, **13**, 323–334.

BYRNE, D., GOLIGHTLY, C., & SHEFFIELD, J. The Repression-Sensitization scale as a measure of adjustment: Relationship with the CPI. *Journal of Consulting Psychology,* 1965, **29,** 586–589.

BYRNE, D., & SHEFFIELD, J. Response to sexually arousing stimuli as a function of repressing and sensitizing defenses. *Journal of Abnormal Psychology,* 1965, **70,** 114–118.

EFRAN, J. S. Some personality determinants of memory for success and failure. Unpublished doctoral dissertation, Ohio State University, 1963.

JOY, V. L. Repression-sensitization and interpersonal behavior. In J. Altrocchi (Chm.), Current research developments with the repression-sensitization personality dimension. Symposium presented at American Psychological Association, Philadelphia, August 1963.

LENARZ, D. M., & VESTRE, N. D. The effect of a course in psychiatric nursing on insight test scores of nursing students. *Journal of Psychiatric Nursing,* 1964, **2,** 137–141.

LIVINGSTON, P. B., & ZIMET, C. N. Death anxiety, authoritarianism and choice of specialty in medical students. *Journal of Nervous and Mental Disease,* 1965, **140,** 222–230.

LOMONT, J. F. The repression-sensitization dimension in relation to anxiety responses. *Journal of Consulting Psychology,* 1965, **29,** 84–86.

ROTTER, J. B. Generalized expectancies for internal versus external control of reinforcement. *Psychological Monographs,* 1966, **80**(1, Whole No. 609).

SCHULBERG, H. C. Insight, authoritarianism and tendency to agree. *Journal of Nervous and Mental Disease,* 1962, **135,** 481–488.

TOLOR, A. The relationship between insight and intraception. *Journal of Clinical Psychology,* 1961, **17,** 188–189.

TOLOR, A., & REZNIKOFF, M. A new approach to insight: A preliminary report. *Journal of Nervous and Mental Disease,* 1960, **130,** 286–296.

ULLMANN, L. P. An empirically derived MMPI scale which measures facilitation-inhibition of recognition of threatening stimuli. *Journal of Clinical Psychology,* 1962, **18,** 123–132.

ULLMANN, L. P., & McREYNOLDS, P. Differential perceptual recognition in psychiatric patients: Empirical findings and theoretical formulation. In J. Altrocchi (Chm.), Current research developments with the repression-sensitization personality dimension. Symposium presented at American Psychological Association, Philadelphia, August 1963.

ZUCKERMAN, M. The development of an affect adjective check list for the measurement of anxiety. *Journal of Consulting Psychology,* 1960, **24,** 457–462.

School Phobia and the Fear of Death

Walter Tietz, M.D.

It has been known for some time that
the psychodynamics in school phobia could
be best understood as a variant of separation anxiety.[9] Furthermore, it has also
been observed that school phobia is part
of a natural history of depressive disorder
and that there seems to be a depressive
family constellation in the school phobic,
occurring in successive generations.[1] The
prognosis in school phobia seems somewhat dependent on age. It is relatively
good in children prior to adolescence and
relatively poor in older children.[7] In
younger children the dynamics of separation anxiety are prominent: whereas in
older children there is more widespread
insidious characteriologic family disorder
where a depressive family constellation
dominates. It is the purpose of this paper
to present a series of cases of school phobia
occurring in adolescents from 11–15 years
old, all associated with death in the family,

where the schol phobia served as a façade for the real fear which was fear of death. An attempt will be made to understand this in the theoretical framework provided by Bowlby.

Case Histories

Case 1

Patient is a 14-year old white female, who developed psychosomatic complaints and school phobia shortly after her maternal grandmother's death, which was coincidentally followed by a move of the family to a new section of the country where there was no extended family. The mother was an intensely phobic woman always fearing the death of her own mother and was extremely overprotective to her children because she had always feared some harm might come to them. The patient became obsessed with fear of her own mother's demise and became afraid she too would die.

Case 2

Patient is a 15-year old white male, who became acutely disturbed about two months after a serious accident where he was severely crushed, incurring a fracture of the arm. He began to feel weak, helpless, and felt he could not exist without his mother being constantly with him, resulting in his failure to go to school. The patient literally felt he would die if he were not with his parents. Furthermore, the father also was obsessed with the fear of death.

Case 3

Patient is a 14-year old white female, who developed psychosomatic complaints and intense school phobia when, one and a half years after her grandfather died, her maternal grandmother who was dying of cancer moved into her home. She was afraid that her mother might also die, leaving her alone, susceptible to death. As a result, she was afraid to go to sleep, equating sleep with death, and afraid to go to school because then her mother might die.

Case 4

Patient is a 12-year old white female, who became acutely upset when her mother had to leave for the East to attend the funeral of the maternal grandmother. She began to develop various psychosomatic complaints, and finally would not go to school at all.

Case 5

Patient is a 12-year old white male, who had been extremely anxious for the past four months, since his paternal grandfather died in Israel. The father had gone to Israel and stayed there for a month. Upon his return, the father became irritable, anxious and depressed. About two weeks after the father's return, the boy became frightened, had various psychosomatic complaints, and refused to be left alone. He always wanted one of his parents to be at home with him, and he refused to go to school. He verbalized the fact that he was afraid something might happen to them, especially his father. When the parents would leave him, he would go into the room with his sister in order not to be alone.

Case 6

Patient is an 11-year old white male, who had had a school phobia ever since he started school. When he started school at age six, his father had been dead for one year, following a bleeding duodenal ulcer. His mother and paternal grandmother, who moved in with them, constantly reminded him of his father's death. The death of the remaining two brothers of his father over the ensuing years only intensified the feelings of loss of his father. Furthermore, the family belonged to a religious sect which predicted the death and destruction of mankind in the next few years. The boy was constantly afraid his mother might die and that this would leave him helpless and weak. He became depressed and developed suicidal ideation, while at the same time he was afraid of his own death and destruction.

Discussion

Thus, it can be seen that death, or fear of death can be a precipitating event in the genesis of a school phobia. In all the cases presented here, there was not only a school phobia, an active death or fear of death of the parent, but it was also always associated with a fear of the child's own death.

How can this best be understood? Johnson [9] and her co-workers have suggested that the syndrome of school phobia be redefined in terms of an etiologic diagnosis, namely, separation anxiety. Johnson has defined separation anxiety [9] "As a pathological emotional state in which child and parent are involved in a relationship characterized by an intense need on the part of both to be in close physical proximity." Sperling [10] sees school phobia as a neurosis characterized by fixation at the anal-sadistic level, the time where individuation and separation should occur. It thus represents a failure to resolve the normal infantile symbiotic relationship the mother has with the child, and is interpreted as an acute separation threat which has the implied meaning of impending death.

The problem of separation anxiety and its relationship to grief and mourning has been studied intensively by Bowlby. According to Bowlby,[2] the child develops a tie to the mother as a direct outcome of the activation of a number of instinctual response systems among which are crying, smiling, sucking, clinging and following. When these instinctual response systems are activated and the mother figure is temporarily not available, the response is one of separation anxiety.[3] When the mother figure appears to be permanently absent, the response is one of grief and mourning.[4]

Thus, the relationship of separation anxiety and mourning is determined by the temporary or permanent absence of the mother figure. Viewed in this light the clinical observance of the association of school phobia in the child and depression and depressive constellation in the family, can be readily understood.

Furthermore, if one feels that the attachment behavior to the mother is basically instinctual and has survival value, failure to resolve this attachment and separate successfully, would cast doubt on one's ability to exist autonomously. Thus, failure to dissolve this pre-oedipal bond means failure of ego autonomy and implies ego dissolution.

The relationship of depression to separation of the infant from the mother figure had earlier been described by Spitz.[11] He described a syndrome occurring in infants in the second half of the first year of life at which time the infants were separated from their mothers for a period of three months or more. The infants lost their means of emotional support and therefore developed an "anaclitic depression" manifested by sadness, withdrawal, slowness of movement, loss of appetite, and loss of weight. This became very serious and actually had a high mortality with it. In addition to the high mortality, followup studies on these infants showed some retardation of development.

It is possible that in the cases of school phobia described in this paper, the feared loss of the mother figure was not only manifested by separation anxiety and school phobia, but also by an "anaclitic depression," in Spitz's sense. The fear of their own death which all these cases showed, may be a direct outcome of an "anaclitic depression." Thus, the feared loss of the mother figure on which to lean on or depend on, caused a feeling of vulnerability, manifested by their fear of their own death.

As a result of a number of studies,[5, 6, 8] it has been postulated that the effects of early separation are hidden, and later repeated experiences of loss reactivate the processes originating in the earlier loss. Bowlby feels that studies reporting an association between childhood mourning and later depressive states are significant because of the similarity he discerns between grief and mourning in an adult and the despair phase of response to separation in an infant. He feels that the defensive detachment following the despair phase of childhood mourning precludes a healthy working through of grief in the child and later predisposes him to depressive reactions.

In the cases reported here, the association of separation anxiety, manifested by the school phobia in the child, and a death in the family were concomitant. The death tended to start the process of grief and mourning and in a circular fashion reactivate the feelings of anxiety associated with separation. The sequence of events was the exact reverse of the usual manner grief and mourning proceed.

There, as described by Bowlby,[3, 4] the phase of protest, separation anxiety, is succeeded by a phase of despair, or grief. In these cases reported here grief occurs first, and then is followed by separation anxiety, manifested by school phobia.

It should be noted that the cases presented are mostly in the older age group which is associated with a poorer prognosis. The association of school phobia and death in the family may be fortuitous and may not be causally related, but it does seem to affect the prognosis when school phobia does develop. It seems fairly obvious that school phobia will not inevitably develop in every child when an actual death occurs in a family. Bowlby has felt that the effect of the mother's disappearance or death is related to a critical time in the child's development, namely from six months to three years.[3, 4] If the mother is absent in that period a serious characterologic effect may appear in the child. Nevertheless, it would be interesting to study children where death has occurred in the family and no school phobia develops. In this way the coping mechanisms can be better understood.

Summary

Six cases of school phobia occurring in adolescents ranging in age from 11 to 15 years old are presented. In all the cases there is an association of school phobia, an active or feared death in the family, and a fear of the adolescent's own death. Using the frame of reference provided by Bowlby, school phobia can be understood as failure to resolve the normal attachment behavior. Its failure becomes linked up symbolically with failure to exist as an independent person, resulting in a school phobia. The presence of an active death in the family does seem to affect the prognosis once a school phobia does develop.

REFERENCES

1. Agras, S. The Relationship of School Phobia to Childhood Depression, Amer. J. Psychiat., 116: 533–536, 1969.

2. Bowlby, J. The Nature of the Child's Tie to His Mother, Int. J. Psycho-Anal., 39:350–373, 1958.

3. Bowlby, J. Separation Anxiety, Int. J. Psycho-Anal., 41:89–111, 1960.

4. Bowlby, J. Processes of Mourning, Int. J. Psycho-Anal., 42:317–339, 1961.

5. Dennehy, C. Childhood Bereavement and Psychiatric Illness, Brit. J. Psychiat., 112:1049–1069, 1966.

6. Earle, A. M. and Earle, B. U. Early Maternal Deprivation and Later Psychiatric Illness, Am. J. Orthopsychiat., 31:181–186, 1961.

7. Eisenberg, L. School Phobia: Diagnosis, Genesis and Clinical Management, Ped. Clin. N. Amer.,

5:645–666, 1958.

8. Greer, S. The Relationship Between Parental Loss and Attempted Suicide, A Control Study, Brit. J. Psychiat., 110:698–705, 1964.

9. Johnson, A. M., Falstein, E. I., Szurek, S. A., and Svendsen, M. School Phobia, Amer. J. Orthopsychiat., 11:702–711, 1941.

10. Sperling, M. School Phobias; Classification, Dynamics and Treatment, Psycho-Anal. Study Child, 22:375–401, 1967.

11. Spitz, R. A. Anaclitic Depression, An Inquiry into the Genesis of Psychiatric Conditions in Early Childhood, Psycho-Anal. Study Child, 2:313-342, 1946.

RELIGIOSITY, GENERALIZED ANXIETY, AND APPREHENSION CONCERNING DEATH

ROBERT L. WILLIAMS AND SPURGEON COLE

A. PROBLEM

Since the pioneering efforts of Freud (8), psychologists have made some attempt to appraise experimentally the psychological efficacy of religion. Freud construed religion as an attempt to resolve the father-child conflict, a means of abrogating the terrors of nature, and a psychic rationalization for the inequities of fate. Religion was presumed to be an outgrowth of insecurity, and God a personification of the father image who ultimately would provide for man's needs and punish him for his misdeeds. Freud affirmed that above all else the prospect of death impels man to fabricate divine beings to protect himself from the ultimate threat of nature. Religion therefore was considered to be a prime symptom of neurosis and a product of paranoid minds (7). Reasoning from Freud's postulations, one would expect both prevailing insecurity and preoccupation with death to be characteristic of the highly religious. Present evidence is somewhat contradictory relative to both dimensions of insecurity (1, 3, 4, 5, 6, 9, 10, 12, 13, 14, 16). Two possible sources of inconsistency in previous research are the definition of "religiosity" (2, 18) and the method of delineating "general insecurity" and "fear of death" (1, 5).

In the present study, the experimenters (Es) have operationally defined religiosity as the magnitude of religious activity reported by the subjects and have attempted to relate these religiosity indices to two dimensions of insecurity.

B. METHOD

1. Subjects

The subjects (Ss) were taken from introductory psychology classes at a state college in the South. From the total sample of 161 students three groups were constituted: high religiosity ($N = 29$), intermediate religiosity ($N = 23$), and low religiosity ($N = 24$).

141

2. Instruments

Four self-report inventories were utilized in the assessment of religiosity and security level: The Religious Participation Scale, The Security-Insecurity (S-I) Inventory, The Minnesota Multiphasic Personality Inventory (MMPI), and The Perception of Death Scale. The Religious Participation Scale, an expanded form of Ligon's Religious Participation Questionnaire (11), instructed Ss to indicate the extent of their church attendance, personal prayer, reading of religious material, Sunday school attendance, and church related activity. The S-I Inventory, developed by Maslow (15), consisted of 75 questions to which the Ss responded yes, no, or undecided. High scores were indicative of generalized psychological insecurity. Six Ss chosen at random from each religiosity group were administered the full-scale MMPI. To establish the concurrent validity of the S-I scores, the total number of deviations (T scores of 70 or above) were tabulated for each of the religiosity groups. The Perception of Death Scale, a Likert-type instrument which is an extension of Sarnoff and Corwin's Fear of Death Scale (17), attempted to assess the S's conscious or public orientation toward death via such items as "I am disturbed when I think about the shortness of life."

In a word-recognition task, 15 words, 10 having no obvious emotional connotations and five clearly related to death—"death," "grave," "fatal," "casket," and "dying"—were tachistoscopically presented to each S at intervals varying randomly between 15 and 20 seconds. The 10 neutral words had been equated with the death words with respect to word length and familiarity (19). The stimuli were presented in the order of two neutral words, one death word, two neutral words, etc. Three consecutive trials, or 45 total stimulus presentations, were administered to each S. Amplitude of GSR reactivity to each word was computed by subtracting the mean amplitude of skin conductance during the prestimulus period (the five-second interval immediately preceding the presentation of the stimulus) from the maximum poststimulus conductance level.

3. Procedure

From the 161 Ss originally administered the Religious Participation Scale, those scoring at least 1.0 SD below the mean constituted the low religiosity group, those at least 1.0 SD above the mean the high religiosity group, and those falling between —.14 and +.14 SD from the mean the intermediate religiosity group. All or a random portion of each group was administered the

142

S-I Inventory, the MMPI, the Perception of Death Scale, and the Word Recognition Task.

C. RESULTS

The analysis of results may be divided into two segments: generalized insecurity indices and death-related insecurity. In the first phase of the analysis, the statistical evaluation of the S-I indices for the three religiosity groups revealed that the high and intermediate religiosity groups did not differ in security levels but that both were significantly ($p < .001$) more secure than the low religiosity group ($F = 8.37$, $df = 2/69$). According to the S-I Manual, means of 15.07 and 15.31 for the high and intermediate religiosity groups, respectively, would be indicative of average emotional adjustment and a mean of 26.59 for the low religiosity group indicative of tendencies toward insecurity. The difference obtained in the S-I indices were corroborated by the MMPI scores. The low religiosity Ss ($N = 6$) produced 16 deviations, the intermediate Ss ($N = 6$) three deviations, and the high Ss ($N = 6$) four deviations ($\chi^2 = 13.66$, $p < .005$).

The Ss' generalized, physiological apprehension was appraised via their GSR reactivity to the neutral stimuli throughout the first trial. It was presumed that the more anxious Ss would tend to be threatened by a new task, regardless of how innocuous it might be. The mean GSR arousal for the high, intermediate, and low religiosity groups, respectively, was 1,856, 2,905, and 1,981 ($F = 2.02$, nonsignificant).

The second phase of the investigation dealt with apprehension more specifically related to death. On the Perception of Death Scale the respective mean scores for the high, intermediate, and low religiosity groups were 45.31, 49.56, and 46.29 ($F = 1.26$, n.s.). In the latter segment of the analysis a $3 \times 2 \times 3$ mixed design with religiosity as the between factor and word group (neutral or death-related) and trials as within variables produced two significant findings: a word group main effect ($F = 5.56$, $df = 1/51$, $p < .025$) and a trial main effect ($F = 12.46$, $df = 2/102$, $p < .005$). GSR reactivity was greater for the death-related than for the neutral words, corroborating the presumption that the technique employed provides a valid assessment of underlying physiological anxiety concerning death. The approach failed, however, to differentiate between religiosity groups. The between factor (religiosity) produced a nonsignificant main effect F ratio of 1.65 and no significant interactions.

In résumé, Figure 1 indicates that the intermediate group manifested the

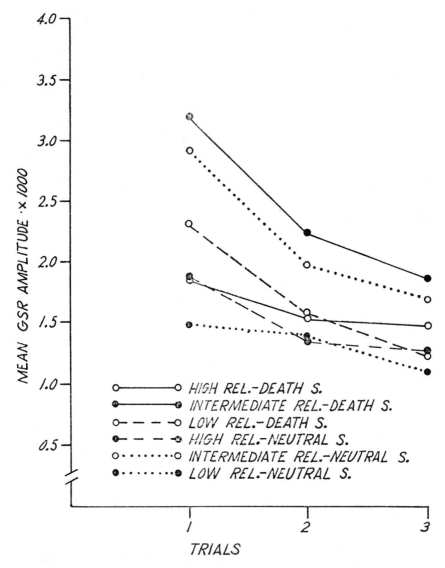

FIGURE 1
GSR Reactivity of Three Religiosity (Rel.) Groups to Death
and Neutral Stimuli (S.)

greatest GSR reactivity to both death and neutral stimuli (S) throughout the experimental trials and that the high group the least responsivity.

D. DISCUSSION

The study has focused on the relationship between two important dimensions of human experience, religion and emotional adjustment. Regardless of one's affinity for religion, it must be admitted that a majority of extinct and contemporary cultures have practiced some form of religious ritual. Freud (8) attributed religion to man's basic insecurity particularly focalized in his perception of death. The present investigation, however, failed to produce any support for the hypothesized Freudian relationship between religion and neurotic inclinations. On all dimensions of anxiety, the active religious Ss manifested the highest level of adjustment.

In the context of psychoanalytic thought, a distinction has been made between overt, conscious anxiety and more covert, repressed insecurities. The present Es found that a group of low religiosity Ss manifested the greatest degree of conscious, prevailing insecurity, whereas the high and intermediate groups did not differ appreciably. Therefore, more secure persons tend to become religious, religion facilitates security, or religious individuals do not openly admit insecurities. At the physiological level the three groups did not differ significantly, although the intermediate group was consistently higher than the high and low Ss.

Perception of death measures failed to produce any significant differences between the religiosity groups. However, on both dimensions the rank order of insecurity scores was intermediate, low, and high. The consistency of the findings suggests that if a larger N or more sensitive experimental manipulations were utilized, the intermediate Ss might exhibit a significantly greater degree of anxiety, particularly at a physiological level. Conceivably, ambivalence in basic religious beliefs and actions may produce more uncertainties and insecurities than being highly religious or nonreligious.

The present study needs to be extended on two counts. First, inasmuch as most of the Ss were from the South, they may generally be more conservative and religious than a sample comprised of students throughout the country. Most expressed a church preference, whereas a sample including a substantial number of Ss possessing absolutely no affinity for religion might have produced different results. On the basis of the present study, we can simply affirm that among students, most of whom have been subjected to some religious influence, the religiously active Ss manifested the least anxiety. A second extension of the study would be to include age as an independent variable. Most of the Ss were

145

college sophomores and juniors, 19 to 21 years of age. It is highly possible that the relationship between religion and insecurity indices may change somewhat as people get older.

E. SUMMARY

On the basis of Religious Participation Scores, Ss were divided into high, intermediate, and low religiosity groups. Reasoning from Freud's affirmation (8) that religion is the product of insecurity, the Es postulated that religiosity and security indices would be negatively related. Two types, generalized anxiety and specific apprehension concerning death, and two levels of insecurity, overt, conscious anxiety and physiological arousal, were assessed for the three religiosity groups. The high religiosity Ss manifested the least anxiety on all dimensions, and the low religiosity group the greatest generalized insecurity ($p < .001$). The intermediate group, though not to a significant degree, yielded the highest scores for the physiological assessment of general anxiety, the self-report concern about death, and physiological arousal to death-related stimuli.

REFERENCES

1. ALEXANDER, I. E., & ALDERSTEIN, A. M. Death and religion. In H. Feifel (Ed.), *The Meaning of Death*. New York: McGraw-Hill, 1959. Pp. 271-283.
2. ALLPORT, G. W. Comment on earlier chapters. In R. May (Ed.), *Existential Psychology*. New York: Random House, 1961. Pp. 94-99.
3. ARNOLD, M. B. Psychology and the image of man. *Relig. Educ.*, 1959, **54**, 30-36.
4. FAUNCE, W. A., & FULTON, R. L. The sociology of death: A neglected area of research. *Soc. Forces*, 1958, **3**, 205-209.
5. FEIFEL, H. Death-relevant variable in psychology. In R. May (Ed.), *Existential Psychology*. New York: Random House, 1961. Pp. 61-74.
6. FEIN, L. G. Religious observance and mental health: A note. *J. Pastoral Care*, 1958, **12**, 99-101.
7. FREUD, S. The Psychopathology of Everyday Life. New York: Norton, 1965.
8. ———. The Future of an Illusion. Garden City, N. J.: Doubleday, 1957.
9. HIRSCHBERG, J. C. Comments on religion and childhood. *Menninger Quart.*, 1956, **10**, 22-24.
10. KLEINER, R. J., TUCHMAN, J., & LAVELL, M. Mental disorder and status based on religious affiliation. *Hum. Relat.*, 1959, **12**, 273-276.
11. LIGON, L. Philosophies of human nature and religious backgrounds. Paper read at Southeastern Psychological Association, Atlanta, Georgia, April, 1965.
12. MARTIN, C., & NICHOLS, R. C. Personality and religious belief. *J. Soc. Psychol.*, 1962, **56**, 3-8.
13. MARTIN, D., & WRIGHTSMAN, L. S. The relationship between religious behavior and concern about death. *J. Soc. Psychol.*, 1965, **65**, 317-323.
14. MARY, W. S. Malidies mentales des religieuses. *Suppl. Vie. Spir.*, 1959, **12**, 295-305.
15. MASLOW, A. H. Security-Insecurity Inventory: Manual. Palo Alto, Calif.: Consult. Psychol. Press, 1952.

16. MOBERG, D. O. Religious activities and personal adjustment in old age. *J. Soc. Psychol.*, 1956, **43**, 261-267.

17. SARNOFF, I., & CORWIN, S. Castration anxiety and fear of death. *J. Personal.*, 1959, **27**, 374-385.

18. SWENSON, W. Attitudes toward death in an aged population. *J. Geront.*, 1961, **16**, 56-66.

19. THORNDIKE, E. L., & LORGE, I. The Teacher's Word Book of 30,000 Words. New York: Columbia Univ. Press, 1944.

Attitudes Toward Death in Chronically Ill or Dying Patients

The Psychosocial Aspects of Advanced Cancer

Teaching Simple Interviewing Techniques and Record Keeping

Edmund C. Payne, Jr., MD, and Melvin J. Krant, MD

Failure to obtain psychological and social information regarding a patient with a lethal long-term illness and his family may lead to inappropriate medical decision-making and treatment, and thus result in failure to meet the patient's major needs. The use of simple interviewing techniques by nonpsychiatrist physicians and medical students can yield important information concerned with patient care. This information should become part of the medical record in order to document the data as any other pertinent historical or physical data, to transmit this information to other physicians who may review the medical record, and to serve as a self-imposed discipline as the physician learns to expand his communication with the patient.

The care of a patient with a long-term illness that is debilitating and progressing towards death, such as advancing cancer, is difficult for the physician, for other members of the health professions, and quite obviously for the family as well. Decisions must often be made that are pertinent to the management of the patient, but may not be directly related to a physical problem; frequently a patient may present with complaints that emanate from psychologic or social dimensions but come disguised as somatic problems. As Engel has observed,[1]

Medical students not only have little opportunity to gain an understanding of the unity of psychosomatic interrelationships, few ever acquire the techniques to make appropriate psychological observations. The average medical school graduate has had so little guidance in the technique of interview and so little understanding of what constitutes meaningful psychological data that he is virtually incapable of eliciting, much less recognizing, any but the most blatant examples of psychological distress.

This issue is not simply one of the physician's kindness nor of his sympathetic concern with the patient and family, as important as these qualities are in medical care. The physician as well as other health team members are interested both in the best medical care and medical decision for the patient and in handling the complaints and symptoms manifested by the patient. Failure to comprehend the psychological concerns of the patient and family may well produce unnecessary and even ill-programmed therapies that cannot succeed in alleviating the patient's complaints, much less the associated anxieties.

The physician's response to a patient's anxiety cannot routinely be a psychiatric consultation. Every patient undergoing an important change from health to disease experiences some degree of anxiety and concern. There will never be enough psychiatrists available to deal with this universal human suffering and distress. Comprehensive care of the patient with a serious medical illness must remain the responsibility of the internist or surgeon, and this care must include recognition and management of the social and psychological dimensions.

A review of the typical hospital ward medical record often reveals a dearth of information relative to psychologic factors at play in patients, and this absence is clearly a reflection of the lack of appreciation for the importance of these data in arriving at intelligent medical decisions in which concern both for the disease process and for the entire patient are reflected. A survey of 15 randomly selected charts of patients treated for metastatic cancer in a teaching hospital showed that in only two instances did the physician record in the chart what the patient had been told about the illness. One of the notes (written after two years of treatment and the only one of its kind in the record) read as follows: "Much of this patient's trouble is concern about her illness. She demands to know her diagnosis, and I tried to answer her in a roundabout way." In only seven instances was any reference made to the patient's emotional state. In four instances this was confined to a word or phrase, eg, "the patient appears depressed." Only in three cases was there any indication of an attempt to appreciate and alleviate the patient's unhappiness. Reichard, too, has observed:

> The startling fact is that medical doctors seldom record on a chart any observations of psychological events . . . The medical chart of today offers convincing evidence that the tradition of medicine is strongly antagonistic to treating psychological data in the systematic, scientific manner that is accorded to physiological data.[2]

Doctors put into their charts that which they consider to be important. So do physicians who become authors. A review of several major textbooks concerned with the cancer problem and the management of patients failed to reveal any discussion concerned with the psychological or social implications of disease.

A program for fourth-year medical students, focusing on their approach to seriously ill patients, and particularly those with cancer, was inaugurated three years ago in the Oncology Division of the Lemuel Shattuck Hospital to study problems in and methods for improving communication and management. A consulting psychiatrist as well as the senior physicians of the Oncology Division met weekly with a group of four to six students to discuss attitudes in patient care.

The fourth-year students were assigned to the medical units of the hospital for a two- to three-month period. Patients with chronic diseases of many types are referred to these medical wards from private physicians and from other hospitals in the Boston vicinity. Many patients with advancing cancer were included in these ward units. The fourth-year student was involved in direct patient examination and care, and worked alongside medical residents, the senior ward physician at his visit, and had consultation visits in various specialties, including oncology.

The conferences were conducted in an area apart

from the ward units and participants included the students, social service workers, student nurses, ward nurses, the consultant psychiatrist, and the oncology physicians. The students selected a case for presentation (not necessarily a cancer patient, although these tended to predominate). The case was usually selected because of a problem in discussing an issue with an individual, or else, because of some difficulty in management. During the first few sessions of each student rotation period, the psychiatrist interviewed the patient, but gradually the student proceeded with the interview himself. A lengthy discussion period followed these interviews. These sessions usually revealed that problems existed in the student's and the physician's on-the-ward history taking, which in turn reflected important defects in conceptualization of the patient's situation. Almost without exception, the students failed to obtain crucial information concerning the patients' reactions to disease, the patients' relation to important people in their lives, and the patients' concepts of the physician and the hospital. In looking at the medical record and in discussing the issue with the students, a similar, widespread lack of information on the part of more senior physicians was evident. The lack of the senior staff's attention to this area obviously results in a deficiency of appropriate instruction of the students.

These conferences demonstrated for the students that every patient with a serious illness has some knowledge of the pathological processes occurring in his body. This knowledge is organized on several levels of awareness. The type of knowledge and the way in which it is organized depend on the symptoms produced by the disease and their effect on the patient's functioning, on the specific informational feedback (either explicit or nonverbal) which he receives from his physician, friends, and family members, and on his own methods of dealing with threatening information. Most patients seen in the oncology conferences had been referred by an outside physician, and many had seen several physicians during the course of the illness. Some information about their illness, realistic or distorted, bluntly stated or euphemistic, had been transmitted to all of these patients by their previous physician.

From the interviews, it was apparent that the majority of the cancer patients whose disease had been regarded as potentially curable had been given some indication that they had a malignancy. Those patients with inoperable conditions reported receiving more varied information from their physicians. In a minority of cases, the physician had given the diagnosis more or less directly, although, to protect the patient, the ultimately fatal import of the condition was generally controverted, softened, or not dealt with at all. Other physicians had conveyed a diffused and euphemistic picture of the condition to their patients: "a tumor," "premalignant changes," "a mass," etc. Some patients reported that their physicians had avoided any discussion of diagnosis whatsoever, a strategy which the patients, almost without exception, avoided challenging with questions but to which they reacted with anxiety.

The reactions of these patients whom the students interviewed to the information which they had received from their physicians and from their own perceptions of changes in their bodies also showed a range that was determined by their characteristic style of dealing with danger and by the stage they believed assumed by their doctors. At one end of the spectrum was the unusual patient who seemed to have assimilated a relatively undistorted understanding of the nature of his illness and its implications. This response was never solely the product of complete frankness by the physician. Always the patient had taken the further step of intergrating the information available to him and drawing his own conclusions. More commonly seen was the acceptance of the diagnosis, but a wishful reliance on the hospital for further treatment, or on the current physician to reverse the verdict. Still other patients clung to euphemistic designations of their disease, floated in vague concepts of the illness unmarked by any clear delineation of its nature. Some few patients evaded any questions which directed their attention to this problem.

The initial observations indicated that the spontaneous approach of students and most ward physicians (including residents and senior physicians) was to avoid any discussion with the patients about the nature of the disease. The referral note transmitted information as to the patient's diagnosis and prior therapy, but almost never was mention made of the psychological impact of diagnosis or therapy on the patient, and seldom would the transfer note indicate what information had been transmitted to the patient or family. With very few exceptions, the patients, once admitted to the Lemuel Shattuck Hospital, were not asked what they had been told about their illness, and in no instance was this information recorded on the patient's record. A discussion with the patient of his emotional reactions to the illness was equally avoided. Questions were not asked about what the patient thought was wrong with him, whether he was worried, frightened, or discouraged, or what he expected of the hospital.

The interviews in the teaching conferences revealed that most of the patients were deeply concerned about dying. Most were depressed and frightened, but tenuously warded off these affects by clinging to an unrealistic hope that they would be restored to health in the hospital. These attitudes were generally on the surface of the patient's awareness and easily elicited. Most patients indeed responded gratefully and eagerly to an expression of interest in their feelings and to an opportunity to express them. At times the patients revealed easily obtainable information that cast light upon a physical problem. This was exemplified by the woman with spinal metastases from a breast carcinoma, who had been told that her spine was affected by the cancer and who was presented because she could not be persuaded to move from a supine position. Neurological examination had revealed no abnormalities sufficient to account for this seeming paralysis. When questioned, she quickly revealed a belief of delusional intensity that her spine had been eaten away and that any movement that she made would cause her to break in two. As this belief was revealed to be unfounded and the patient was convinced that motion was freely possible without injury, she was persuaded to sit up and gradually became ambulant.

Communication between physician and patient as to the psychologic impact of disease and about the patient's conception of the illness is important if the physician aspires to more than a mechanistic standard of medical management. Neglect in this area deprives that patient of a most valuable source of emotional support, and exposes him to potential delusions, conceptions, or experiences most disruptive to his life's activities. The potential for the latter is exemplified by a 53-year-old woman with metastatic carcinoma admitted for consideration of

155

further treatment. At the time of the conference interview, she had been in the hospital undergoing tests for a week. She was to be discharged in two days, following a decision that no further treatment should be offered at the time. The physician presenting her case had commented on her bland, cheerful attitude during her hospital stay. When questioned he said that he had not discussed discharge with her but assumed that someone had.

In the teaching conference, the patient quickly responded to the interest that was being shown in her personal views and feelings by telling how frightened she was feeling. She suspected that her illness was a very bad one, perhaps cancer, but had never discussed this either with her physician at home or with the doctors in the hospital. She had felt a deep despair before coming to the hospital but became more optimistic when plans for hospitalization were made. She had heard of the hospital, knew that the doctors were very good, and believed that she could and would be helped. She had not allowed herself to consider the possibility of not being helped, and did not know what she would do in that event. At present, she said, she was patiently waiting for treatment to begin and did not suspect that her discharge was imminent.

The undisturbed misconceptions concerning treatment and care under which this woman had labored during her hospitalization demonstrate the extent to which communication had failed. An abrupt discharge from the hospital in which she had placed all her hopes, without further clarification and before she made some new adjustment with her doctor's assistance, could have been catastrophic. Lengthy preparation for discharge was obviously necessary.

Communication between patient and physician serves a number of vital functions. Without information about the patient's fears, superstitions, and degree of knowledge, the physician's planning cannot help but be clumsy and often inappropriate. It is also important for the patient to have information about his medical situation. Appropriate information permits him to mobilize his more mature capabilities, to partake in the management of his illness, and to adapt more effectively even to extremely grave situations. He may selectively develop denial regarding the disease but this is not predictable ahead of time. Conversely, an informational vacuum blocks more active attempts at adjustment and encourages more primitive and infantile methods of seeking security. The physician must make some assessment of the person he is treating in order to give this information in an appropriate and acceptable form. The physician possesses great authority and influence with his patient which increases proportionately with the seriousness of the illness and the sick person's relative helplessness in the face of the threat of his bodily integrity and to his life. The patient can obtain a sense of security and comfort from the relationship with the physician, even though the physician may in fact be unable to eradicate the disease. The sense of security, perhaps unfounded in reality but very real in its effect, is analogous to the security that a child obtains from a confident relationship with his parents. For it to develop, however, and for it to be utilized sensitively and effectively, there must be an exchange in which the patient knows that the physician is aware of his concerns and the physician directs his support and clarifications to the specific needs which the patient reveals to him.

For most people, dying is an isolated and lonely experience. Friends and family are uncomfortable with a lethally ill person, avoid him, and when with him, frequently assume an air of artificial cheerfulness that blocks any communication in the area of most concern to the patient, namely, his distress and his illness. Similar avoidance by the physician intensifies this isolation; sensitive inquiry into these areas of concern helps alleviate it.[3] The purpose of these conferences was to demonstrate that open discussion with patients is possible, and that information acquired can be used for medical planning.

The physician frequently fails to obtain necessary information about another important area, the patient's relationship with the people closest to him. Attention to these relationships, however, can be decisive in planning successful medical management. Any patient with a prolonged illness, especially if it is progressing toward a fatal termination, suffers an impairment of his self-sufficiency and is dependent on his environment, to varying degrees, for physical and emotional support. The physician must assess the extent to which the spouse or other central family member can provide this support.

A person responds to the serious illness or threatened death of a spouse, a parent, or a child with a complex mixture of painful emotions consisting of grief, anxiety, fear of loss of accustomed support, depression, and at times even anger. At the same time that the greatest demands are being made to give nursing care and emotional sustenance to the patient, the central family member may be immersed in this personal upheaval. This difficult situation is often compounded by the breakdown of communication that occurs even with the couples who had achieved an intimate and open relationship prior to the illness.

The physician must evaluate the strengths and weaknesses of the family before sending his patient home from the hospital. In some instances it is obvious that such a plan would overtax the family's emotional resources, and that some alternative, such as a nursing home or a hospital for prolonged care, must be considered. Frequently, auxiliary services such as the Visiting Nurse Association, homemaker services, or a skillful social worker can provide the needed support. The physician cannot make these decisions wisely, however, without a careful initial and continuing discussion of the reactions with the family members. In addition to providing information, this assessment is an important source of support. Joint discussions with patient and spouse can sometimes offer a model of frankness that makes subsequent communication between them easier and freer.

The reluctance of students and physicians to investigate their patients' knowledge of and reaction to illness, and their consistent (wishful) tendency to underestimate the degree of patients' distress in the face of life-threatening illness seem related to a variety of factors.[1] Two, however, stand out. The most easily discernible motive is to protect themselves from sharing their patient's painful feelings. Communication of an effectual message is mediated to an important degree by means of empathy and identification ("I understand what you feel because I can share your feelings"). The physician exposes himself to a milder and time-limited degree when opening and exposing the patient's feelings of anxiety, fear, depression, and helplessness. This is not only painful in itself but may also activate the physician's unresolved conflicts concerning death, mutilation, and loss. A student physician who was most adamantly opposed to any inquiry into patients' feelings and who openly advocated a completely mechanistic approach to medical management eventually blurted out that he had experienced a series of personal losses and such an exploration was for him too painful to consider. A thoughtful observation of his own reactions to his patient can help the physician recognize his own reasons for avoiding these issues and learn to deal with them more effectively.

The second most important reason for avoidance is simply lack of knowledge of how to conduct such a discussion with patients. Few students, or indeed house officers or senior physicians, had seen a tactful inquiry into these areas, and feared such an investigation would evoke emotions in their patients which would get out of control and thereby damage their patients.

Demonstration interviews with cancer patients. conducted initially by the instructor and increasingly taken over by the students, were effective in helping students overcome their apprehension and successfully include these areas in their history-taking. The important factors were: (1) discussing the relevance of this material; (2) demonstrating how it could be applied to patient management; and (3) the most essential step, demonstrating the simple interviewing methods by which this information could be obtained within the context of the medical history. Although the long-range effects of their care of patients cannot as yet be determined, they did discuss these matters with patients, often for the first time, and discovered that the questions can be asked without excess trauma for doctor or patient, and that useful information can be obtained. Further, the information thus obtained could be documented on the patient's chart. Once recorded, changes in affect, in attitude to disease and treatment, and other psychologic or social factors could be noted as part of the follow-up notes, and the information would thus become available to the next reader of the chart.

In conclusion, several recommendations seem relevant. First, training programs in simple psychological interviewing should be made available for physicians at all levels of function. Psychiatrists may well take the lead and initiative in developing such a program in both university and community hospitals, but active participation by respected instructors in medicine and surgery is essential for success. Instruction in interviewing principles will help physicians cope with their difficulties in dealing with patients. Second, information obtained in patient-interviews should be considered as important as the routine history and physical examination, and should be entered onto the medical record. It is certainly insufficient to check off "depressed" or "not depressed." We would suggest that the following information be recorded in the charts as an important and useful part of the medical record.

1. What has the patient been told about his illness (by previous and present physicians)?

2. What conclusions has the patient reached about his illness (these obviously include his misconceptions)?

3. How is he coping with his illness? Can a degree of functional incapacity due to psychological factors be recognized? How much fear and depression does the patient experience?

4. What has the central family member been told regarding the illness? Has different information been given to different people (patient and spouse), and has the family been instructed or advised as to ways of dealing with the patient?

5. What is the family reaction to the illness? Will there be areas of difficulty or instability that should be supported or attended to?

6. What supplementary support does the physician regard as necessary to maintain the family?

In effect, these questions must be posed as questions needing discussion and not organized into a yes-no check-off list. If given an opportunity, physicians will abbreviate discussion in areas of discomfort to the point of ritual, which may well prevent any real commitment to the needs of patients and families. These questions are offered as a guideline that each physician or student will modify depending on personal styles.

Well-documented information in the medical record serves as a means of communicating information about a patient. In the same way as in dealing with a physical complaint, appropriate therapeutic steps can be taken to either correct a psychological impression or to make decisions based upon an awareness of the disease's impact. These should be functions of each and every physician and should not be seen as areas of concern solely for a psychiatrist or a social worker. In so accepting this responsibility, the physician should be in a better position to administer care and make judgements concerning patient and family.

This investigation was supported in part by Public Health Service grant 10391 from the National Institute of Mental Health.

References

1. Engel, G.L.: Medical Education and the Psychosomatic Approach, *J Psychosom Res* 11:77-85 (June) 1967.

2. Reichard, J.F.: "Teaching Principles of Medical Psychology to Medical House Officers: Methods and Problems," in N. E. Zinberg (ed.): *Psychiatry and Medical Practice in a General Hospital*, New York: International Universities Press, Inc., 1964, pp 169-204.

3. Payne, E.C.: "The Physician and the Dying Patient," in Levin, S., and Kahana, R.J. (eds.): *Psychodynamic Studies on Aging: Creativity, Reminiscing, and Dying in the Aged*," New York: International Universities Press, Inc., 1967, pp 111-163.

4. Payne, E.C.: "Teaching Medical Psychotherapy in Special Clinic Settings." in N. E. Zinberg (ed.): *Psychiatry and Medical Practice in a General Hospital*, New York: International Universities Press, Inc., 1964, pp 135-168.

PATIENTS' REACTIONS TO DEATH IN A
CORONARY CARE UNIT

JOHN G. BRUHN, A. EUGENE THURMAN, JR.,
BETTY C. CHANDLER and THOMAS A. BRUCE

HOSPITALS equipped with coronary care units have reduced their mortality rate from heart attacks by about one-third [1]. In addition to the advantages of continuous monitoring and the ability to apply immediate life-saving techniques, the environment of the coronary care unit provides a close physician and nurse relationship with the patient [2–4]. Yet there is evidence which indicates that while there are clinical advantages, the environment of the unit also has certain psychological stresses which impinge on the patient. These hazards include the nature of the equipment used, and the fact that patients witness cardiac arrest and resuscitation and observe the clinical progress and decline of other patients [5]. Although the intensity of the physician and nurse interaction with the patient in the unit is advantageous, the disruption of this relationship by transfer to the ward has been shown to be associated with increased catechol excretion and certain cardiovascular complications [6]. The relationship between disturbances in the environment of a metabolic ward and certain physiologic changes has also been reported [7, 8]. These findings seem to indicate the need for further research regarding the relationship between physiological factors and psychological stresses in a coronary care unit

The present paper reports the results of a study which focused primarily on the physiological and psychological responses of patients who witnessed deaths in a coronary care unit.

METHOD

Description of the coronary care unit

The Coronary Care Unit (CCU) at the University of Oklahoma Hospital contains four beds spaced 4–6 ft apart which are separated by draw curtains, the only means of isolating patients from each other. Each bed is equipped with an ECG monitor located outside the curtain. Along the opposite wall is a nurse's desk with an oscilloscope for monitoring continuous ECG tracings, a supply closet and a "crash cart" for emergency use.

Generally patients can observe who enters and leaves the unit. They are acutely aware of the movement and presence of mechanical devices such as the Bird respirator. Because the unit is small, conversation must be subdued in order not to be overheard. A sudden influx of numerous medical personnel concentrated around a particular patient is a signal to the other patients that either an emergency has arisen or a cardiac arrest has occurred. Death is later well-defined by the presence of an empty bed. Visitors are permitted for periods of 5 min each hour. Frequent visitors may be either an indication of close family ties or a decline in the clinical status of a patient.

This study was supported in part by Grant No. 1-K4-HE-38, 912-01 from the U.S. Public Health Service, National Heart Institute.

Patients rarely spend the entire period of their hospitalization in the unit and are usually transferred to the ward when their status has stabilized. The amount of time a patient spends in the unit before transfer or discharge is often used by other patients as a means of assessing their own clinical progress.

PROCEDURE

All patients admitted to the CCU ($N = 48$) over a period of 3 months were observed by one of the authors (A.E.T.) who kept a diary of daily events, noting staff interrelationships, admissions, discharges, cardiac arrests and patterns of communication between patients. The observations were made each day at random periods from 7 a.m. to 12 a.m. In addition, the nurses' notes provided documentation of medication, clinical routine, systolic blood pressure and pulse for 24 hr periods as well as events occurring from midnight to 7 a.m. The exact time of death of patients in the unit was recorded, and this determined the time period for the study of two physiological indices of anxiety, namely, increase in systolic blood pressure and heart rate [9] and assessment of mood.

Sample

Subsequent to the three month observation a sample ($N = 29$) of the 48 patients was chosen for study according to the following criteria: two or more patients who spent a continuous 24 hr period of time together in the unit during which, (a) a death was witnessed (study group $N = 17$); and (b) a period of no critical events (control group, $N = 12$). This design allowed for two control comparisons. Each patient served as his own control (within group comparison), as well as a between group comparison (study group vs. control group).

The mean ages of the study and control groups were 61.0 and 52.4 respectively. There were no significant differences in age between the two groups ($t = 1.49$, NS). Although there were significantly more males ($N = 9$) than females ($N = 3$) among the controls, ($X^2 = 4.77$, 1 df, $p < 0.05$) compared to the study group (7 males; 10 females), it was felt that differences in sex between the two samples would not be a variable that might influence the physiological indices. There were no significant differences between groups in the distribution of clinical diagnoses. Therefore, it was felt that diagnosis did not bias the results obtained.

Determination of variables

Time segments. Because of the possible variation in systolic blood pressure and heart rate due to the diurnal–nocturnal cycle, it was deemed essential to control for the time of day. As mentioned previously, the time of death of a patient in the unit determined the critical time segment which became the focus of investigation. The study was purposely designed to minimize disruption of ward routine and also to allow, as far as possible, that the events and observations be representative of the unit. Therefore, the time recorded by the nurse on the patients' charts just before the death period and just subsequent to it was the source of data for systolic blood pressure, heart rate and pertinent clinical comments. The sicker patients generally had more frequent readings of their vital signs; however, recordings were made for all patients in four hour intervals. Thus, the beginning and end of the four hour interval within which the death occurred delineated the time sample studied.

Several time controls were incorporated into the study. First each patient in the study group was compared with himself before and after a death (Day I), and again the same four hour interval was examined exactly 48 hr later (Day III). Death occurred at random intervals and, therefore, the 24 hr day was adequately sampled. In the control group a random sample of any 24 hr was used for the first observation, and the same procedure was followed as with the study group.

Systolic blood pressure and heart rate. The direction of change (increase, decrease or no change) in systolic blood pressure and heart rate was assessed by comparing the nurses' recordings before and after the occurrence of a death for the study group. The identical information was obtained for the same time period 48 hr later. Then the two directions of change were compared with each other. The same procedure was followed for the control group except that the first observation was determined on a random basis.

Mood. The head nurse on the two day shifts rated each patient daily on anxiety, depression, hostility, anger and fear on a four point scale (0 = absent, 1 = mildly present, 2 = moderately present and 3 = markedly present). In addition, any of the patient's verbalizations about his clinical progress or CCU events were noted. The same two nurses provided the observations and ratings throughout the study.

Because of the methodological difficulties in precisely correlating ECG changes with CCU events, and because all patients were not monitored continuously each day while in the unit, ECG's were not included in the present analysis.

Drug effects. Because of the diversity of medications and diets, it was not possible to study changes in the urinary excretion of certain metabolites such as was done in the carefully controlled study by

163

Schottstaedt [7]. However, it was deemed necessary to examine carefully the drugs administered to both the study and control groups to rule out the possibility of drug effects. There were a limited number of drugs used routinely in the CCU, as opposed to a general ward because, as to be expected, most of the patients had cardiovascular disease. Both groups of patients received either the same or equivalent drugs. And in fact, although phenobarb is reported to depress slightly both blood pressure and heart rate, as in sleep [11], three of the five patients in the study group receiving this drug still showed an increase in systolic blood pressure. Aminophylin tends to increase blood pressure, but in the instance where the drug was used there was a greater increase in systolic blood pressure than could be accounted for by the drug alone [11]. It was, therefore, concluded that drugs would not effect any significant differences found between the groups.

RESULTS

The quantitative data were analyzed by Marsh's method for testing the significance of the difference between proportions [10] and were two-tailed tests.

Systolic blood pressure and heart rate

The distribution of the patients as to changes in systolic blood pressure and heart rate may be found in Tables 1 and 2. It was found that within the Study Group a significantly greater proportion of patients showed an increase in systolic blood pressure subsequent to witnessing a death ($p < .01$) than they did 48 hr later. The same time period 48 hr later shows a greater proportion of patients with a decrease in systolic blood pressure. Although following a death in the CCU the proportion of patients showing an increase or decrease in heart rate is fairly evenly distributed, 48 hr later the trend for the Study Group is a decrease in rate ($p = 0.05$). However, in the Control Group no significant differences were found between Day I and Day III on systolic blood pressure or heart rate. The findings related to systolic blood pressure, particularly, suggest that witnessing a death has physiological effects on patients.

TABLE 1.—WITHIN GROUP COMPARISONS OF CHANGES IN SYSTOLIC BLOOD PRESSURE AND HEART RATE*

Group		Systolic blood pressure		p	Heart rate		p
		Increase N =	Decrease N =		Increase N =	Decrease N =	
Study group	Day I	10	3	< 0.01	6	7	< 0.05
	Day III	4	10		2	13	
Control group	Day I	4	7	NS	5	6	NS
	Day III	3	6		2	5	

* Patients exhibiting no change were excluded from the analysis.

TABLE 2.—BETWEEN GROUPS COMPARISONS OF CHANGES IN SYSTOLIC BLOOD PRESSURE AND HEART RATE*

Day of observation		Systolic blood pressure		p	Heart rate		p
		Increase N =	Decrease N =		Increase N =	Decrease N =	
Day I	Study group	10	3	< 0.05	6	7	NS
	Control group	4	7		5	6	
Day III	Study group	4	10	NS	2	13	NS
	Control group	3	6		2	5	

* Patients exhibiting no change were excluded from the analysis.

In the between groups comparison (Table 2), only on Day I is there a significant difference between the Study and Control groups ($p < 0.05$) on systolic blood pressure, with more of the Study Group showing an increase; no differences were found on heart rate. By way of contrast, 48 hr later both groups of patients are quite similar in the distribution of direction of change in systolic blood pressure and heart rate.

These findings suggest that increase in systolic blood pressure may not only indicate the clinical state of the patient but also a change in his psychological state.

Mood

To control for judge, the same nurse's rating of patient's mood was used from the shift (7–3 and/or 3–11) just prior to a death and compared with her rating of the same patient 24 hr later. Because of the demands on the nursing staff of the CCU this was the best and closest approximation of time and assessment of mood that could be made surrounding a death in the unit. A similar procedure was used surrounding the Day I time period for the Control Group.

The nurses were not told that the occurrence of a death in the unit was the time segment which would be the focus of the investigation. When an emergency arose, all of the nurses' efforts had to be concentrated on attempts to resuscitate. It was not possible for them to assess the effects of a critical event upon the other patients at the time of an arrest. Therefore, it was hoped that by not informing the nurses that the study was concerned with the effects of death upon the patients, that they would not be biased and look for changes of mood in relationship to that event.

Of the moods rated, namely, anxiety, depression, hostility, anger and fear, only change of rate in anxiety occurred often enough to warrant statistical analysis. As can be seen in Table 3, the Study Group had a statistically significantly greater proportion of patients who were assessed 24 hr later as exhibiting increase in anxiety than did the control group ($p < 0.01$). This is an interesting finding in that, even with two equally critically ill groups, one might expect anxiety to decrease generally following the passage of time in the hospital as the patient became accustomed to it.

TABLE 3.—BETWEEN GROUPS COMPARISON OF CHANGES IN RATING OF ANXIETY

Group	Anxiety		p
	Increase N =	Decrease or No Change N =	
Study group	9	8	< 0.01
Control group	1	11	

Descriptive data

The following two brief patient summaries illustrate the patients' psychological responses to death in the CCU: This was the sixth hospitalization for Mr. A., a white, 60 yr old fry cook. He was admitted to the hospital in coronary heart failure and with vascular insufficiency to the lower extremities. An electrocardiogram on admission showed evidence of an old anterioseptal and recent inferior wall myocardial infarction. His father and mother had both died of heart attacks at age 64 and 69 respectively. Three days after admission he was transferred to the CCU because of frequent PVC's. He was not apprehensive upon admission; however, the second day in the CCU a patient died and the nurse noted that Mr. A. became depressed and was afraid that he would never be better. He also said that he was afraid to go to sleep because he might never wake up. The two days following the death he seemed less depressed and hopeless. However, on the fifth day in the CCU another patient died. Mr. A. became more tense, hostile and agitated and asked to be moved to another room. He again said that he was afraid to go to sleep because he was afraid that he would die.

This was the second hospital admission for Mr. B., an obese 63 year old white farmer with a history of having had two myocardial infarctions. He was seen in the emergency room where he complained of chest pain and shortness of breath. His pulse rate was 200 and an electrocardiogram showed first degree heart block with recurrent ventricular extrasystole. Nine hours after Mr. B. was admitted to the CCU, a patient in the unit died and Mr. B. was noticeably depressed by the death. However, during the next five days he was cheerful, talkative and ambulatory and no PVC's were noted. During the afternoon of the sixth day in the unit, Mr. B. was observed talking in his sleep of dying. The monitor showed normal sinus rhythm with PVC's; his blood pressure was 176/120, pulse 100 and respiration 36. Upon awakening he complained of cold feet. PVC's were noted throughout the afternoon and evening. The next two days were uneventful.

Other events. Although the present study focused primarily around patients' reaction to death, data were also obtained, through interviews and observations, regarding patients' reactions to other aspects of the environment of the CCU. Patients frequently complained about disturbances by other patients. Moaning, crying and at times shouting, were cited as countering a restful environment. Perhaps the most dramatic example was that of Mrs. C., who was abruptly awakened one night by an elderly, disoriented patient in the adjoining bed who emptied a bedside pitcher of cold water on her. Figure 1 shows the significant changes in Mrs. C.'s blood pressure and the onset of PVC's that surrounded this event. Disturbances also included admissions and transfers. Newly admitted patients were frequently vocal in their expressions of pain. The transfer of patients out of the unit

165

sometimes meant that remaining patients would be moved to another bed in the unit. One white female patient objected to being moved beside a Negro male patient. Thus, the general environment was one that necessitated continual adjustment for the patients.

The monotonous clicking of the Bird respirator was an additional source of disruption. There was relatively little concern about the presence or sound of monitors. However, some patients expressed a fear of the monitor leads because they were in contact with electricity.

The continual parade of visitors was a disturbing influence to those patients who did not have visitors. However, these patients desired some type of interaction with others as evidenced by the fact

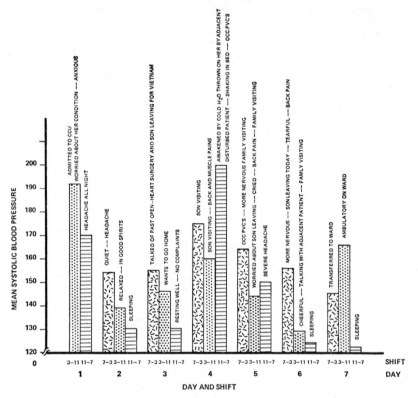

Fig. 1.—Changes in the mean systolic blood pressure associated with environmental events occurring during the CCU stay of a 60 yr old white, female patient with chronic rheumatic heart disease.

that they were more talkative with the interviewer, and at times, requested that he return to talk further. With numerous visitors, staff and the activity surrounding an admission, transfer or arrest, the unit was often noisy and disruptive.

When patients were interviewed following their transfer to the ward, the majority expressed relief at having left the unit.

COMMENT

The findings of the present study support the notion that patients in CCU units would be more comfortable in separate rooms. Despite the fact that patients might be given explanations about CCU procedures and the use of mechanical devices, the ability to observe the clinical progress and decline of adjacent patients and to witness cardiac arrests presents psychological hazards to the patients. Although death might be considered routine by the staff in the care of acutely ill patients, the impact of witnessing this event on patients has been shown in the present study to manifest itself in increases in systolic blood pressure and psychological symptoms of anxiety. The importance of a carefully monitored and restful environment for cardiac patients is well-recognized. In addition, however, the patient's attitude toward his own illness and recovery is strongly influenced by the medical care environment. The structure and organization of a CCU unit determines to a large extent the type of psychological stress to which patients will be exposed. While it is impossible to protect patients against all stressful conditions, it would seem crucial to minimize their exposure to them at a time when their own survival is threatened.

Acknowledgements—We are grateful to John M. Kalbfleisch, M.D., for helpful advice. We are especially indebted to Mrs. Mary Ann Mabry, R.N. and Mrs. Mary Lou Greenwald, R.N. who recorded daily observations of patients' mood and behavior throughout the study.

REFERENCES

1. LOWN B. Intensive Heart Care, *Scient. Am.* **219**, 19–27 (1968).
2. DAY H. W. An Intensive Coronary Care Area. *Dis. Chest* **44**, 423–427 (1963).
3. DAY H. W. Early Experiences in an Acute Coronary Care Area. *Lancet* **83**, 53–55 (1963).
4. DAY H. W. Effectiveness of an Intensive Coronary Care Area. *Am. J. Cardiol.* **15**, 51–54 (1965).
5. Hackett T. P., CASSEM N. H. and WISHNIE H. A. The Coronary-Care Unit: An Appraisal of Its Psychological Hazards, *New Engl. J. Med.* 279, 1365–1370 (1968).
6. KLEIN R. F., KLINER V. A., ZIPES D. P., TROYER W. G. and WALLACE A. G. Transfer From A Coronary Care Unit: Some Adverse Responses. *Archs Intern. Med.*, **122**, 104–108 (1968).
7. SCHOTTSTAEDT W. W., PINSKY R. H., MACKLEY D. and WOLF S. Sociologic, Psychologic and Metabolic Observations on Patients in the Community of a Metabolic Ward. *Am. J. Med.* **24**, 248–257 (1958).
8. JACKMAN N., SCHOTTSTAEDT W. W., MCPHAIL S. C. and WOLF S. Interaction, Emotion and Physiologic Change. *J. Hlth Hum. Beh.* **4**, 83–87 (1963).
9. CATTELL R. B. Anxiety and Motivation: Theory and Crucial Experiments In C. D. Spielberger. (editor), *Anxiety and Behavior*, Academic Press, New York (1966).
10. MARSH R. W., Tables for Testing the Significance of Difference Between Proportions, *Aust. J. Psychol.* **19**, 223–229 (1967).
11. GOODMAN L. S. and GILMAN A. *The Pharmacological Basis of Therapeutics.* Macmillan, New York (1965).

ATTITUDES TOWARD LIVING AND DYING IN PATIENTS ON CHRONIC HEMODIALYSIS*

Charles E. Norton

Uremia is a fatal illness, for which hemodialysis with the artificial kidney is a palliative. As long as patients are treated regularly two or three times a week for periods of eight to twelve hours at each session, they do not die of their uremia. Presently, some patients have been on hemodialysis for seven years.

It has often been said that it must be very fearful to depend on a machine for one's very life. Such a view tends, however, to miss the nub of the situation. A machine, after all, is as dependable as you make it. Carefully designed and constructed hemodialysis units are now available. Properly used, they are no more fatal than the guns we have around the house or the cars we drive. Improperly used, they provide an easy access to the bloodstream for infection and provide an easy way inadvertently to bleed to death. Carelessness in preparing the dialysate may lead to precipitous changes in blood chemistry, with unfortunate physiologic repercussions.

Patients on the artificial kidney machine do not depend on the apparatus; they depend on people. They depend on those who say, "I will take care of you" or, "Don't worry, that machine will do what it's supposed to do" or, "If there's any trouble, let us know and we'll see that it's taken care of.

In a recent paper[1] I have outlined something of the history of the development of a group of social structures in the Seattle area that have made it possible for patients there to enter into the uncertainties of chronic hemodialysis with relative assurance.

What is new and unknown is likely to upset us. What we have mastered bothers us only occasionally. Adjustment to being on and operating an artificial kidney is not so very much worse than becoming accustomed to driving a car.

The group of 25 patients I shall discuss are all patients at the Seattle Artificial Kidney Center. All are being treated in the center, although several are in the process of training for home dialysis. While the average cost for treatment per patient per year at the center is $10,000, only a few of these patients are paying any sizable part of this out of their own pocket; a substantial proportion is being funded wholly or in part by various insurance policies. A part is funded by government agencies such as the Veterans Administration. Such costs as are not met by these means are partially covered by state aid to the center and a rather considerable remainder by annual state and local fund drives by the center.

For the most part, all of these patients may fairly be considered rehabilitated; that is, from being bedridden and about to die of uremia, they have been returned to relatively active and productive lives, most of them carrying on pretty much as they did before they became ill. Certain new limitations relating to diet, to the use and care of the cannulated limb, and to the actual time involved in dialysis have been placed on their lives and routines. They are liable to certain recurrent physiological ups and downs related to the fact that dialysis is not a totally adequate replacement for a functioning kidney. These limitations can be very annoying, but they are not of the magnitude that would make a person a cripple or an invalid in most cases.

*This research was supported by John A. Hartford Foundation grant No. SD-62.

In a sense, society has done well by these patients. It has attempted to give them the best available medical care. It has provided a means of financial support so that such costs as the patient cannot handle will be covered and such that his ability to support himself and his family will not be impaired. It has arranged things so that, despite the unavoidable inconveniences, these patients have been enabled to live relatively normal lives.

Rationale for the Present Study

As many writers have pointed out, it appears that something in the nature of a social taboo surrounds the subjects of death and dying in our contemporary American culture. Why this should be so is not altogether clear, and many possible reasons have been suggested.

It is obvious that the subject is an unhappy one, and it may be that most people give it only cursory thought because of a distaste for unpleasant matters. It is also true that we are increasingly separated from the actual instances and circumstances of death even of those close to us, so that the natural stimulants to the deepening of our thought in this area are increasingly denied us.

We might then excuse the ordinary man for having little to say on such unpleasant subjects because of the fact that no particularly compelling circumstance has as yet induced him to formulate a philosophy or a point of view on these matters. The other group of people ordinarily considered in discussions of death and dying are those caught in the grip of a terminal illness. During this period, the pressures to deny the fact that one is dying seem very large, and the practical consequences of facing the facts or denying them appear to be relatively small. Whether one admits that one is dying and faces the fact openly or stubbornly denies that one is dying to the bitter end seems to be largely a matter of esthetics. The deathbed does not seem a very opportune place to learn philosophy or to achieve a psychological resolution concerning matters of living or dying.

On the other hand, patients now living by reason of the treatment they are receiving on the artificial kidney might be regarded as facing circumstances conducive to developing a philosophy on such matters while simultaneously being spared the implications of a relatively certain and immediate death. In a properly run program, patients on the artificial kidney are enabled to live generally normal lives. If the program is dependably run, the level of anxiety among the patients is well within tolerable limits. Death is in some ways both very near and very distant. Should the treatment be discontinued, death is certain within the space of a few weeks; as long as treatment continues, death from uremia is forestalled. Assuming the treatment to be dependable, then death for the kidney patient is as remote and unpredictable as it is for the rest of us.

Patients on the Seattle program are carefully screened; in practice, if anyone has been excluded, it has been for the most part for medical reasons. Psychological and social factors are also taken into account, especially if it appears that they would preclude rehabilitation to a useful social existence. Economic factors have operated irregularly, depending on the financial status of the kidney center. What one tends to get, then, is a rather wide range of types of people, all of whom would be classed generally as healthy functioning and productive members of society except for their kidney failure. Of the group studied, one or two patients have less than a high school education. Two or three have postgraduate degrees; one quarter of the others have college degrees; the remainder, or 60 percent, of the sample group, have a high school education.

People on chronic hemodialysis seem to constitute a group who are confronted with death in an unusual way in the sense that they are not in any immediate danger of dying. They have both the occasion and the opportunity to consider the real possibility of dying and to develop an attitude or philosophy toward this inevitable state of affairs. The question before us, under this set of circumstances, is: what sort of attitudes or philosophies toward living and dying do people, our friends and neighbors, the people we meet in the street, evolve?

We have asked ourselves the following additional questions:

1. Is the fear of death and the denial of this fear as pervasive as it is often assumed to be?

2. Does an acute confrontation with death change peoples' attitudes toward life, as the existentialists suggest?

3. Do people wish to be informed if they have a known fatal illness?

Certainly, a common way to ignore the issues involved in being mortal is simply not to give the matter much thought, or at least not enough thought to become emotionally upset. It is, however, not easy to determine who has tiptoed intellectually and gingerly around the subject and who has come emotionally face to face with the whole affair. To be philosophic rather than merely conventional is a relatively high-order achievement and rather uncommon. To be philosophical in this sense is to be able and inclined to confront the larger issues of life in one's imagination directly and face to face. It is an intellectual encounter between an actively aware, thinking person and the often bewildering array of ambiguous issues that surround him. Such an active confrontation with these issues leaves its mark upon a person. His or her thoughts in the area of the confrontation are apt to be more concrete, more detailed, and yet in some way more humble, as though the intricacies and ambiguities of the situation had become more real to him.

In the areas of their conventionality, however, conventional people are more apt to rely on the word of others or on hearsay. Their discussion is inclined to be brief and rather stereotyped. The details and the ambiguities are missing. One has the distinct impression that they are retelling what they have heard or are repeating an old and well-worn standard attitude.

Even under a fairly generous interpretation, only about half of the people in the group surveyed were able to convey the impression that they had given much, if any, independent thought to the subject. The other half gave little or no indication that they had considered or even cared to consider the issues. For the most part, the latter seemed quite unaccustomed to handling subjects at the level of abstraction that would be required to answer at all adequately such a general question as: What does it mean to me to be alive rather than dead? What values do I preserve by being alive?

People may not be philosophic or in the habit of viewing their situation from a generalized and abstract cognitive standpoint for many possible reasons. In some, genetic limitations may play a part. Some gave the impression of suppressing detailed cognitive explorations in a typical hysteric manner. Some identified such thinking as being soft or as wallowing in self-pity. Some appeared never to have progressed much beyond a very concrete level of thinking, wherein they concern themselves almost entirely with the specific details of what occurs without abstracting or generalizing therefrom. Any of these would suffice to prevent a person from thinking very effectively about life's meaning or significance for him; certainly, if a person is unable to generalize about the meaning of life, then he will be even less able to think very clearly about the implications of death or dying.

I would not be surprised if part of what is often called denial in the face of death represents the person's cognitive unreadiness or inability to deal with the generalities of his life. Death is in many respects not a specific entity. It is a generality, a not living any more. It is not a specific such as not going to work on Tuesday or not taking a vacation. It is a generality such as never going to work again or never taking another vacation. If one lives psychologically in a relatively concrete world—for example, "today I put on my shoes, then I went downstairs and ate bacon and eggs for breakfast, then I put on my coat and went to work"—one is apt to deal with death in a like manner—for example, "I did not die this morning, neither did I think or worry about it" or "This afternoon while I was crossing the street, a car suddenly turned the corner and ran into me. I was scared for a brief moment. Now I am in the hospital."

Indeed, one of the stronger impressions made upon this observer is that the great majority of everyday normal people are not particularly inclined to translate the basic assumptions or generalities of their lives into verbal terms. They are not particularly given to thinking explicitly about the larger questions of life: its meaning, its significant values and attributes, or the nature of a life well lived.

Each of the patients interviewed in this study appeared to be completely aware that his own death was at some time inevitable. However, with the process of hemodialysis working as well as it does, in reality they have as little knowledge as the rest of us of when their lives will end or how. The problem of facing up to an imminent and certain death does not arise; consequently, neither does the concept of denial as it is used in the case of people with known fatal and untreatable illnesses.

Denial in the general sense that a person seemed to exclude the possibility that he personally would ever die was not encountered in this group. A more benign denial of a religious nature, in which the person held that he would never quite altogether and completely perish, was very frequently encountered. Indeed, the latter form of adjustment to the inevitabilities of existence appears culturally sanctioned in a high degree, and in the form generally encountered in this group appears to have few practical disadvantages and some fairly evident psychological advantages in terms of personal comfort and esteem. Three quarters of this group claimed to place some, and in a number of instances considerable, stock in the view that the person will find himself involved in some sort of generally pleasant afterlife. None of this group, however, appeared to be in any particular hurry to experience this extraterrestrial existence.

In general, they did not appear to have wrestled with the question of an afterlife as a matter to be dealt with by reasons or proofs. For the most part, they seemed to accept the existence of an afterlife as if it were the conventional and generally acceptable thing to believe. Most had a relatively benign view of the matter and tended to assume that they would go to heaven. They were inclined to brush off questions as to what this afterlife might be as more or less irrelevant, as of little concern to them, or as something they had not considered very deeply.

Only one person in this group expressed any worry as to what might happen to the nature of himself in a life after death. This person had been brought up in a religious tradition and was inclined to take the matter of heaven and hell very seriously. This was the only instance where a practical and potent fear of the afterlife appeared to enter and significantly color daily events. This person suffered the most disruption of early family life of the entire group and showed significant depressive personality traits. It was as though he felt it necessary continually to justify the fact of existing in order to avoid the possibility of dying unjustified and going to hell. Such a capricious and arbitrary damnation would have been but a repetition of what happened in this person's childhood.

Most of these people did not appear to be particularly striving or achievement-oriented. The future did not appear to stretch out before them as a potential arena in which they might hope to develop or become something new or to give birth to some new values. Neither, as far as I can tell, had the future appeared that way to many of them prior to the time of their illness. Death in this context does not appear as much of a tragedy. Life is more a matter of carrying on one's responsibilities, living by the Golden Rule as much as possible, helping where one can be helpful, being cheerful and friendly where and when that is possible, and seeing to it that one's children get off to a good start. Death is no more than an end to this ongoing existence imposed rather willy-nilly by outside forces and circumstances. It is neither tragic nor fearful nor provocative of anxiety.

When asked what it meant to them to be alive rather than dead, perhaps a majority of the patients in this group indicated that they were grateful to be alive. Despite the aspects of conventional etiquette, however, one could not help but feel that, for the most part, the expression of gratitude represented something genuinely felt. When asked why were they grateful to be alive, the more hearty were inclined to answer that they enjoyed living and would be reluctant to stop at this point. In many respects, it struck this observer that this might well be as healthy and happy an answer as one could give to such a question.

A rather more common response related to patients' wishes to be around to watch and to assist their children grow and develop. As biologic creatures, human beings apparently are so constructed that at least in the early and middle portions of life they would rather live than die. Life is perceived as having a certain nonrational attractiveness, a kind of "let's-stick-around-and-see-what-happens" sort of a feeling, a sense of not wishing to let it go for good just yet. Beyond relatively close-at-hand translations of the above feeling, few of these patients appeared to have made much of an attempt to rationalize the feeling of why they wanted to stay alive.

If one takes "philosophical" to mean having the tendency to be verbally explicit about the larger meanings and values in one's life, most of these people were not so oriented. On the other hand, if one means having a tendency to live one's life according to a broad rather than an immediate and entirely local point of view, then a fair number of these people gave the impression of being genuinely, if somewhat inarticulately, philosophical. Faced with an ever-present reminder of the uncertain future, people kept alive by means of the artificial kidney claim not to worry about dying or being dead. This appears most generally as a kind of resignation, a sort of "what will happen will happen" attitude, frequently expressed as "What will happen is not in my hands" or "What will happen is in God's hands" or "When it's my time to go, I'll go."

The medical and physiologic aspects of treatment are outside the competence of most of these people. Intellectually, they probably represent a fair cross section of the population at large. The staff has practiced no secrecy toward these patients; discussions about their condition and their prospects have been open and frank. Except for those few with a medical or nursing background, most of the patients have only a hazy notion of the physiology of even a normal kidney. Although they are apt to know about BUN's and creatinine and potassium levels in relation to the reports of the frequent laboratory tests, very few would have more than a limited understanding of the pathophysiology involved.

In a very real way, then, they are medically at the mercy of or in the hands of others. They would be neither prepared nor able to take over their own complete management even if this became absolutely necessary. The more enterprising of the patients, however, do tend, especially if they are on home dialysis, to look into the technical and mechanical aspects of hemodialysis more closely and to discover

over a period of time what seems to work and what does not by an empirical, trial-and-error, or tinkering process. More to the point, however, is the fact that these persons rely, not so much on one or another particular individual person, as upon an already rather large and growing organization. If anything untoward happens to these patients, it will likely be in the nature of an unforeseen accident or an organizational breakdown or failure. The first can be dealt with only by day-to-day vigilance and care. The second requires the kind of overview into the organizational aspects of the kidney center that few of these patients have.

If pressed, most of these people tended to say that, if the thought of their death were to worry them, they would be concerned about the welfare of those they left behind. This was particularly true when the patients were parents of children who had not as yet left home. Husbands tended to feel a responsibility toward their wives and children, wives more often primarily for their children. Older patients whose children had left home gave a distinct impression of feeling less attached to life than those with younger offspring. The whole experience of having a reprieve from death seemed more casual to those whose families had become able to care for themselves.

Very few of this group would admit to any fear of the process of dying. A large number of this group were relatively close to dying of uremia prior to being dialyzed. A number had been in uremic coma. A number reported from their own experiences that one reaches a certain point in a severe illness at which one is so ill that one does not care whether one lives or dies; one wishes only that it would be decided one way or the other quickly.

One patient reported that he had had concern and anxiety about death and how he would be able to handle it until he caught pneumonia in his teens. During this illness, he experienced great difficulty in breathing and then became comatose for four days. When he recovered, he decided that, if that was all there was to dying, he would have the strength to handle it. In later years, much the same thing happened to him with uremia. This experience only confirmed for him the fact that, if this is what dying was like, then it was not too terrifying.

Since a worry or a fear is a rather difficult entity to quantify, one is rather puzzled to understand what is meant when one is told that a certain person has a fear of dying or that certain people do not entertain such fears. Fears come and go; they are fierce or fleeting. Occasionally, I may feel a fear of being bitten by a dog or of being involved in an accident in an automobile. Would it be meaningful to say I have a fear of dogs or automobiles?

To avoid this dilemma, the patients in this study were presented with a set of ten possible concerns. They were then asked to arrange these in order from those that might worry them the most to those that would worry them the least. Since many claimed not to worry at all, it was frequently necessary to ask them to assume that they were the worrying sort.

After all the patients had ranked these items, a generalized rank ordering was worked out so that in general one could see, over the entire group, how one kind of worry was compared to the others. The list of items in their final order, with the most worrisome item first, is as follows:

1. I will become a burden to others.
2. I will not be able to take care of my responsibilities.
3. I will not be able to accomplish the things I had hoped to achieve.
4. I will run out of money.
5. I will find myself living an unbearable kind of life.
6. The kidney center will not be able to continue caring for me.

173

7. Something that I can do nothing about will go wrong.
8. I will not go to heaven, or I might go to hell.
9. I will die unexpectedly.
10. Tomorrow I may be dead.

The fact of dying or of being dead appears in and of itself to be a relatively minor worry to this group of people. Such worrying as they do appears to revolve about possible unsatisfactory or painful states of being alive or about responsibilities or possible accomplishments projected into the future. Some of the possible worries imply that the patient might die, for instance, as a result of the center's being unable to care for him or that he might run out of money; however, the overall impression of this observer is that the anxiety revolves more about the fact that things will not go well or will go badly than about dying as such.

Dying and fears and worries about dying would seem to take on their content of meaning primarily from the issues of life and living. Dying is in many respects only a negation of living. To a person to whom life means little, death may likewise mean little. To a person attached to life, death will be meaningful as a potential loss that can be delineated only by enumerating his loves, his hopes, and his commitments to life.

In his book, "Modern Man and Mortality," Choron[2] points to a number of historic personages who suffered a marked fear of dying, among them Samuel Johnson, Goethe, and Freud. Perhaps it could be shown that fear of dying is in part proportionate to a person's estimate of his own worth: the greater a person's estimate of his own worth, the greater he might evaluate his loss should he die and the more susceptible he is to the feeling that someone or something might wish for malicious reasons to deprive him of his successes and future potential successes.

Most of the people interviewed in this study did not elevate themselves to this extent. In general, they give the impression of thinking of themselves as just about the same as most other people and maybe a little better off and certainly more fortunate than those who had died of diseases similar to their own.

If a child, while still young, had suffered the loss through death of one or other of the people on whom he had depended, then perhaps death would have been made real to him as an experience of loss to the living; death then acquires a connotation of desertion, destitution, or bitterness and bereavement. Alternatively, death perhaps represents some kind of literal removal to another existence, pleasant, unpleasant, or unknown. In that event, the anxiety might well be related to the proportion of the anticipated unpleasantness or unknown quantity. On the other hand, perhaps, one might feel oneself committed to certain responsibilities or attached to certain people or captivated by the sheer enjoyment of life. In that case, death would be seen as the loss of these goods, as the inability to carry on as one would wish, so that fear of death would have little to do with death as such and would represent rather one's disinclination to give up one's attachments to life.

All of these views and probably more are squeezed together linguistically into a few words such as "death," "dying," and "being dead." It is little wonder that our physiology reacts when these words are mentioned; to fathom that to which our physiology responds is another matter.

If, on the other hand, one views oneself as only a relatively ordinary mortal; if one has not experienced the fearful aspects of death and separation when one was young, impressionable and vulnerable; if one feels the books of one's life to be relatively well balanced, with oneself neither owing nor owed to; if heaven were relatively real and benign and one's conscience were clear—if all these were more or less the case and one claimed not to fear death or to worry or be anxious about its possibility, then shall we call that denial?

174

The question whether a direct confrontation with death has changed a person's view of life was approached by asking these people whether life looked any different to them since they had been ill or since they had been on the artificial kidney.

Of the 21 patients asked this question, 7 reported no change in their view of life. In general, these were among the more concretely or nonconceptually oriented types who gave the impression that issues of living and dying had not really touched their lives. Of the remaining 14, 4 reported changes from previously not considering what life meant to them to thinking about it now, as for example, "I never gave the matter any thought before my illness. Now I appreciate life more." In general, this change in point of view did not appear to have brought with it much, if any, change in the way these persons conducted themselves.

Three of the 14 reported changes in viewpoints that appeared to effect some noticeable changes in their behavior. Most typically, these people reported a tendency to devote more time to interpersonal relationships or to an endeavor to make something of their lives. Three reported changes in their views and ways of life that seemed more related to other aspects of their existence. One had been single before his illness and was now married; another had just entered adolescence and was experiencing a general intellectual awakening; one had grown old and stale at his job prior to his illness, but found a renewed challenge and self-esteem in proving that he could carry on adequately despite his handicap.

One of the 14 reported a radical change that occurred literally overnight when he learned of his fatal illness. Prior to his illness, his business conduct had diverged from his religions and normal values. His conversion to a more integrated life was of the sort that would warm the heart of any lover of Dickens' "A Christmas Carol." Two were people in their forties who had for one reason or another already faced the issues of life and death earlier in their lives and whose experience with kidney disease only reinforced earlier philosophic attitudes. One reported a marked increase in frustration because his illness continually interfered with his habit of making and carrying out long-range business plans.

In general, it would be hard to determine how much the quality of these people's lives has been changed by their experience. The tendency would, however, appear to be in the direction of an increased appreciation of what they already had and a tendency to elevate the value of interpersonal relationships as compared to the possession of material goods. When this group was asked whether they would wish to be informed if it should happen that they fell victim to another fatal illness not related to their present disease—for instance, cancer—80 percent said they would want to be told.

If, as I am inclined to assume, this small group represented for the most part a random selection of our great middle class, then of this class I would say that, in the face of death postponed, it is inclined to be stoic, resigned, and more or less self-satisfied. The group as a whole is inclined to feel that worrying is useless, that the best thing to do is to keep going as well as one is able, to carry out one's ordinary tasks and responsibilities, to enjoy life if that is possible, and where possible to avoid becoming a burden to others. On the whole, they appear to take the world about them at face value, accepting it as it appears to be without being either skeptical or curious.

Elaborate justifications, rationalizations, and intellectual inquiry of the adolescent or philosophical sort are in general conspicuous by their absence. Only a few appear to be asking themselves, "Is this whole undertaking worth the effort involved?" Few inquired how the project came about or who is operating it. Few appear to have examined explicitly the values encompassed in their lives, the implications of their views on the afterlife, or the possible social or psychological implications of the experiment in prolonging life in which they were participating.

On the other hand, talking about the issues of life and death with several of these people was for this observer a moving experience. These people gave the impression of being on comfortable and friendly terms with life. Death for them was but one of the innumerable comings and goings of life, to be neither dreaded nor denied. For them, the earth was good mother, trustworthy, calm, compassionate. It seems quite clear that a more than ordinary intellectual accomplishment is not a necessary precondition for psychological health or for the attainment of a perfectly workable view on matters of living and dying.

REFERENCES

1. NORTON, C. E. 1967. Chronic hemodialysis as a medical and social experiment. Ann. Intern. Med. **66**: 1267.
2. CHORON, J. 1964. Modern Man and Mortality. The Macmillan Co., New York, N.Y.

DISCUSSION OF THE PAPER

DR. OTTO MARGOLIS (Affiliation Unavailable): What are the criteria that one would use in distinguishing between a lack of anxiety—in fact, sometimes even a lack of concern with death—and what you might consider to be a denial of death?

DR. NORTON: I would be very unhappy to be compelled to answer that question. However, I have the feeling that, if one approaches the whole question from too limited a framework, then many things that might not be denial are labeled as denial. It was my intention to see whether I could distinguish some of these things.

DR. MARGOLIS: I know what the psychiatric definition of denial is; it's a feeling that what is actually true isn't true. That would be a fairly severe definition, and certainly it very seldom comes up in that strict sense.

DR. RICHARD ELGOSIN (Affiliation Unavailable): I wonder if you found in this group of patients any who sought death actively by seeking mistreatment or who in any way wanted to die rather than live?

DR. NORTON: Not in this particular group of 25. Now, I might mention the Scribner group's overall rate of mortality. So far, they've had experience with 71 patients, and over the whole time of their program have lost 8, none of these defined as suicide. That means that all of the rest of the people we've had experience with are still living. Several people, I felt, were unhappy or not sure that their way of living was quite worth the effort, but I encountered no one who in any way gave me the impression that he was seriously thinking of suicide or might attempt it.

DR. NORBERT BURLIS (Affiliation Unavailable): Is there a difference between patients on home dialysis and those who come to the clinic?

DR. NORTON: I can't answer that. I've been in contact with both, but this particular study was done entirely with inpatients.

DR. GIFFORD: Perhaps I should say how I felt about the question of denial. I admit that it's used in a very loose and general way. I think it conveys more the meaning of knowing intellectually, but not believing in a deeper sense, and I thought that I would have to interpret the very bland, comfortable picture that your patients gave as an evidence of how successful their denial was. That list of the ten concerns, of which the tenth was, "I may not be living tomorrow," was a perfect example of this. I have some things to discuss about a colleague of mine who has been working with a kind of group therapy with spouses of patients on home dialysis; he found that this was very helpful to them, mainly in dealing with their guilty and hostile feelings about the sick person. They revealed such fears as making a mistake with a machine or deliberately killing their spouse. I wondered if you have had similar encounters.

DR. NORTON: We have not had a regular program of therapy or group therapy. On several occasions, the nurses brought together a group of wives and, from their report, what eventuated was this: since the patients were being cared for directly there were feelings of being left out, and that because there is a lot of psychological and social activity invested in the Center by the patients. A sort of in-group phenomena takes place.

I'd like to go back to the question of denial, not because I consider myself an expert, but only to share my thought, a hypothesis that recurs to me, that this question may well be very distinctly a matter of the presuppositions that the observer brings. After all, the observer thinks that this treatment should be onerous. When the patient denies this, the observer says, "I certainly think it is; therefore, you're denying it." I don't know how you can get around that. I can say only that, the longer I've been with the program, the more I have the feeling that in some sense the adaptation to such procedures is genuine. You see it in some patients in psychotherapy—for example, the great fear they have of driving a car. They have never driven a car. They postponed it in the 30's and 40's; finally, they started with a great deal of anxiety and after a while they emerged, in a sense feeling that they had mastered it. If that's denial, then in a sense we're all continually denying. I don't know how we're going to resolve that.

DR. SENESCU: Do you have any information about the period between the time the patient is an applicant and the time he is selected for dialysis? Second, I'd like to make one comment about denial, which we've been discussing here as an aside. Having struggled with the concept for a long time now, I think it is too gross. I think that it must be measured in behavioral terms. People say they get impaled on this issue because they rely on what the patient admits. I've gotten in trouble myself many times on this. If the individual does not take care of himself, only then can you begin to speak of denial.

DR. HOLLAND: What is your selection rate? You generalized in saying that you thought that this was perhaps applicable to the general American middle class, but initially stated that these were 25 patients who were selected for their cooperativeness and general suitability for the program. Selected from what size population? Also, how long must they wait?

DR. NORTON: A lot of issues have been made about the selection process in the Seattle area, they have been quite careful, especially at the center. They have two committees. They have a medical advisory committee, composed largely of doctors, which rules on what you might call medical criteria. These criteria are: no heart disease and relatively good physiologic condition—aside from kidney disease. Age also enters to some extent there; if you're getting too old, that would be called a medical criterion. Then a second committee, which is anonymous, evaluates people on their social use; this group has actually functioned very little and has been called on to decide only on those relatively rare occasions that occurred earlier when there were two people and room for only one. In general, when there are enough places available, that committee has tended to approve routinely.

As far as I can see, most of the selection process must go through informal channels outside the system—that is, with regard to who is initially referred to the Center. Everybody is supposed to be referred by a doctor. We don't get large numbers of welfare-type patients, so we haven't had to turn them down; neither have we had to make financial commitments to these people. Actually, few people have been rejected. When I last checked into the whole experience of the center—the center now has some thirty-odd patients— they had turned down only seven or eight people and a number of these people had gone elsewhere, some to the Veterans Administration. Obviously, the selection process is not severe.

DR. RACY: Dr. Norton's description of these patients and his matter-of-fact approach to their treatment is very reassuring, but I am disturbed by this question: Do you have the feeling that your group was, psychologically speaking, hypernormal?

DR. NORTON: I wish that I could say that. No, not really. As a matter of fact, I was interested in the study because I am trying to evaluate for myself what the man in the street is like psychologically; I was rather assuming that these people were just randomly selected in regard to psychological strengths and weaknesses.

DR. RACY: Yet, if you consider psychiatric surveys and studies elsewhere, you would think that, even in a population as small as this, the incidence of psychopathology, quite apart from whether the kidney is functioning or not, would be higher than this. You have given a remarkably idyllic picture of a very fine group of people.

DR. NORTON: This is not to say that there is no psychopathology; I could recognize a great deal. Nothing of psychotic proportions, however; in this group no severe character disorders are evident, but there are many neurotic disorders and many neurotic characters. There are a number who seem to me to be quite clearly hysterical, and there are a number of neurotics whom anybody working in the center could easily identify, because they give their associates such a hard time.

DR. RACY: But this did not seem to affect the treatment or the response to the possibility of death?

DR. NORTON: I mentioned earlier the trouble that some of the staff had with people with what we would call neurotic character disorders of a fairly adamant type. In this setting it becomes perfectly clear that, even with this larger sanction of death, there are some people who will keep their neurotic perspective on life, and they'll continue to have the severest headaches and pains month after month until they decide that it would perhaps be in their best interest to change.

DR. RACY: The following speculation is implicit in my question: I wonder if something about the setup and its implications is not conducive to a massive form of denial that may affect the study. I'm not saying this is adaptive or bad, but these people may have a vested interest in presenting this as very successful.

DR. NORTON: I wouldn't argue the proposition; I think it may well be. Other factors also have occurred to me. These people have been selected in a most extraordinary way to be treated well. They have the sense of being cared for. It's not often that you find people who will subsidize you to the extent of $10,000 a year for the rest of your life, especially if you're a barber or a day laborer or a Boeing mechanic; we have a number of these. It seems to me that this would be extremely comforting and esteem-building.

DR. HOLLAND: Is the transference to Dr. Scribner at a Godlike level?

DR. NORTON: Dr. Scribner enters almost not at all into the life of the patients at the kidney center. Dr. Pendras is the physician in charge of the center, and they look to him as their physician. They never see Dr. Scribner.

DR. HOLLAND: Is he beatified?

DR. NORTON: I wouldn't say so, not there. He may be crucified elsewhere!

UNIDENTIFIED SPEAKER: I wonder what the feelings of these people are toward the artificial kidney and kidney transplants and whether they entertain any hope for the improvement of transplants?

DR. NORTON: I haven't asked everybody, but the general opinion that I pick up is that these people generally tend to look forward to a transplant as a possible way out of having to spend the rest of their lives on dialysis. From my point of view, this is somewhat unrealistic; people with a broader medical background don't necessarily visualize this possibility. The man in the street, our average patient, seems to have that hope. I think perhaps that one of the reasons for this is that we've had no first-hand experience in Seattle with transplants; consequently, none of these patients has been shocked by the trials and tribulations of the procedure.

DR. HOLLAND: Have you at any time seen depression break through this rather complacent facade? I have a feeling that it would be unrealistic to expect patients over many many months to maintain this kind of equanimity in the face of considerable stress.

DR. NORTON: This possibility always exists. I wouldn't be surprised if one lady I mentioned in my paper became depressed, because she's that type, but as yet she has not. Another lady, a fairly normal person, nonphilosophical in the verbal sense, who has always lived on a farm and is very much in tune with reality, seems to fit in this category. She has been very unhappy because her farm and her family are way off in Montana; in order to get this treatment, she's had to be separated and uprooted. You get a recurrent feeling in talking to her that she is weighing this cost. However, that's a case of being separated from one's family and loved ones; it's not a matter of putting up with the discomfort of the treatment.

DR. HOLLAND: All the reports I have read about chronic dialysis speak of the appearance of neuropathy—a new disease that carries with it pain and discomfort. You have not mentioned this or any other adverse effects. Is the hostility that may be related to getting an impairment of the use of hands or feet, for example, displaced to this syndrome? Or is it ascribed to dialysis? Or does this not occur in Seattle?

DR. NORTON: Neuropathy and bad neuropathy occurred early in the program; patients still have residual effects. Empirically, it seems to be a result of insufficient dialysis. Anyway, neuropathy has not continued. Apparently this is because the word has gone out to physicians that, if they consider sending someone for treatment, they should send them relatively early before they get this, and then we'll treat them adequately so that they may avoid this complication.

DR. HOLLAND: Would another possible interpretation be that the neuropathy occurs late in the course of uremia and dialysis, and that the patients will all eventually get neuropathy? What I have seen is not ascribed to the uremia as such, but rather to the dialysis.

DR. NORTON: I shall not pretend to be a pathophysiologist. I can say only that the experience of the group seemed to be the opposite. We had people who started out with a bad neuropathy, which has improved; none are presently getting worse, and the new people are not contracting it.

MR. PRITCHARD: This is another indication of how little the professionals really know about patients. I'd like to emphasize this by discussing denial and the expression by patients of the wish to die. Let's assume that anxiety exists. If it's on the patient's side, he may have instinctive or cultural ways of handling it. If it's on the doctor's side, he may also have his own ways of handling it. In the hospital I was in, the interns and residents often asked me to visit patients they thought were going to die and probe their reactions, because they themselves could not talk to them. Their view was that the patients were denying that they were dying. It occurred to me that perhaps the patient was trying to bolster the physician's morale because he realized how upset the doctor was, how personally he took the impending loss of the patient. To give an example of this, the last words of one man in the hospital were, "Did I play it right, Doc?"

With regard to the wish to die, I wonder if we could not view this as a more diffuse phenomenon. I was thinking of comparing suicidal and pseudosuicidal intention with the cry for help. If a person says, "I want to die," depending on the way he says it, he may in fact be saying, "I don't want to die." Nevertheless, the doctor may take this as an expression of his wish to die and begin to doubt the possibility of saving him. In a mixed society, people from different ethnic and cultural backgrounds express themselves differently. South Europeans, for example, are inclined to dramatize and express their worries freely. This is a way of disposing of a situation by overdramatizing it. Anglo-Saxons from the Northern countries tend to hold things in and thus try to neutralize a situation. Thus, I think we may be missing many pointers given to us by patients by tending to take the profession's definition of denial.

DR. NORTON: Although I've had experience only in Seattle, I've read the literature and talked to some of the people at other places. I have the distinct impression that many ways of running a program don't work out very well. A number of people have had trouble running a program staffed by rotating interns and residents and a center manned by people who change every month. This would create, I think, a tremendous anxiety in everybody concerned. By way of contrast, both of the nurses at the center have been with Dr. Scribner's program practically since its inception seven years ago. Dr. Pendras was then a fellow and is now running the program; I think he's been acquainted with dialysis for almost as long a time. Everybody is definitely as experienced as one can be in this work—it's a professionally committed field. It may make some of the psychiatrists shudder to be told that the nurse I mentioned before was single and took a liking to one of our patients and married him. This girl is very cognizant of death and dying and talks about it frequently. However, if he didn't have a kidney disease, I would say that the husband would be an entirely suitable mate. He's a college professor of physics, a very nice man who has done some work on the kidney machine, figuring out its mathematics. In that sense it's not pathological, except as you may not like the idea of the nurse's going ahead with the situation even with her eyes open.

Psychological Aspects of Chronic Haemodialysis

A. HARARI, H. MUNITZ, H. WIJSENBEEK, J. LEVI, M. STEINER AND M. ROSENBAUM

INTRODUCTION

This study concerns some of the psychosocial problems of patients undergoing chronic haemodialysis. More specifically, we investigated changes and problems in the areas of work, finances, sexual and social activity and family relations. A person undergoing dialysis is often unable to work regularly, due to impairment of his physical and mental abilities. He may suffer from complications which limit his physical abilities. Furthermore, Shea et al. (6) noted that disturbances in memory and concentration and general irritability are characteristic of such patients.

The nature and frequency of the treatment appear to be most crucial in affecting the patients' work habits. They must lose hours of work at least twice a week when they are being dialysed. This problem is only partially alleviated by night dialysis. In addition, after dialysis most patients suffer from headaches, nausea and general weakness that further impair their working capacities (8). In many cases also the patients have to change jobs or occupations in order to move closer to the renal unit (7).

The inability to work regularly has significant implications for the financial status of the patients. The cost of dialysis may be a further financial drain. Although in Israel the actual cost of dialysis is taken care of by the Health Insurance Scheme (most of our patients are insured in the Workers' Sick Fund of the General Federation of Labour), there are additional expenses. These expenses involve travel, medical care and blood for transfusions. Sand et al. (3) describe the emotional stress suffered by patients due to the loss of income. McNamara (2) mentions a case in which it took 150 hours for social workers to deal with the patient's financial problems. The dialysis may considerably restrict the patient's social activities. In addition to his physical disabilities, a patient often loses interest in social activities due to feelings of shame, guilt and anxiety. The family on the other hand may be so overprotective as to prevent the patient from

181

any activity. Shea et al. (6) describe how such patients establish new social groups in which they meet together and extend emotional help to each other.

The family is perhaps most affected when one of its members undergoes haemodialysis. Certain difficulties and stress emerge between the patient and his close relations. Cramond (1) ascribes these to the fact that when the mother is absent from home twice a week, there are many members of the family at home who help and that because of this shunt, the mother is afraid to love her children. When the father undergoes dialysis, the irritability caused by his loss of earning capacity may affect his relationship to his children. Generally, the parent–child relationships are more affected when the mother than when the father is a patient, since the mother is better able to regulate the relations at home than the father. Physical and psychosocial factors strongly influence the relationships between the patient and the marital partner.

Schreiner (4) found testicular atrophy in all patients suffering from chronic uraemia. Those patients who were on chronic dialysis suffered from amenorrhoea and impotence. Shambauch et al. (5) mentioned impotence and lack of libido as causing stress in the relationships between the patients and their spouses. The men felt their loss of masculinity while the wives were tense due to lack of sexual gratification. Further, since the wife often becomes the main provider there is an additional loss in the husband's self-esteem and feeling of masculinity.

Shambaugh et al. (op. cit.), who examined 18 patients and their families, reported that all partners believed that the illness would lead to absolute disability or death. Some of their subjects even wondered why their partners had not committed suicide. In some cases strong dependency feelings developed, when the patients viewed their partners as doctors. This was particularly noted in home dialysis. Shambaugh et al. (op. cit.) reported a case in which the partner developed a depressive episode after his spouse underwent successful transplantation.

METHOD

Subjects

Nineteen patients, 11 from the Beilinson Hospital (Petah Tikwah), and 8 from Ichilov Hospital (Tel Aviv), took part in the survey. Of the Beilinson patients 6 were dialysed at night and 5 in the daytime. In the Ichilov Hospital all dialyses were performed in the daytime. Each patient was dialysed twice a week.

The mean age of the patients was 37 years, ranging from 18–67 years; 16 patients were males and 3 were females; 12 patients were married with children, 6 males were single and 1 female was a widow. The mean time in dialysis for all patients was 16 months, ranging from 3–48 months. With the exception of the 2 youngest patients all patients had been born outside Israel.

Procedure

Each patient was interviewed twice in a half-open interview, each interview lasting 1 hour. Since many patients hoped for transplantation and thus might have suspected that the interviewing process was part of a selection programme, it was explained to them that the purpose of the survey was to gather information for the establishment of new renal units. Thus the patients were prevented from giving "good answers". The interview questions referred to five main areas: work, finances, social and sexual activity and family relationships. The subject was asked to state whether changes had occurred in these areas in the four following periods: before the start of the illness, during illness, in early phase of dialysis and during dialysis. In addition, the subjects were asked about their expectations for the future.

RESULTS AND DISCUSSION

Table 1 shows the number of patients who reported either decline, no change or improvement during the illness, and in the early phase of dialysis, and their expectations for future changes in the areas of work, finances, social activity, family relationships and sexual activity.

TABLE 1

THE NUMBER OF PATIENTS WHO REPORTED EITHER DECLINE, NO CHANGE, OR IMPROVEMENT DURING ILLNESS, IN THE EARLY PHASE OF DIALYSIS, DURING DIALYSIS, AND THEIR EXPECTATIONS FOR FUTURE CHANGES IN THE AREAS OF WORK, FINANCES, SOCIAL AND SEXUAL ACTIVITY AND FAMILY RELATIONSHIPS

| | | Work | Finances | Social activity | Interfamilial relations | | Sexual activity |
					to spouse or parent	to children	
During[a] illness	decline	13	8	6	1	1	11
	no change	2	7	9	4	5	5
	improvement	1	1	1	11	4	0
Early phase of dialysis	decline	9	12	7	1	2	10
	no change	9	6	12	5	7	8
	improvement	1	1	0	12	4	1
During dialysis	decline	1	5	2	3	1	2
	no change	10	8	14	9	8	10
	improvement	8	6	3	6	4	7
Expectations	decline	1	6	1	1	1	0
	no change	3	3	15	14	11	9
	improvement	15	10	3	3	1	10

[a] Three patients started immediately with dialysis.

Most patients showed a strong decline in their ability to work during illness and the early phase of dialysis. However, during dialysis there was improvement in about 50% of the patients. Nearly all patients hoped that their ability to work would improve. They associated the improvement with an improvement in physical condition and

183

hopes of transplantation. All patients changed their occupations to lighter ones or stopped working.

Most patients were economically affected by their illness. In all but 4 cases the main reason for financial decline was the patient's inability to work. In the 4 exceptional cases the decline was due to hospital fees, payments for blood and travel expenses. Most of the financial declines occurred during the illness (in 8 patients) and at the start of dialysis (in 12 patients). In 5 patients there was a continuous decline all through their illness. Except for 1 patient, who had been ill for 20 years, there was no reported financial improvement at the start of dialysis. However, during dialysis there was improvement in 6 patients and 5 out of these expected further improvement. The 6th expected no change. The main reasons for improvement were pensions, insurance or government help. A few patients remarked that they needed to pay less for blood transfusions. Ten patients expected future improvement with better health, which would enable them to work more. Social activities tended to decline especially during illness and the early phase of dialysis. Eight patients ascribed this decline to their physical weakness. Many noted fatigue within 1 hour or less of contact with people. Others complained they could not dance. One patient was overprotected by his wife, who did not even let him go to the cinema (though he was able to do so physically). Three patients isolated themselves because they did not wish others to learn about their illness. One of these found himself a different set of friends, none of whom knew about his illness. Five patients were socially isolated even before the onset of the disease.

Two patients blamed society for their decline in social activities. Partial social recovery was noted in only 2 patients; most patients showed no recovery. Very few patients expected any recovery in social activities. Of the 3 who did, two noted an improvement during dialysis. Most patients reported improvement in the relationships to their spouses or their parents during the illness, before dialysis, and at the start of dialysis. However, during treatment only one-third of the patients indicated improvement in this area, and 3 patients actually noted a decline. As to the future, the majority believed that no changes would occur in their relations with the family. It appears that, as the patients fell ill, the family became more united. On the other hand, during dialysis the family became somewhat accustomed to the state of illness, and less improvement in interfamilial relations was noted.

Thirteen of the patients examined had children. Nine were parents of children under 18, while 4 had older children. Only 2 patients reported a decline in their relationships with their children. They ascribed this to their growing impatience with their children. Over 50 % of patients reported no change in the relations. Four patients reported improvement. It seems that the patients tried to protect the children from the adverse effects of the illness.

Nearly all patients showed some decline in libido and sexual activity. This was not uniform in all patients. Some reported less frequent intercourse, others lack of ejaculation or lessening of sexual interest. Less than half of the patients reported some improvement during dialysis, but only 2 females reported that there was no substantial decline in their sexual activity. Four patients refrained from sexual intercourse though they claimed they were able to do so, physically. One couple feared another pregnancy. One patient severed contact with his girl friend lest she learned about his illness. Two patients thought their kidneys might be adversely affected by sexual intercourse.

SUMMARY

The authors examined the changes that occurred at selected times in the course of the illness in chronically dialysed patients. Each patient (the total number was 19) was interviewed twice in an half-open interview, each interview lasting 1 hour. Five main areas were covered: work, finances, social activity, family relationships and sexual activity.

During the illness there is a trend towards a decline in the parameters of work, finance, social and sexual activity.

In the early phase of dialysis this trend seems to continue. During dialysis, this trend seems to stop and even shows some improvement.

The family relationship is the one parameter which seems to improve with the illness; this improvement seems to continue all through the illness.

REFERENCES

1. CRAMOND, W. A., Renal homotransplantation. Some observations on recipients and donors, *Brit. J. Psychiat.*, 113 (1967) 1223–1230.
2. McNAMARA, M., Psychosocial problems in a renal unit, *Brit. J. Psychiat.*, 113 (1967) 1231–1236.
3. SAND, P., LIVINGSTONE, G. AND WRIGHT, R., Psychological assessment of candidates for a hemo-dialyis program, *Ann. intern. Med.*, 64 (1966) 603–610.
4. SCHREINER, G. E., Hemodialysis for chronic renal failure, Part 3 (Medical, moral, ethical and socioeconomical problems), *Ann. intern. Med.*, 62 (1965) 551–557.
5. SHAMBAUGH, P. W., HAMPERS, C. L., BAILEY, G. L., SNYDER, D. AND MERRIL, J. P., Hemodialysis in the home-emotional impact on the spouse, *Trans. Amer. Soc. artif. Organs*, 13 (1967) 41–45.
6. SHEA, E. J., BOGDAN, D. F., FREEMAN, R. F. AND SCHREINER, G. E., Hemodialysis for chronic renal failure, Part 4 (Psychological considerations), *Ann. intern. Med.*, 62 (1965) 558–563.
7. WRIGHT, R., SAND, P. AND LIVINGSTONE, G., Psychological stress during hemodialysis for chronic renal failure, *Ann. intern. Med.*, 64 (1966) 611–621.
8. WIJSENBEEK, H. AND MUNITZ, H., Group treatment in a hemodialysis center, *Psychiat. Neurol. Neurochir.*, 73 (1970) 213–220.

Group Treatment in a Hemodialysis Center

H. WIJSENBEEK AND H. MUNITZ

INTRODUCTION

Although recommended, group therapy is seldom discussed *per se* in the pertinent literature on the treatment of chronic renal failure in an intermittent hemodialysis program.

The authors treated a small group of such patients during one year in weekly sessions. Frequent topics, discussed in the groups were family problems, death problems, aggression and submission, the shunt as a visible reminder of the disease and changes in the body image.

The task of the psychiatrist in the unit towards the patients and the medical staff was discussed. It seemed that his task was more to add to modern technology a human understanding than assisting the medical staff in the selection of patients, although the authors do not exclude a scientific way of finding the right patients for such a program.

Patients will receive and work with a psychiatrist in their group in a better understanding, knowing that he is not a member of a selection committee. This knowledge will improve the doctor-patient relationship.

It is too early to evaluate the results of this form of treatment. The account which follows deals with psychiatric group treatment under exceptional circumstances, with a group of patients who are undergoing intermittent hemodialysis.

This is a group of people who live under continuous, extraordinary stress. Their lives are wholly dependent upon recent technological advances in medicine. This very progress, however, raises new problems for the patient as well as the physician; the mechanisation of medicine.

The patient is required to cooperate not only with medical personnel, but with a machine as well. This is a natural outgrowth of increased sophistication in laboratory techniques, and it is also in tune with our computerized technology. The introduction of the computer in medicine, however, is not only a means to precision in data processing. Many physicians tend to use the machine as a defense against human contact with the patient.

The physician, educated to exert all his powers toward the saving of human lives, is now faced by a contradiction: economic considerations force him to limit the number of patients who may benefit from this therapy. In effect, then, the physician must choose: not who will live, but who will die. His position is made still more difficult since the definition of death is changing. We have reached an era when technology permits us to prolong an individual life by providing him with the healthy organs of another individual. Some of these organs, however, have been the focus of human emotion and imagination as the kidneys in the Old Testament and the heart as the site of love and courage, and not merely a specialized muscle to be transplanted. It is to be expected that these factors as well as others will lead us to revise our approach to death.

It is not surprising then that in some centers group therapy is being carried out not with the patients but with the medical staff itself (3).

We divided the problems of the patients in a renal unit as follows: (i) problems of the chronically ill; (ii) specific problems of hemodialysis; (iii) the problems of the person permanently threatened by death. We concentrated in this paper on points (ii) and (iii).

The psychological reactions of these patients vary both in form and in intensity.

In the last years interest has grown in the psychiatric aspects of chronic renal failure. The psychiatrist may be called upon to aid in the selection of patients, or to treat them. Sometimes he fulfils both functions. It seems to us that anyone dealing with the selection of patients must ask himself: "Am I able to foretell accurately how a person will withstand hemodialysis and/or renal transplantation?".

An extensive review of the literature on the psychological aspects of chronic hemodialysis was published recently by MacAfee Husek (2). Most of the papers reviewed here were studied by us but we feel that her review relieves us from again discussing several separate papers. From her review it becomes clear that the criteria for selecting patients for a dialysis program is still wide open for further deliberation. We want to point out that the patients forming our group were not selected per se and we started our work only after the patients were received in the unit. This relieved us, perhaps, from the severe guilt feelings between members of the staff, as described by Kaplan De-Nour and Czaczkes (3). Nowhere in the literature we found the observation about the difficulties connected with selecting patients in a small country. In Israel these difficulties are obvious because everyone knows everyone and this leads to personal relations building up unscientific pressures on members of the staff. This again is connected to socio-economic factors and possible changes in familial patterns and interaction between the patient, the doctor, the family of the patient and his role in society. These interactions were examined by Harari from our Department (1). Most authors feel that group therapy is the most beneficial therapeutic approach to help counteracting the stress experienced by these patients (2). But we did not find a more detailed report of working in a group of patients in the literature.

Group therapy is well suited to a group of patients faced by a genuine threat, as opposed to a neurotic fear. This was well understood by the medical non-psychiatric members of the unit and led to the request put to us for psychiatric group work in the unit. Our impression was that the medical staff felt that by giving care to the patients will help the staff to cope better with their own problems. We understood that they, and later on we ourselves, feel that the death of one patient under its care means also the death of another, the patient who had not been chosen for care — but if he had, might then have lived. We accepted their invitation with mixed feelings and only after prolonged consideration.

The presence of the group diminishes the threat of a psychiatrist. The group's dynamics reflected their position in society and the ability to interact successfully within the group enhanced the individual's adjustment outside the group.

Within the group patients were able to express their anxieties freely. The group atmosphere also accepted their aggression and encouraged them to verbalize it. They were treated as people and not as patients. Within the group they learned from one another how to cope with certain of their difficulties. They also had direct communication with the nephrologist attending the sessions, and a simple clarification from him could reduce anxiety and resolve many daily problems.

Some of the patients felt the need for psychiatric assistance. However, others perceived the psychiatrist as a compounded threat: *i.e.* expressing danger to sanity as well as life. This fear, however, disappeared very quickly, and they initiated contact. On the other hand, the nursing staff felt that their patients were being taken from them and that the going-on in the group seemed mysterious. These feelings led to a certain measure of resistance in the nurses.

COMPOSITION OF THE GROUP

The group under treatment is comprised of the patients, the psychiatrist, the nephrologist and a secretary, writing protocol. There were 8 patients, in age ranging from 17 till 57, 7 males and 1 married female. They met once a week for one year in the unit. After the meeting in the late afternoon hours, they were connected to the machine. Many times we went then to the treatment room and talked with the patients separately. An interesting aspect was the psychiatric atmosphere in real "clinical surroundings", something like a psychiatrist in an operation theatre. A second group of patients who were not participating in the therapeutic meetings became aware of the therapy group. The mere existence of the therapy group influenced this second group. A closer examination of such a secondary group seems indicated.

MATERIAL

The material brought up in group meetings may be divided into 3 parts, distinguished by the time and the topics of conversation. In the first stage patients confined their discussion to very superficial problems, such as those concerned with employment. Any attempt to touch upon their personal problems was warded off.

In the second stage the central topic was the medical regime and its effects upon the patient's life. Matters such as the diet, the shunt and the machine were discussed.

At this stage patients were helped to overcome their difficulties in self-expression. They also used this opportunity to verbalize a large measure of aggression against the medical staff.

In the third stage the patients discussed the place of the patient within his family, his feelings as a sick individual, and the reactions of the family to the patient's illness. They described the problem of overprotective attitudes within their families. Others, on the contrary, voiced fears that their families would neglect them. One patient remarked that families could be divided into ". . . . those who don't want to hear about the patient, and those who protect him too much . . . .". He added " . . . . actually all families do some of one and some of the other . . . .". Some patients used denial as a defence against their feelings of illness: these patients expressed a feeling of illness only when connected to the machine. Most patients, however, acknowledged a constant feeling of illness.

The patients describe stages in their feelings. When they first learn of the severity of their illness they often develop a condition similar to a reactive depression. They withdraw from social activities, remain at home, and welcome the family's protectiveness.

One of our patients told us that since he became ill he feels he has lost social status, and that his worth as a human being has diminished.

The next stage is a compensatory one. The patients attempt activities outside the home. They try to learn to live with the illness. Their efforts meet varying degrees of success. Often the family refuses to accept the possibility that a "sick" person can maintain activity. It seems to us that this conflict is the problem preventing the establishment of family equilibrium. The third stage is one of acceptance and leading to integration: "we learn that we are ill, we must live and accept our fate".

We should now like to discuss specific problems raised during group meetings. The following points were raised.

Family problems

These are complex; not only is the patient chronically ill, but there is the compounded threat that another family member will be asked to donate a kidney. The patients requested that their families be interviewed and be provided with psychiatric support as well. All described their own families as overprotective, but declared that "other" families would be rejecting. One patient stated: "my parents wrap me in cotton until I cannot move". Another described his elderly father of 70 snatching a heavy hoe away from him every time he began to work.

All the patients felt considerable resistance to the familial attitude of overprotection. At the same time, some added that they did indeed need some measure of protection since they were, in fact, sick. Some individuals tried to overcome their families' protective attitudes by initiating a deconditioning-like process. They would increase their activities gradually, and in turn the family would become accustomed to the new level of activity and cease objecting. Occasionally the patients would rebel. This could take the form of a sudden disappearance from home or neglect of their diet. One patient married when he learned the nature of his illness. He explained that he was seeking someone who would protect him.

Death problems

A major problem, of course, is the fact that these persons are living in the shadow of death. All of them are aware of this. There is an unofficial organization of renal patients: they know one another, and even know patients in other medical centers. Some patients regularly read the obituary notices in the newspapers. They respond to the death of another renal patient with increased anxiety, feelings of aggression and sometimes with attempts at suicide. Their awareness of the closeness of death dominates their thinking: a member of the group expressed it by saying: "whenever I go for a walk, I take my little daughter with me in case something should happen to me". It is well known that patients with chronic, life-threatening diseases such as diabetes may use their illness as a means to suicide. Our group shows similar tendencies. We have seen patients attempt suicide by violating their diet requirements. Alternatively, they may neglect the shunt, hoping for infection and complication. They may suddenly cease taking medication. When these acts are discussed with the patients, it becomes clear to them that some are instances of suicide attempts. One patient explained that he takes revenge on the doctor by suicidal acts which involve disobeying medical orders. We believe that some sudden deaths in this group may have resulted from such suicidal acts.

Aggressive feelings

All our patients expressed aggressive feelings towards the medical profession. They felt improper care had led to their illness. They reason further that since the medical profession failed them it is now obliged to save them. They feel, accordingly, a large measure of aggression toward the medical personnel. This leads to a psychological dilemma, since they are dependent upon medical aid and therefore inhibited from expressing their anger and rage. As a result, they face a threat that if they manifest their hostility they will be rejected. Their aggression is displaced into petty quarrels between patient and fellow-patient, and patient and nurse. In turn, the staff finds it difficult to tolerate their " ingratitude", and there are occasionally outbursts of hostility.

After the death of 2 members of the group, the remaining patients were aggressive against the doctor and also against the whole group. There was no mention of the deceased patients, but the group atmosphere became tense.

An important place in therapy was the formation of normal outlets and working through the material.

Shunt

In the beginning of treatment, most of our patients had an external shunt. Lately, however, there has been a shift to the use of an internal shunt and most of the patients in the group now have an internal shunt.

The patients regard the shunt as the symbol of their illness, the tangible evidence that they require constant and highly specialized care. Many try to conceal it with appropriate garments or in some other way. A difficult thing to do in our subtropic climate. They fear an accident to the shunt, resulting in blood loss; or they imagine the shunt will be caught up by some object and be torn out of their body. The patients are aware that change of colour in the shunt is an indication of blood clots, and yet they are reluctant to wash it out, fearing the pain. They repeatedly inspect the shunt to reassure themselves that it is in good condition. Fears concerning the shunt are experienced not only by the patients but by their families as well. This is still another source of family problems. The shunt becomes part of the patient's body, and at the same time symbolizes his illness and his pain. It is a weak point as well, a possible focus for infections. It is understandable, then, that psychological problems associated with the shunt are numerous, and that much of the patient's anger is directed at it.

It is interesting to compare above problems with similar problems encountered after amputation of limbs. The shunt having become a part of the patient's body, becomes in addition a part of his body image. The extent to which it is integrated into his body image can be seen in an example: Jewish ritual law dictates that a body be buried with all its organs in place; and one of our patients asked a rabbi whether his shunt should be buried with him too.

An internal shunt is a source of tension prior to the puncture by needles, particularly if this procedure has caused difficulty on preceding occasions.

Life with the artificial kidney

Patients have to live with the machine for 28 hours each week. Initially, the process of connection to the machine rouses tension and fear. Patients have fantasies of mechanical breakdowns, bursting pipes through which all their blood will drain away, or less specific but equally catastrophic fears of accidents to the machine and thus to them. Many are disgusted by the sight of their blood flowing out of their bodies.

We noticed that simple technical explanations by the nephrologist in the group helped the patients to understand what is going on and to relieve their fears.

The patients at first lie motionless, fearing that the needle will be disturbed in the blood vessel by the slightest motion. In the course of time they learn that they do have some freedom of movement, though limited. The connection to the machine renders the patient completely dependent on the medical staff, and increases his anxiety. Some patients prefer not to undergo hemodialysis at night because the number of nurses is smaller on the night shift. This dependency on the machine can be seen in one of our patients who felt increased anxiety as he walked away from the machine and the hospital. Moreover, most patients are unable to sleep while undergoing dialysis spending all their time anxiously observing the machine to be certain that nothing has gone wrong with it. The same we observed during night flights in a plane, where anxious people don't sleep, fearing that sleeping they will loose control.

In the course of time these reactions decrease in intensity, and eventually some may disappear.

Diet

Keeping the prescribed diet poses difficulties. They learn to know the exact composition of their food. After some time in the group they will discuss food in technical and nutritional terms. In addition, the fact of keeping a diet stresses their exceptional status. Social occasions become problematical. At home they must weigh all food and drink consumed. It is not surprising that rebellion against the illness, the staff or the family may take the form of overeating. Patients observed that in periods of stress they reacted with a tendency to bulaemia, sometimes leading to serious consequences. In the group it became clear that some of these episodes were frank suicidal attempts; others arose from aggression directed against the staff. Nearly all the patients remarked that they experienced food fads. Some ate prohibited foods before coming to the unit.

Food restrictions make the patient increasingly dependent. He strives naturally to free himself of this dependency and as inevitably, he fails. Coping mechanisms were frequently discussed in the group.

Body image

We suggest that the attachment to the machine and the concomitant flowing of blood outside the natural boundaries of the body are potent causes of disturbances of the integrity of the body image. In addition, the failure of kidney function is sometimes accompanied by fantasies in which patients imagine empty space in the place of the kidneys. Unlike healthy individuals, the patients are highly conscious of the renal area. The absence of urine leads to sexual fears and fantasies which may be very disturbing. Some patients fear that sexual intercourse may harm their kidneys. The prospect of transplanting a healthy kidney is always in the mind of the patient and in case when the donor is a family member can add to disturbances in the body image. We know of a case in which a kidney was transplanted from mother to son, and subsequently a pathological relationship developed between them. This case will be reported separately.

Depressive and psychotic reactions

We saw reactive depressions after failure of transplantation, frustrations at work and at home, or in times of exacerbation of the renal state. Antidepressive drugs were effective. Some patients experienced psychotic states at the time of dialysis. These were exogenous psychoses.

All the patients showed signs of lethargy, poor attention span, and disturbances in the ability to concentrate, to work and to maintain consciousness. These were most marked on the day of dialysis and the day following. This was still more conspicuous if there was a drastic fall of blood urea. These conditions may develop to the point of exogenous psychosis. Symptomatology may include disturbances in the level of consciousness, visual and auditory hallucinations and paranoid thinking.

These clinical manifestations are probable evidence of a chronic brain syndrome as described by Menzies and Stewart (*4*). More renal insufficiency may also cause disturbances in the sleep cycle, suffering insomnia at night and sleeping by day. We have already mentioned the patient who dares no fall asleep while connected to the machine. Some patients suffer insomnia under normal circumstances as well. We presume that biochemical and psychological factors are responsible.

RESULTS

As in any group treatment it is difficult to evaluate the results. It seems to us that this form of treatment helps the patient to work through his problems together with fellow-sufferers. We noticed that group therapy improved to a great deal the atmosphere in the unit until it became a real therapeutic community. This does not exclude the possibility or advisability of separate encounters between doctor and patient.

After one year of work in the unit we found that every patient and his family are in need of psychiatric assistance and that group therapy was appreciated by the patients and the medical staff as the best form of treating the manifold coping mechanisms of the patient and his therapist.

ACKNOWLEDGEMENTS

We wish to express our thanks to the physician-in-chief Dr. J. Rosenfeld and Dr. J. Robson, nurses and technicians of the Dialysing Unit of the Beilinson Hospital for their kind cooperation and help in this study.

SUMMARY

Group treatment in a hemodialysis center is discussed in this paper. Eight patients were under treatment and they met with the psychiatrist and the nephrologist once a week during one year, some hours before they were connected to the machine. Special attention was paid to the specific problems of hemodialysis and the problems of a person, permanently threatened by death. The material brought up and worked through was centered around complex family problems, death problems, coping with aggression, the shunt as the externalized symbol of illness, life with the artificial kidney, body image and psychiatric reactions.

After one year of work we found, after we studied the reactions of patients, their families and staff members, that this form of therapy is highly recommended in treating the coping mechanisms of the patient, his family and his therapist.

REFERENCES

1. HARARI, A., *Psychosocial Examination of Patients and Families during Hemodialysis*, Doctoral Thesis, Medical School of Tel Aviv University, 1969.
2. HUSEK, J. A., *Psychological Aspects of Chronic Hemodialysis; a Summary and Review of the Literature; Suggestions for Further Research*, School of Public Health, University of California, Los Angeles, Calif., 1966.
3. KAPLAN DE-NOUR, A. AND CZACZKES, J. W., Emotional problems and reactions of the medical team in a chronic haemodialysis unit, *Lancet*, ii (1968) 987–991.
4. MENZIES, I. C. AND STEWART, W. K., Psychiatric observations on patients with regular dialysis treatment, *Brit. med. J.*, i (1968) 544–547.

DENIAL AS A FACTOR
IN
PATIENTS WITH HEART DISEASE AND CANCER

T. P. Hackett and A. D. Weisman

In previous studies[1-3] we observed that the denial of stress appears to serve the best interest of the coronary patient both by reducing anxiety and by bolstering hope. In contrast, the terminal cancer patient's attempt to deny the imminent peril of his illness seems to heighter his sense of lonely apprehension. In order to verify this observation and to better understand it, we set up a comparison study between 20 patients hospitalized with acute myocardial infarction and 20 patients dying of cancer.

The process of denial begins when the patient is told of his condition. The doctor sets the stage with the information he conveys and the way in which he imparts it. Consequently, the first item chosen for comparison was the information each patient had been given by his physician. We predicted that the cancer group would be told less than the cardiac group.

Assimilating the facts of an illness and accommodating to them depend upon the patient's capacity for accepting information, but this is also heavily influenced by the setting in which the exchange occurs. Since the atmosphere of the cardiac ward was supportive, optimistic, and tended to favor denial, we believed that the cardiac patient would not be encouraged to face the full impact of his illness. As a consequence, the coronary patient would assimilate less information about his disease, would be less accepting of its limitations, and would be more apt to make unrealistic plans. Because the aura around the terminal cancer case in a general hospital is cheerless and constrained, denial would be less effective. As a result, the cancer patient would assimilate more information about his condition, and his concern with his death would be much more apparent than in his cardiac counterpart.

Based on the difference in caretaking, we postulated that the affect of the cardiac group would be one of mild to moderate anxiety, while depression would characterize the cancer patients.

We also predicted that the interpersonal relationship between staff and patient would be friendly, sustaining, and encouraging for the cardiac group, while ambivalence, uncertainty, and unintentional subversion would be commonly found with the cancer group.

Finally, we anticipated that the predominant concern of the cancer patient would be relief from his symptoms; his interest in the future would be confined to the immediate. Cardiac patients would be future-oriented, with a major interest in their capacity to return to work.

Material

Forty cases were selected from patients seen in the last ten years during our work with the critically ill patient. They ranged in age from 27 to 74 years. There were 14 females and 26 males. Pairs of cancer patients and cardiac patients were matched according to age and sex. In most instances, they were of similar religious and socioeconomic backgrounds.

All 20 cancer patients were hospitalized for terminal care when first interviewed.

One or both authors followed each patient in daily, weekly, or biweekly visits, depending upon the need, until the time of death. Throughout this period, the investigators worked closely with the hospital personnel responsible for the patient's care. In most instances, the patient's relatives were seen. The cardiac patients were interviewed two or three times during the first two weeks of their admission and were followed until discharge.

Method

Twenty questions were devised to investigate denial. They fall into the following five categories:

(1) What the patient is told by his doctor (Question 1).
(2) How the patient assimilates this information (Question 2–12).
(3) Staff-patient relationship (Questions 13-16).
(4) Predominant concerns and orientations toward the future (Questions 17-18).
(5) Physical discomfort and need for medication (Questions 19-20).

Question 1. What has he been told? (a) true diagnosis and prognosis, (b) some information but inexact and/or incomplete, (c) very little to nothing.

Data for Question 1 were obtained by direct questioning of the physician. An (a) response indicated that the myocardial infarction (MI) patient was told that he was on the danger list.

Question 2. What does he seem to know of his condition? (a) true diagnosis and prognosis, (b) some information, but inexact or incomplete, (c) very little to nothing.

Data on Question 2 were obtained by asking the patient what he knew about his illness. Cardiac patients were scored (a) if they told us that they were or had been aware of being in the immediate danger of death. This is not the same as knowing they were on the danger list, because this could be construed as a hospital routine rather than a comment on the patient's condition.

Question 3. Does he accept the limitations of his diagnosis? (a) yes, (b) no, (c) mixed.

To accept limitations of a myocardial infarction, the patient must remain in bed as he is told, must not smoke or exercise, and must remain on a strict diet. The terminal cancer patient who no longer asks for or expects a cure has accepted the limitation of his illness. The mixed response refers to individuals who tend to be realistic, but who occasionally err in the direction of wish fulfillment. They are, however, always willing to accept a correction for this error.

Question 4. Does he make unrealistic plans? (a) yes, (b) no, (c) mixed.

Unrealistic plans for the cancer group refer to setting up schemes that can never be realized because the patient will be dead. In the cardiac group, any plan that fails to acknowledge coronary disease would be unrealistic. This includes returning to the same pattern of life that might have helped precipitate the coronary.

Question 5. Does he make references to his own death? (a) direct, (b) indirect, (c) none.

If the patient spontaneously refers to the possibility or certainty that he will die soon as the result of his present illness, the response is recorded as direct. An indirect response means that it comes in answer to a question from the examiner or is in the form of a veiled reference to his death.

Question 6. Does he know he will soon die? (In MI, does he know that his life is in imminent danger?) (a) direct, (b) indirect, (c) no.

195

We consider that a patient knows he is to die when he tells us either spontaneously or in answer to our question that he will die soon. Such comments or replies are considered as direct responses. In the cardiac group, a patient who states directly or in response to a question that his life is in serious jeopardy is regarded as a direct responder. In both groups, the indirect response is one in which the patient mentions his own death, but does so as if it were one of a number of alternatives. The indirect response may be cloaked in humor or delivered as a third-person story. The indirect response is one in which the possibility, more than the fact, of death is acknowledged.

Question 7. Does he spontaneously express fear of dying? (a) yes, (b) no.

Spontaneous expression of the fear of death is counted positive if the examiner or nurse or another doctor reports it.

Question 8. Predominant affect as observed by others. (a) anxious, (b) depressed, (c) mixed anxiety and depression, (d) euphoric/depressed, (e) normal.

Reports of the patient's affect are compiled from nurses' notes, doctors' notes, and the social workers' observations. They rarely disagree with the opinion of the examiners. The term "norma7" is the one most frequently used by the staff in describing a patient who is not noticeably anxious or depressed, whose responses are appropriate, and who usually has a sense of humor about his illness.

Question 9. Does he complain of anxiety or depression? (a) frequently, (b) occasionally, (c) never.

Only unsolicited complaints are recorded. "Frequently" means an average of once per day or more. "Occasionally" refers to once every few days or every week.

Question 10. Does he complain of loneliness or vague fears? (a) frequently, (b) occasionally, (c) never.

Only unsolicited complaints are recorded. "Frequently" means an average of once per day or more. "Occasionally" refers to once every few days or every week.

Question 11. When asked, does he admit to anxiety, depression, or vague fears? (a) readily, (b) reluctantly, (c) denies.

Question 12. Does he ask for reassurance about his illness? (a) yes, (b) no.

We did not include subtle, indirect requests, but confined our data to those people who asked the examiners directly what they could look forward to in the immediate future.

Question 13. Does he complain about the staff? (a) frequently, (b) occasionally, (c) never.

Data were obtained by consulting our notes, nurses' notes, doctors' notes, and social workers' notes.

Question 14. Does the staff complain about him? (a) frequently, (b) occasionally, (c) never.

Data were obtained by consulting our notes, nurses' notes, doctors' notes, and social workers' notes.

Question 15. Does the staff like him? (a) yes, (b) no.

To score this question, we spoke with the staff and referred to the chart.

Question 16. Does the behavior of his relatives antagonize the staff? (a) yes, (b) no.

To score this question, we spoke with the staff and referred to the chart.

Question 17. Is he interested in discussing the future? (a) no interest, (b) interest in immediate future, (c) preferred to talk more about the distant future.

Response (a) means that the patient would discuss nothing except his feelings at the very time of the interview. In cancer patients, response (b) related to their interest in the possibility that symptomatic relief might be obtained. In cardiac patients, it refers to whether there would be a return of function or strength,

196

enabling them to increase their range of activity. A statement such as "I'm just living from day to day" characterizes response (b). Response (c) refers to the interest in planning and discussing the future at a distance in time when they could begin to function as they had before becoming ill.

Question 18. Predominant concern of the patient. (a) fear of death, (b) concern about the relief of symptoms, (c) fear of inability of work, (d) fear of leaving spouse and/or children, (e) none.

Data for this question were obtained from our interview with the patient. Certain recurrent themes or preoccupations were part of each patient's dialogue. We chose the most prominent one. There was no instance in which two such themes vied with each other for predominance; the one listed always dominated the others.

Question 19. Physical discomfort. (a) pain, (b) dyspnea, (c) nausea, (d) weakness, (e) miscellaneous.

Data were obtained by reviewing the patient's chart.

Question 20. Medication. (a) narcotics, (b) analgesics, (c) tranquilizers, (d) hypnotics, (e) antidepressants.

Data were obtained from the patient's chart.

Findings

Cancer patients are not told the full truth as often as are patients with myocardial infarction. Seventeen of the latter were given a full understanding of their condition, although it was couched in overly optimistic terms. Three were not given a complete explanation, but no one in this group was told nothing. Only seven cancer patients were fully informed, while ten were given partial explanations, and three were told little or nothing of their condition.

Despite the relative paucity of information given them, ten cancer patients knew their diagnosis and prognosis, and five more were reasonably well along the way to obtaining full knowledge. Only five were relatively unaware of what was happening to them. In the myocardial infarction group, nine spoke with sufficient knowledge to convince us they knew the full extent of their illness, whereas eleven seemed not to have wholly assimilated the information given them.

The answers to Questions 3 and 4 about the acceptance of limitation and unrealistic plan-making showed no significant difference between the two groups.

More cancer patients (10) than cardiac patients (5) make direct references to own deaths. However, more cardiac patients (10) than cancer patients (7) make indirect reference to their deaths. Eleven cancer patients knew that their deaths were likely to occur in the immediate future and spoke about this spontaneously. When questioned about it, five answered that they would be dead in the near future. Fourteen of the cardiac patients stated they knew their lives were in serious danger during the acute period of their coronary occlusion. Furthermore, they remained aware of their critical states throughout their stay on the acute cardiac service. Only six coronary patients gave indirect evidence of their awareness of being critically ill. Only one patient in each group spoke spontaneously of being frightened to death.

The affect of the cancer patient as described by observers other than investigators tended to be more depressed than that of the cardiac patient. Seven were openly depressed, nine were described as having a mixture of apprehensiveness or anxiety, alternating with or concomitant with depression. Fourteen of the cardiac patients were described as having a normal affect by their nurses and physicians. Only two of the cancer patients complained frequently of anxiety and depression;

TABLE 1
RESULTS OF QUESTIONING CANCER (CA) PATIENTS
AND MYOCARDIAL INFARCTION (MI) PATIENTS

Questions	CA	MI
1. What has he been told of his condition?		
a) True diagnosis and prognosis	7	17
b) Some information, but inexact and/or incomplete	10	3
c) Very little to nothing	3	0
2. What does he seem to know of his condition?		
a) True diagnosis and prognosis	10	9
b) Some information, but inexact or incomplete	5	11
c) Very little to nothing	5	0
3. Does he accept limitations of diagnosis?		
a) Yes	9	10
b) No	6	6
c) Mixed	5	4
4. Does he make unrealistic plans?		
a) Yes	6	5
b) No	9	12
c) Mixed	5	3
5. Does he make references to his own death?		
a) Direct	10	5
b) Indirect	7	10
c) None	3	5
6. Does he know he will soon die? (In M.I.: Does he know his life is in imminent danger?)		
a) Direct	11	14
b) Indirect	5	6
c) No	4	0
7. Does he spontaneously express fear of dying?		
a) Yes	1	1
b) No	19	19
8. Predominant affect as observed by others		
a) Anxious	0	2
b) Depressed	7	2
c) Mixed (anxiety and depression)	9	2
d) Euphoric/depressed	2	0
e) Normal	2	14
9. Does he complain of anxiety or depression?		
a) Frequently	2	1
b) Occasionally	7	2
c) Never	11	17
10. Does he complain of loneliness or vague fears?		
a) Frequently	2	1
b) Occasionally	9	2
c) Never	9	17

TABLE 1 *(Continued)*

Questions	CA	MI
11. When asked, does he admit to anxiety, depression, or vague fears?		
a) Readily admits	9	3
b) Reluctantly admits	2	8
c) Denies	9	9
12. Does he ask for reassurance about his illness?		
a) Yes	7	1
b) No	13	19
13. Does he complain about the staff?		
a) Frequently	5	0
b) Occasionally	6	1
c) Never	9	19
14. Does the staff complain of him?		
a) Frequently	2	0
b) Occasionally	2	0
c) Never	16	20
15. Does the staff like him?		
a) Yes	16	20
b) No	4	0
16. Does the behavior of his relatives antagonize the staff?		
a) Yes	5	0
b) No	15	20
17. Is he interested in discussing the future?		
a) No interest	9	1
b) Interest in immediate future	10	10
c) Preferred to talk more about the distant future	1	9
18. Prominent concern of the patient		
a) Fear of death	1	1
b) Concern about the relief of symptoms	18	0
c) Fear of inability to work	1	11
d) Fear of leaving spouse and/or children	0	3
e) None	9	5
19. Physical Discomfort (symptoms persisting more than 2 days after admission)		
a) Pain	20	3
b) Dyspnea	8	2
c) Nausea	14	0
d) Weakness	20	3
e) Miscellaneous	20	4
20. Medication		
a) Narcotics	20	3
b) Analgesics	20	6
c) Tranquilizers	20	4
d) Hypnotics	20	16
e) Antidepressants	12	0

seven complained occasionally of it. The remaining eleven never complained of anxiety or depression. The distribution was the same in answer to Question 10.

When asked by the examiner if they were depressed, anxious or uneasy, nine of the cancer patients readily admitted that they were, and nine denied that these emotions troubled them. In the cardiac group, three readily admitted anxiety and depression, eight reluctantly admitted it, and nine denied it. Seven cancer patients asked reassurance of the examiner; thirteen did not make this request. Only one cardiac patient asked reassurance of the examiner.

Eighteen cancer patients had as their predominant concern the fear that their symptoms could not be controlled. No cardiac patient had this fear. Eleven in the cardiac group were principally concerned about being unable to go back to work; five claimed they had no fear at all. Three of the cardiac group were concerned about leaving their spouses or children.

In the area of interpersonal relation, there is a marked difference in the responses of the two groups. Five cancer patients complained frequently about the staff, and six complained occasionally. Nine never complained. No cardiac patient complained frequently, and only one complained occasionally about the staff. There were no staff complaints about the patients in the cardiac group. Two cancer cases elicited complaints from the staff and two brought forth occasional staff complaints. All cardiac patients were liked by the staff; four cancer patients were disliked. None of the relatives of the cardiac patients antagonized the staff, whereas relatives of five cancer cases antagonized the staff.

Nine cancer patients were totally uninterested in discussing their future. Ten were willing to discuss the immediate future; one preferred to discuss the distant future. One cardiac patient was uninterested in discussing the future. Ten preferred to talk of the immediate future only; nine preferred to talk of the more distant future.

Without exception, there was far more physical discomfort in the cancer group and a commensurately greater use of narcotics, analgesics, tranquilizers, hypnotics, and antidepressants.

The results of the investigation were summarized in TABLE 1.

Discussion

One of the surprises of this investigation was the relative uniformity of responses between the cancer and cardiac groups. When we drew up the twenty items for comparison, our expectation was that notable differences would exist between the groups on nearly every count. Tabulation reveals that these matching pairs resembled each other more than they differed. This was especially surprising because we had long considered these two groups of patients as opposites in most respects.

As we predicted, the cancer patient is told less by his physician than the cardiac patient, but ends up appearing to know more about his condition. Perhaps the most likely reason for this can be found in the type of care each group receives. A conspiracy of silence surrounds the dying cancer patient. The physician and relatives, in their efforts to keep the patient ignorant of his fate, generally blunder when they try to disguise the facts; their attitude alone betrays them. The persistence and eventual worsening of symptoms adds to the patient's sense of decline. Nurses, especially students, often dread contact with terminal cases, as they fear being embarrassed by being asked questions they cannot answer. As a consequence, the aura around the sickbed is not conducive to bolstering the patient's denial. Instead, this atmosphere is more likely to heighten his awareness of being ill. The fact that cardiac patients are essentially asymptomatic after their initial symptoms have subsided its undoubtedly a significant factor in their convalescence. If they are so inclined, it allows them to minimize the seriousness of their illness. Furthermore, the cardiac ward atmosphere tends to be optmistic and hopeful, with a uniformity of response from nurses, relatives, and physicians that ensures a consistent buffer for the denial of full awareness.

Despite the favorable atmosphere on the cardiac wards, there was less evidence of denial by our cardiac patients than we anticipated. They accepted the limitations of illness as readily as the cancer patients and had no greater tendency to make unrealistic plans. References to death tended to be more indirect when given by the cardiac group, but roughly the same number of cardiac as cancer cases made no mention of death. Again, knowledge of imminent death was equally represented in both groups, as was the lack of spontaneous expression of the fear of dying.

In previous work[3] with coronary patients, we had been especially impressed with what could best be described as their "normal" affect. They seemed to face the adversity of their illness with equanimity. We use the term "normal" because their mood drew no attention from others. An observer would have had difficulty in determining that these cardiac patients were involved in a life and death struggle. It was the consistency and sturdiness of this affect that originally caused us to think that the myocardial infarction patient was able to deny effectively. The present study bears out our impression of affect. Fourteen of the cardiac group had normal affect, while eighteen of the cancer patients were depressed and anxious. Furthermore, the cardiac patient complained less than the cancer patient of anxiety, depression, loneliness, and vague fears, and he asked less for reassurance. Up to this point, our contention about the cardiac's denial is well supported. However, the responses to Question 11 force us to reconsider this belief. When directly questioned, the same number of cardiac patients as cancer patients admitted to having suffered these unpleasant emotions. That only three of the cardiac responses were readily offered is hardly significant in light of the fact that 11 did admit to being apprehensive, however reluctantly. This means that, despite the hopefulness and enthusiastic push for optimism on the cardiac ward, the patient is unable to deny emotional stress as much as he appears to.

Probably the main reason for the normal affect seen in the fourteen cardiac patients had to do with the attitude of the staff. The patient is expected to behave as if he were fully confident of a favorable outcome and is encouraged to conform to this behavior pattern by a variety of open and covert persuasions. The important feature is that the ward's influence in promoting denial is essentially reasonable and benign; it does little more than channel the patient's own tendency in that direction. Consequently, he does not balk at being gently nudged into the role of the noncomplaining, normal-appearing optimist. Our data indicate that it would be a mistake to assume that that affect was a genuine reflection of the patient's state of mind. Despite his normal appearance, the cardiac patient's dialogue is apt to contain at least as many references to death as does that of the terminal cancer patient. To interpret this finding is another matter. It could be regarded as isolation of affect, on the one hand, or inadequate denial, on the other. It is also perfectly reasonable to consider the response altogether appropriate, that is, simply the case of a man who prefers to appear calm despite what he feels. A more practical question is whether these inadmissible or unspoken fears represent a source of psychological tension that could harmfully alter the individual's adaptation to stress. To answer this will require biochemical, neurophysiological, and psychological indices that are beyond the scope of this presentation. There is, however, little doubt that future investigations will be obliged to correlate their clinical impressions with some type of measurement that reflects alterations in chemistry and the physiology of stress.

Our questions on the staff-patient relationship brought forth a disappointingly small amount of data. The main difficulty was in obtaining sufficient material to answer the questions. There is so little revelatory information in a hospital chart on the attitude of doctors and nurses toward a patient that we had to settle for less than we expected. In addition, the verbal accounts of professional personnel about their attitudes toward patients were, in our opinion, unreliable because of their reluctance to divulge negative feelings. There was more interaction between the cancer patients and the staff because they required more care over a longer period of time than their cardiac counterparts. It has been the experience of most that, the more dependent a patient becomes, the more apt friction is to develop between him and his caretakers; such is the case with cancer. The four cases that drew hostility from the staff had long-term malignancies and were demanding and essentially ungrateful.

The responses to the question of past, present, or future orientation were in part predictable, in part provocative. As could be expected, only one of the terminal cancer patients was interested in the distant future. This was understandable because they are preoccupied with the control of the symptoms about which their life progressively centers as their illness advances. As they grow more sick and enfeebled, they become fiercely aware of discomfort. Unless symptomatic relief is automatically obtained, their horizon is limited to the next narcotic injection. The same, however, is not true of the myocardial infarction patients. They usually have few if any physical symptoms. Why, then, should ten of them be as concerned with the immediate future as the same number of cancer patients? These ten coronary patients had no more symptomatic distress than did the others in their group. Their heart disease was not more severe and their prognoses were no worse than those of the other ten. Age was not a factor, as its distribution ran from 36 to 74, with no clustering. We expected most of the cardiac group to be especially interested in the more distant future, when they would face the problems of returning to work. Perhaps this finding further demonstrates the fact that the cardiac patient is more cautious in outlook than his affect and attitude would suggest. Despite his manifest confidence and optimism, he measures his progress warily from day to day, more attuned to the threat of recurrence than he admits.

It is significant that only one cancer and one cardiac patient were concerned predominantly with the fact of death. This finding is in agreement with the responses obtained from Question 7 and corroborates in earlier observation of ours[4] and of others[5] that the fear of death is not common in the dying. Fear of death and dying is a more predominant concern of the healthy than of the terminally ill.

The fact that 18 of 20 cancer patients were principally concerned about the control of their symptoms is not surprising when one examines the responses to Questions 19 and 20. All of the cancer patients were physically uncomfortable; pain, present in varying degrees in all cases, was the chief source of distress. In contrast, the cardiac group were essentially symptom-free, although a few had troubles, as listed in TABLE 1. Going over the hospital records to list these symptoms made us more aware than ever the most important difference between cardiac and cancer patients is not merely in the *type* of somatic distress each has, but in the *amount* of physical discomfort. The cancer patient in this study is far more sick from symptoms than is the patient with a coronary occlusion. As a consequence, medication was perhaps the main topic of conversation in the doctor-cancer patient dialogue. That the control of symptoms through drugs eclipsed the patient's concern for his family is not surprising when one takes into account the intensity, chronicity, and ultimate significance these symptoms have for the sufferer. Furthermore, there is another element that is very difficult to catalogue or quantify. It is the physician's attitude toward dispensing medication, which is independent of his interest or lack of interest in handling the problems of the dying. Why doctors are inclined to be stingy in issuing narcotics, hypnotics, and tranquilizers to the dying is not a question to be answered in this paper. The fact is that more physicians are niggardly when ordering these drugs than either logic or common sense would admit. A peculiar Puritan morality that doctors are inclined to pick up at some stage of their training causes them to frown upon the liberal use of narcotics, even when the need is most apparent. The disapproval that results from having to dispense these drugs is visible, more often than not, to the patient, and it can add considerably to his torment. Once again, the heart patient seldom experiences this sort of conflict in the doctor-patient relationship.

Aside from demonstrating a few of the important variables that separate the patient dying of cancer from the cardiac patient who may be dying of his illness, our most significant finding has to do with the similarity in response to the threat of death between two groups of patients who are treated in remarkably different ways by the medical profession. Both groups appear capable of arriving at a correct assessment of their medical situation, despite what they have been told by doctors. Cancer patients, who are told very little about their diagnoses and prognoses, manage to find the truth by themselves. Cardiac patients, who are told a great deal about their condition in a way designed to encourage optimism, end by behaving as though they had accepted the information in the way it was intended, but still appear to realize their peril, although they may not directly acknowledge it.

References

1. BROWNE I. W. & T. P. HACKETT. 1967. Emotional reactions to threat of impending death: Study of patients on monitor cardiac pacemaker. Irish J. Med. Sci. 6: 177-187.
2. HACKETT, T. P., NED CASSEM & W. A. WISHNIE. 1968. The coronary care unit: An appraisal of its psychologic hazards. New Eng. J. Med. 279: 1365-1370.
3. HACKETT, T. P. & A. D. WEISMAN. 1964. Reactions to the imminence of death. In The Threat of Impending disaster. G. H. Grosser, H. Wechsler & M. Greenblat, Eds. M.I.T. Press, Cambridge, Mass.
4. WEISMAN, A. D. & T. P. HACKETT. 1961. Predilection to death: Death and dying as psychiatric problems. Psychosom. Med. 23: 232-256.
5. FEIFEL HERMAN 1959. The Meaning of Death, McGraw-Hill Book Co. New York, N.Y.

DISCUSSION OF THE PAPER

CHAPLAIN FITZGERALD (Affiliation Unavailable): It would seem that, with the cardiac patient, there is more of the ability to respond and to respect his individuality. With the cancer patient, there seems to be more of a regression to earlier stages. I'm thinking as a layman, of course, and my understanding of medicine comes from life. You often hear, "If I'm going to die, I'd rather die of a heart attack than of cancer." I wonder if it would make any difference if those who are involved, were themselves helped by psychotheraphy to ascertain their own feelings in working with a cancer patient. Would this change the environment, as it seems to have with the cardiac patients? Or is this a matter of respecting the patient as he is, granting him regression to the infantile? Is it a matter of responding to the patient where he is? Can something be done in terms of the environment?

DR. HACKETT: It is much easier, I think, to administer to the cardiac patient than to the terminal cancer patient. One of the troubles is that we talk a great deal, of course, to nurses and to aids. However, the paramount figure who determines policy is the doctor, and we have less contact with doctors than we have with social workers, nurses, and others. The doctors still want to be silent. For the most part, they aren't open with their cancer patients; until we can get to them, which we must do in medical school, we're at a great disadvantage.

What I'm saying in this paper is that, despite the fact that the cardiac wards operate at optimum—I think they do very well in encouraging denial in a proper way—they still don't get to it. Something is missing. However, if you then reorient yourself simply with symptomatic care, you also find that physicians are gravely in error in the way they medicate dying terminal patients. We haven't even gotten to that stage yet. Sometimes, when you order narcotics in increasing doses, you encounter people who complain to the director that you are addicting this patient, as if addiction were a problem in the last month of a person's life. That is an insane concept, and yet it happens all the time. Usually you give a drug such as thorazine, 25 mg about four times a day. If you give 200 mg six times a day, people who aren't acquainted with that dose will complain.

When you're dealing primarily with pain problems, you must reorient your system of therapeutic values and face the problem. That is, you give the drug in sufficient dose to help the symptom, not in the dose the textbooks recommend. In a word, we haven't even come to the point of being able to approach what you were asking. We can do this on the cardiac wards because there you tell a patient that he has had a heart attack and you smile and say that you're going to save him. For the same reason, dermatologists tell most of their patients that they have a cancer because they're usually basal cell cancers that are eminently curable. However, the gynecology men are less frank because they have much more serious conditions with the cervix and breast.

With the cardiac patient your chances, if they survive the first ten hours, are quite good; the longer they survive, the more optimistic you can be. However, it's pretty hard to pretend an optimism that you don't feel. The same person who can be effusive, pleasant, and encouraging in cardiac failure, where there is a slight chance, loses this ability when he faces a terminal cancer patient, who has no chance. Nevertheless, we behave as though we could, with this policy of silence that assumes that all of us are very good liars, which we are not.

DR. SENESCU: We're really concerned with the whole problem of our relationship to patients. We're not good at it, and it seems to me we're using the fatally ill patient or seriously ill patient as a means of illustrating this. It's rather dramatic, and we like our drama, I suppose—all of us. The problem seems to be that, when people are helpless and childlike, we do very badly. We are angry at them, we run away from them. This point is so fundamental that we should not be distracted from it. Actually, in general the coronary is rather notorious for his inability to admit any helplessness or childishness; he likes to work. To return to the issue of patients' regressing, we don't give them the kind of care they need, a care which does smack somewhat of the parent-child relation. Then they get more frightened, and they retreat.

DR. HACKETT: Well, you certainly get more demands with the cancer patient because of variety of symptoms and also because of the depression. Essentially, however, the largest demand doesn't come from the patient; it arises from the setting in which he finds himself and that is one of dishonesty and untruth.

I usually give two talks a week to the student nurses and graduate nurses at the hospital as new ones come in. Invariably the problem of caring for the terminal patient arises. I am always stymied. I can tell them what I do. I can cite references about what people have done. I can tell them about individual cases, but I always end up by saying, "Unfortunately, you're on the firing line, and it depends on what the doctor wants. If you feel that a patient needs to be told and isn't being told, then tell the doctor; if he won't do it, tell your supervisor. If nothing happens, go to the director of the hospital, right up the line. Don't let them off the hook." I firmly believe that. I just can't consider that regression is the principal issue—not so much the regression that you see, because certainly you see regression in all kinds of illnesses. It is probably no different in other patients than the cancer patient, but the cancer patient is in a unique situation because rarely has the whole profession combined to perpetrate such a hoax as it has on him. I don't know when it began, but I think it was relatively recent, probably at the turn of the century; up until that time people were certainly quite forthright in discussing prognoses. At least you get that impression in reading the literature. Somewhere along the line of advance in medical technology, where the impetus was all on saving life, we began to back away from, to minimize, and to shun the dying patient. Dying in itself is not considered treatable. It's the level of symptomatic treatment that we should excel at. We don't.

DR. LADIMER: I'd like to ask a question that you did not discuss, perhaps Dr. Feifel or any others who have done actual studies of patient reactions, responses, attitudes, and feeling will also comment. Have any of the patients at this stage in their illness commented on the possible contribution that they might be making to research or science or medicine in general?

DR. HACKETT: I have worked with terminal cancer patients on the project for the last 12 years with a total of 70 patients. I have never heard one mention the possibility that his position as a guinea pig would contribute to medical progress. I tend to doubt those who say otherwise.

DR. FEIFEL: As a matter of fact, that was one of the motivational devices we did use in trying to get patients to cooperate with us, we told them that the information that we would gather might not be specifically applicable to their conditions, but that it might be of use to other people. I think this perhaps contributed to persuade them to cooperate.

DR. HACKETT: It wasn't the sole reason they did it, however. There must have been something else; there was the possibility of gaining something. What we did find after a while, of course, was that, in the research context, we were affording the patient the very thing about which we are complaining today. That is, this was an entryway through which they could break the isolation in the conspiracy of silence that Dr. LeShan mentioned earlier as something we the living impose upon the dying. I must admit that, when I started my research, I was very much humbled because I had not anticipated this extraordinary discovery that the patients would thank me and my colleagues for affording them the opportunity to discuss their feelings, their thoughts, their fears, even their hopes about dying and death. This is what they said: "It's you, the living, who erect an iron curtain and prevent us from saying what we honestly feel." Actually, many patients will tell you that they play the role, that they enter into the charade which we impose upon them. Many times, alas, we mistake the role, the shadow for the substance. This is what I tried to indicate; I think perhaps Dr. Standard alluded to this earlier: that too many of our theories of dying are the creations and product of the living and are not based or rooted in the patient himself. Too much of the information we have is rooted in the physician and the psychologist. This does not mean that we the living, the professional people with skills or resources, should not contribute to the overall matrix of how to handle the dying patient. What I suggest is that we could all make a much weightier contribution to this multiple regression equation.

DR. LADIMER: Let me clear something up. When I was speaking before of volunteering, I had one thing specifically in mind. It was surgical patients for surgical techniques.

GENERAL DISCUSSION

CHAPLAIN KEARNEY (Affiliation Unavailable): My comments and questions are directly largely to Dr. Hackett although the rest of you may wish to discuss them. I have the fascinating but frustrating task of having to visit patients before surgery on a number of units such as neurological service before surgery for brain damage or, hopefully, repair of seizure problems, Parkinson's disease, head and neck cancer, and open heart surgery for the heart patient. I'm impressed at the varied reactions of these groups. The heart patient tends to be fatalistic. His chances are six in ten he'll make it and he says, "I'll die anyway if I don't, so let's go ahead with minimum amount of anxiety."

The head and neck cancer patient may be assured of total removal of tumorous growth but is uncertain of the future and tremendously anxious. The neurological patient feels he is not living much of a life anyway and wants the surgery.

My questions are: Is there a component of hope involved here? Does this make a difference, say in our contrast of heart and cancer patients? Does a cancer patient see himself slipping away inch by inch, with the direction he's going his major concern, as compared with the heart patient who slips away suddenly and hopefully holds level and perhaps goes uphill? Is hope a component as you see it?

DR. HACKETT: A very strong component. I think that it makes all of the difference in the world. It certainly prompts the cardiac wards to continue on as they have been. With the cancer patient I think one can maintain far more hope for them than previously but I don't think one should give encouragement in a deceptive or dishonest way. In other words, if you're talking about someone's being totally cured of, let's say, a lung tumor with metastases, you wouldn't discuss his vacation plans and so forth. Whereas once the issue has been broached, one may offer him a number of legitimate things, such as a pain-free course, and doing as much as possible to get to a cure. I think that one never loses hope. If you lose hope in treatment, I think you lose faith in yourself. But, a more realistic hope is, I suppose, what I'm talking about. You begin with what you can do and then go on from there.

DR. MELLETTE (Affiliation Unavailable): One very vital factor that I feel circumvents some of this regression and that provides some hope and fulfillment is the patients' participation in their illness. In other words, although the physician makes the major decisions, they also have a role. The patient can decide whether or not he wants milk of magnesia or Alophen. He can participate in the evaluation of his symptoms. He actually can play a part in the course of his illness. This may take many directions. It may result in his being happy to have experimental treatment. It may go as far as his actually requesting a postmortem because of the feeling that this will give him a degree of continuity. The important thing here is that the patient has to feel worked *with* and not worked *on*.

DR. HOLLAND: I agree with Dr. Hackett in terms of the problems one encounters caring for cancer patients in a general hospital. I'd like to offer the suggestion that what Dr. Hackett really would like to see is a coronary care unit kind of atmosphere around his cancer patient, with more concern over, and more care of, symptoms. The only place that I think one sees this today is in the kind of unit Dr. Amiel has in France where, indeed, this may engender problems for the staff, too. I think, perhaps, that where you see cancer patients brought together in a group (and, unfortunately, nowadays the only reason for bringing them together is essentially for research efforts), there is a general absence of depression among them and an overall feeling on the staff's part that indeed there are things that still can be done.

DR. STANDARD (Affiliation Unavailable): I'd like to make two remarks, one on the question of death and the other on the question of research. First, on the question of death, the point I would like to stress is that it is not a "unit thing" and that dying is not a "unit thing." Someone mentioned Socrates approaching his death and how he felt before he started with his cup of hemlock. This has nothing to do with what we're talking about. He was a man in the prime of his life, thinking well, feeling that society had injured him. He was a member of the Athens community and he himself had something to do with creating its laws. He was given an opportunity to live if he would leave Athens, but he decided to die. It is different from an ill man who is dying, who is nearly dead before he dies and continues to die a little bit as he goes along. I think the relationship between these two situations should not be mistaken.

Second, when we speak of research, we speak of momentarily forgetting the immediately sick man, with an eye toward the man who will be sick tomorrow, hoping we'll take better care of them both then. I think once a man decides he's going to go into research, he somehow comes out on a separate pedestal, particularly considering the ease with which he can get money for his work, as well as the prestige it offers him in society. He begins to be treated in a far too special manner, and it is then that his situation becomes somewhat equivocal with regard to the laws of our general society, and, thus, he can become immoral or unethical. My point about research is that it's important. Without it we are not doing our job. I think research should be done in addition to caring for the ill, today and not used as a substitute for it, I think that it is easy for us to make people understand almost everything we want them to. The reason they don't understand is because we do try to obfuscate a little bit in doing it, and this applies even to those of us who are honest. I think it should be explained to a patient that he is being asked to do something not just for himself but also for the future. And very often he will want to cooperate.

Someone spoke here about a man dying and mention was made that his last contribution to society was that he would die for the good of future society. I think there may be people like that. In my experience I have not seen them.

DR. SENESCU: I'd like to say something about the research problem, too, about patients wanting to help mankind and science. I think they do want this. And, I think the reason they do is that in so doing that they are treated as valuable, worthwhile, useful human beings. Those who have worked in state hospitals and have done research there see this happen all the time. One of the problems we have is how can we convey to the terminally ill, or seriously ill patient that he is valuable and worthwhile? Obviously we can't do it if we don't think it and feel it. This is a question that we're beginning to explore with more and more honesty, namely, that people who are nearing death are not often treated as if they were valuable, worthwhile human beings.

DR. LADIMER: I asked a question before about research. I'd like to ask one about clinical management. When I was at the clinical center at NIH, I was impressed by certain diversionary aspects and I wonder whether any of you people use these techniques. Fatally ill patients have time to kill. Do you interest them in other things? These people used to approach me about a variety of problems—selling real estate, husband-wife relationships, taking care of children, a whole host of matters. But, it turned out to be an extremely valuable use of time, and I would say it might even be helpful psychotherapeutically. What do you think?

MRS. GEROWITZ: What we tried to do in connection with some of the problems you've raised was to cut through on two fronts. With the relatives of the dying patient we developed group meetings to help them at least discuss and ventilate their feelings. We encouraged them to talk about the problems of the dying and to give the dying hope in terms of what they have done in their lives, what kind of positive contributions have they made. They've had families, they have grown children, some are grandparents, some are mothers, and we've tried to help them utilize all of their faculties as long as possible.

Now, sometimes it's pretty hard, and we're not always successful, but at least we've made an attempt. We're doing the same thing with out-patients in the Cancer Clinic, so that these people come together to be able to discuss quite frankly that they do have cancer. I think an interesting sidelight is the physician who attempted to obfuscate his patient's diagnosis, with the patient realizing it subsequently. This took quite a time, but I think we're making some sense through the use of groups to help people deal with some of the problems that they're facing and to prepare themselves for death. Does not a patient have the right to make some preparation for his future? Isn't this, indeed, a thing that he's quite capable of doing in many instances, and if we obfuscate the issue, we deprive him of this privilege.

On the question that Dr. Hackett raises in terms of the atmosphere of the ward on your myocardial infarct, I would wonder what a patient feels like who is no longer receiving medication and who is still in the hospital. He thinks, what in heavens name is happening to me? Here I am. Nobody's treating me, but I'm still here. I would be concerned. There are many factors in this kind of research: the number of hospital days that each group of these patients is experiencing as part of the whole picture; how many days does each one of these patients spend in the hospital? Is the cardiac patient moved from an intensive unit into a general unit, and what is his feeling in the move? Is this hope? And, doesn't this change the atmosphere? And, finally, what effect does the intensity of the treatment have?

DR. LeSHAN: One issue that's been emerging here is our concern over dishonesty with the patient, conspiracy of silence and obfuscating the diagnosis. We speak of regress and we ask what can we do about it. Isn't it perfectly plain that one of the things we do is depress the patient into a regression and then wonder what to do about it? Just coming into the hospital itself can rob you of adulthood. Being an adult means you've had to fight pretty hard, means you can make your own decisions on what you eat, what you wear and where you go and whether you can go to the bathroom alone. And, if you think this isn't pressed down in a hospital, I suggest you do what I do. Fight with some floor nurses in order to have the newspaper and the floor sweeper knock before entering the room where a 60-year-old woman may be using a bedpan. The regression is pressed in.

Then, to make matters worse, we hide information. How many of you have seen those wonderful little conferences outside the patient's room where the patient's relatives and the doctor are discussing things that are withheld from the patient. If we don't want the regression, then we have to treat the patient, as has been suggested, as an adult, as a human being who has a right to take some hand in his life.

DR. WALTER PANKY (Affiliation Unavailable): I'd like to comment on something Dr. Hackett raised. He advocated adequate pain relief in the dying patient and also the importance of alert consciousness in the person who is dying. Now these seem contradictory, and I would like to ask Dr. Hackett which he thinks is more important? Alert consciousness or adequate pain relief, and how does one resolve this dichotomy?

DR. HACKETT: It depends on the patient first of all and if he wants to be under. If so, then you do so. But, what I was trying to argue against was the uniform practice of simply increasing everything—narcotics, hypnotics, tranquilizers. Some people don't like to be drugged. As I said in the talk, they don't like the feeling of chemical lethargy that comes on them. And I also think that you can achieve a good deal of pain relief by adding something like methedrine or a cerebral stimulant and still keep them fairly well alert. So it depends primarily on the patient.

DR. STAFFORD-CLARK: I'm not going to talk directly about the dying for a moment. I'm going to talk about children with a good expectation of life who were treated in two different groups. Twenty years ago I did some research in Boston in the Children's Hospital, again, with a matched group, this time not on myocardial infarction and cancer, but on rheumatic heart disease and an orthopedic ward. In the rheumatic heart disease ward the children felt all right. They were over the fever. But, the physicians and the nurses were terrified if they were overactive (children are prone to be in a hospital, of course, during the day) before they had recovered because they then might incur permanent heart damage. And, the weapon used quite unconsciously by the staff to keep the kids in bed and lying still was anxiety, *adult* anxiety, which is very threatening indeed. So the children all thought there was something terribly the matter with them, and when asked what they had wrong with them, they often replied, "cancer of the heart." At that time cancer and heart disease were as they still are, the two major illnesses for which one should donate money. Hence, the children's logic was inevitable.

In the Orthopedic Ward, as an example, everyone said, "Why little Jimmy is great. We took his leg off last week for osteogenic sarcoma, and today he said when he grew up he was going to be a baseball player." We then were contriving another kind of denial. In both cases the physicians and the nurses together created a situation and then stood back and either admired or deplored it. This is the responsibility that brings us back to the doctor. And, in bringing it back to the doctor, we can quote from Francis Bacon in this respect who commented on this a long time ago. He said, "I consider it the office of the physician," and by that he was including surgeons for he was a generous man, "not only to restore health but to mitigate the pain and the dolorous suffering. And not only when such a mitigation may conduce to recovery, but also when it may serve to make a fair and easy passage."

Long-Term Adjustment, Prognosis, and Death in Irreversible Diffuse Obstructive Pulmonary Syndromes

DONALD L. DUDLEY, MD, JOSEPH W. VERHEY, MD,
MINORU MASUDA, PhD, C. J. MARTIN, MD, and
THOMAS H. HOLMES, MD

Forty subjects with severe debilitating irreversible diffuse obstructive pulmonary syndrome were studied over a 4-year period. They were found to utilize denial, repression, and isolation to protect their failing respiratory systems from environmental inputs. Failure of these defenses led to physiologic and psychologic deterioration. Psychosocial assets were found to be as important as the physiologic assets in the treatment of these patients. Patients with high psychosocial assets were found to be more effective in protecting themselves from dangerous symptoms or behaviors and were more likely to proceed with realistic, appropriate treatment programs. The probability of dying was increased in the presence of both low psychosocial and low physiologic assets. Dying was found to be a specific goal-directed adaptive behavior which was reported as being comfortable and relatively devoid of threat. Emotional upsets accompanying death were largely related to problems with family, friends, and hospital staff.

IN OUR SOCIETY'S DESIRE to ignore and avoid death, practical studies and educa-

Supported in part by US Public Health Service Undergraduate Training Grant in Psychiatry 5-T2-MH-5939-16; USPHS Undergraduate Training in Human Behavior Grant 5-T2-MH-7871-05; State of Washington Initiative 171 Funds for Research in Biology and Medicine; O'Donnell Psychiatric Research Fund; and Firland Research Fund.

The authors wish to thank Robert Forsgren, MD, and E. Mansell Pattison, MD, for assistance in the collection of data.

cation about death are almost nonexistent. Most physicians, despite having to deal with death frequently, have little concept of what the dying patient is experiencing. This lack of knowledge of dying behavior is traceable to the lack of systematic studies of the natural history of death. Because of a lack of objective data, reliance is placed on magical beliefs and defensive maneuvering.

The present study was carried out in order to help bring some objectivity into the area of dying behavior and its antecedents. The irreversible diffuse obstructive pulmonary syndrome (DOPS or clinical emphysema) is a chronic lung failure in which long-term close medical attention is a must. These patients are thereby relatively easy to follow and provide a good population for the study of long-term adjustment. In addition, DOPS is a disease entity in which the mortality can be predicted for mild, moderate, and severe abnormalities.[1] The patients in the "severe" category have a 5-year mortality of over 70%. It was largely from this group that patients were drawn for this study.

Methods

Subjects

Forty subjects with DOPS, between the ages of 25 and 81 (mean 58), were studied over a 48-month period. The subjects were all initially hospitalized and represented a sample of convenience. The only criteria for entrance into the study were the physician's judgment that the patients were critically ill with DOPS and their own willingness to participate. Of the 40 subjects, only one refused to participate fully.

The DOPS was rated according to the criteria suggested by Martin et al.[1] There were 9 patients in Group III (moderate disability and insufficiency) and 31 in Group IV (severe disability and insufficiency).

In addition, 6 medical students volunteered to serve as control subjects in a head pain experiment.

Physiologic Variables

Initially, all patients were clinically stable. In the month prior to the study, baseline blood gas and gross ventilatory measurements were collected on all subjects. The gross ventilatory measurements consisted of the vital capacity (VC), the maximal breathing capacity (MBC), and maximal expiratory flow rate (MEF) before and after bronchodilators.[2] The vital capacity is the maximal volume, expressed in liters, that can be expired from the lungs after a maximal inspiration. The maximal breathing capacity is the maximal volume of air that can be breathed in 15 sec converted to liters per minute. Both of these variables were measured with a Collins 9-liter respirometer. The maximal expiratory flow rate, a single breath test, represents the maximal air flow during forced expiration.[3] It correlates well with the maximal breathing capacity.[4] Predicted values for the maximal breathing capacity and vital capacity were those of Baldwin, et al.[5]

The partial pressure in arterial blood of oxygen (Pa_{O_2} in mm Hg), carbon dioxide (Pa_{CO_2} in mm Hg), and the pH was measured on each subject with a Beckman physiologic gas analyzer. The Pa_{CO_2} has a normal value of 40 ± 2 mm Hg, and the pH is 7.4 ± 0.2 in this laboratory. The Pa_{O_2} varies with age.[6]

Measurements of respiratory rate (RR), minute ventilation ($\dot{V}$), and end tidal concentration of alveolar carbon dioxide were made by using a pneumotachograph and an infrared carbon dioxide analyzer.[7, 8] Intermittently, the anatomic dead space (V_D) was measured by graphic analysis of the expired carbon dioxide (or nitrogen) and volume curves.[9] The measuring instruments were connected to a four-channel, direct-writing pen recorder. The respiratory rate, minute ventilation, alveolar ventilation (V_A), fractional concentration of alveolar carbon dioxide (FA_{CO_2}), oxygen uptake (V_{O_2}), and carbon dioxide production (V_{CO_2}) are

212

presented in the figures and tables which follow.

The anatomic dead space is the amount of air in the conducting system of the lungs. The alveolar ventilation is the amount of air reaching the alveoli and is calculated by subtracting the minute dead space volume from the minute volume. The end tidal carbon dioxide concentration is the fractional concentration of alveolar carbon dioxide at end expiration and represents the alveolar value (FA_{CO_2}). This value is higher than the mean FA_{CO_2}. However, for comparison purposes in the same individual it is an adequate estimation. The carbon dioxide production is the amount of carbon dioxide expired each minute, and the oxygen uptake is the amount of oxygen removed from the inspired air per minute. In calculating these variables, the fractional concentrations of oxygen and carbon dioxide in expired gas were measured using a Scholander gas analyzer. These values, with the volume of gas expired per minute, were used to compute the oxygen consumption and carbon dioxide production.[7] The respiratory quotient (RQ), which represents the ratio between carbon dioxide production and oxygen consumption, was also computed for some subjects.

3-Methoxy-4-hydroxymandelic acid (VMA), normetadrenaline (NMA), metadrenaline (MA), and creatinine were measured by methods previously reported by Masuda.[10]

Psychosocial Variables

The Berle Index is a test which furnishes a quantitative assessment of total psychosocial assets.[11] The test has three parts: Berle I is composed of objective data (worth 20 points); Berle II is concerned with facts about the patient's family and interpersonal relationships (30 points for females, 28 points for males); and Berle III is an evaluation of past performance, personality structure, and attitude of patient toward his illness (40 points). In general, patients scoring below 60% have not shown symptomatic improvement. The final ratings of the Berle Index were made by an investigator who had no knowledge of the clinical outcome or the physiologic data. Data on which to score the test were derived from the initial estimate by the ward physician and the patient's subsequent performance.

In addition, all subjects were followed with psychiatric observations while conducting their daily routine, and those deteriorating were studied more intensively during the process of dying.

Results

Long-Term Adjustment

General Observations

As a group, these subjects utilized the whole range of mental mechanisms but most consistently used denial, repression, and isolation as defense mechanisms. Their attempts to insulate themselves psychologically from their surroundings led to numerous misunderstandings with the staff, relatives, and friends, which in turn led to greater use of the defenses. A breakdown of the defenses was associated with increasing symptoms and physiologic deterioration.

Noxious Head Stimulation

The effectiveness of the psychologic defense mechanisms in reducing the impact of environmental stimuli was demonstrated in 6 DOPS patients (all Group IV). Their response was compared with the response of 6 medical students who served as controls. The subjects were stimulated with a headband which was known to produce a severe headache and respiratory hyperfunction in normals. As illustrated in Table 1, the DOPS subjects and controls had significantly different responses. Hyperventilation with psychologic activation was seen in the controls, and a mild hypoventilation with psychologic withdrawal was seen in the DOPS subjects (Table 2).

Subject 1 was a 25-year-old white male married medical student. Prior to the experiment, he felt apprehensive, and his hands were cold and moist. He felt he had volunteered only out of obligation to the Department of Psychiatry. Once the headband was placed and the experiment begun, his apprehension left.

After the first tightening of the headband, he said that the pain was tolerable. He felt uncomfortable and tense, but indicated that he was able to put up with it. After 20 min he "felt like grasping the damned clamp and throwing it off." He was very irritable and uncomfortable and said he just wanted to get out of the situation. Just before the headband was removed he said, "I was getting mad as hell." During the head pain, this subject hyperventilated and had an increased oxygen consumption. He tolerated the headband for 25 min. After removal he felt relieved and relaxed (Fig. 1).

Subject 2 was a 25-year-old divorced laborer who presented with far advanced clinical emphysema and bronchial asthma. He also had pulmonary tuberculosis from which he was recovering. He denied any feeling about the pain experiment and volunteered for unstated reasons. During the experiment, he said, "It did not seem to bother me a bit. . . . I felt depressed. . . . Pain don't bother me emotional." He said that he did not feel like doing anything about the pain— that there was nothing that could be done about such things. He stopped the experiment because "I thought I'd had enough." He denied ever being activated by pain, and said, if anything, it made him feel depressed and lonely (Fig 2).

COMMENT. The lack of activation during headband stimulation in patients with severe clinical emphysema was interpreted as being secondary to the successful use of denial and repression. An additional physiological load was thereby shunted from a failing organ system. This is illustrated by Subject 2. With

215

TABLE 1. HEAD PAIN: MEAN CHANGE FROM CONTROL VALUES
(6 DOPS SUBJECTS COMPARED WITH 6 CONTROL SUBJECTS)

	ΔRR	$\Delta \dot{V}$ (1/min)	$\Delta \dot{V}_A$ (1/min)	ΔF_{ACO_2} (%)	$\Delta \dot{V}_{O_2}$ (ml/min)
DOPS subjects	−1.5	−0.8	−0.8	−0.1	−14
Control subjects	+4.3*	+4.9†	+3.9†	−0.8*	+95*

Means differ by Student's t test (one-tailed).
* p < 0.05.
† p < 0.025.

TABLE 2. RESPONSE TO NOXIOUS HEAD STIMULATION

	RR	$\dot{V}$ (1/min)	$\dot{V}_A$ (1/min)	F_{ACO_2} (%)	$\dot{V}_{O_2}$ (ml/min)
Control subjects (6)					
Control	9	6.8	5.7	5.9	319
Pain	13	11.7*	9.6†	5.1*	414†
DOPS subjects (6)					
Control	20	8.2	5.9	5.0	303
Pain	19	7.4†	5.1†	4.9	289

Student's t test (one-tailed).
* p < 0.01.
† p < 0.02.

216

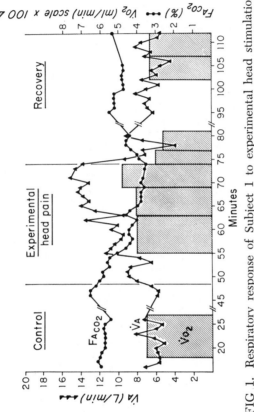

FIG. 1. Respiratory response of Subject 1 to experimental head stimulation.

217

the degree of pulmonary insufficiency exhibited by this patient (MEF = 100), a physiologic response of the magnitude displayed by Subject 1 may have precipitated a respiratory crisis.

Group Therapy

As a further step in testing the defense system, 12 subjects with DOPS were asked to participate in an intensive group therapy experience in which strong emotional reactions occurred in the course of the group interaction. Seven subjects were unable to tolerate the therapy. The emotional changes in these subjects were associated with physiologic decompensation and increased respiratory symptoms to which they could not adjust. In defiance of their physicians' orders, these patients refused to attend the group psychotherapy meetings. As shown in Table 3, the subjects who could not tolerate the therapy had significantly more obstructive airway syndrome (MBC + MEF) and fewer psychosocial assets (Berle Index).

Subject 3 was a 62-year-old white male married grocery clerk who was hospitalized for the first time with severe DOPS. The patient had had mild to moderate exertional dyspnea and a chronic productive cough as long as he could remember. He had been in the hospital continuously since his admission 4 years prior to this study.

The patient had been married, divorced, and remarried 30 years prior to admission. His first wife later married a dentist, and she and the patient's son had no further contact with him. His second wife had always been independent and self-supporting. They had no children. The patient was a chronic alcoholic until 2 years prior to admission, when he was rehabilitated. For the year preceding and up to 5 days prior to admission, he had worked as a grocery clerk. He and his wife had been sepa-

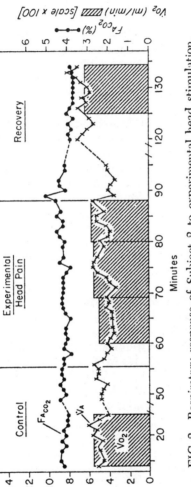

FIG 2. Respiratory response of Subject 2 to experimental head stimulation.

rated for 2 years, and she had been planning to divorce him at the time he was admitted. On admission he was insolvent with no source of income.

Over the 4 years of his hospitalization, he formed a close attachment to the hospital. When asked about going home he would say, "This is my home," and made it clear that he wished to stay in the hospital. When confronted with discharge, he became angry and anxious, and developed increased respiratory failure. Atttempts to overcome his dependency and mobilize him were met with the same response. During his hospitalization, he received a veteran's pension and social security benefits. During this same period, his wife retired. They were reconciled during the hospitalization, and the wife became dependent upon him for financial help for the first time in their life together. The patient, on the other hand, was dependent upon his wife for emotional support. However, she did not want him home, and he did not want to return home. His wife was his only visitor. After the completion of the study, he transferred to another hospital where he died of respiratory failure.

Prior to the study, his VC was 1.6 (47% of normal), his MBC 19 (20% of normal), his MEF 40, pH 7.41. Pa_{CO_2} 43, and Pa_{O_2} 65. He attended five group therapy meetings and then refused to attend any more. After attending two group meetings, his arterial pH was 7.39, Pa_{CO_2} 50, and Pa_{O_2} 34. After leaving the group, his pH was 7.41, Pa_{CO_2} 52, and Pa_{O_2} 50. One year after the start of the group, his pH was 7.39, Pa_{CO_2} 50, and Pa_{O_2} 50.

In the group he would actively and passively try to avoid emotionally laden topics and was openly rejecting and destructive in his comments. He quit the group because "It cannot do any good." At that time, he appeared to be deteriorating physiologically. This was

220

TABLE 3. COMPARISON OF PATIENTS WHO HAD A POSITIVE GROUP PARTICIPATION
AND PATIENTS WHO HAD A NEGATIVE GROUP PARTICIPATION*

	Berle Index	%VC	% MBC	MEF	pH	Paco₂	Pao₂
Patients with positive group participation (5)	68	92	62	128	7.44	41	64
Patients with negative group participation (7)	44†	61	36‡	73§	7.43	44	59

Student's *t* test (one-tailed).
* Data collected with the assistance of E. Mansell Pattison, MD, Department of Psychiatry, University of Washington.
† p = < 0.005.
‡ p = < 0.05.
§ p = < 0.025.

221

reflected in the blood gas values shown after participating in two group meetings.

COMMENT. When his defenses were overcome and he tried to discuss psychologically charged topics, he experienced increasing dyspnea and was observed to develop cyanosis. After several episodes of respiratory embarrassment, during sessions which evoked strong emotions, he refused to cooperate and responded to emotional probing by the group with denial and destructive comments. He was not able to return to the group despite encouragement and urging by four physicians including the chief ward physician. He made it very clear to all that he could not tolerate the increased respiratory symptoms associated with group psychotherapy.

Prognosis

At the termination of an 18-month observation period, 24 subjects were alive and 16 were deceased. Of the 24 living subjects, 14 had been discharged and 10 remained hospitalized. When the mean physiologic and psychosocial values of the deceased group were compared with those of the entire living group and with the hospitalized group, significant differences were limited to the elevated Pa_{CO_2} in the deceased group. When the deceased group was compared to the discharged group, significant differences were limited to the Berle III and the total Berle. At the end of 48 months, 29 subjects were deceased, and only one of the 11 living subjects still remained in the hospital from the original hospitalization. When the deceased subjects were compared to the living subjects, significant differences were limited to the %VC, the Berle II and III, and the total Berle. This is illustrated in Tables 4 and 5.

In a further analysis utilizing chi-square, the %MBC was chosen as the one physiologic variable which best reflected total pulmonary performance. The total Berle was used as the best reflection of psychosocial assets. Using this type of analysis, the only significant difference between the deceased and living group was the %MBC at the 18 month follow-up period. There were no significant differences in the deceased and discharged group. Both the Berle and %MBC, however, gave trends in the direction of a low Berle and %MBC being associated with death and a high Berle and %MBC being associated with remaining alive. The Berle and MBC values, therefore, were added. Using this value, significant differences were found between deceased and living subjects at 18 and 48 months, and between the deceased and discharged at 18 months (Table 6).

COMMENT. Although of little predictive significance when used independently, %MBC and the Berle Index were found to be additive factors. This is seen as best representing reality. Except in extreme cases, it is doubtful if any single physiologic or psychosocial factor by itself provides good predictive data for an individual. It is the interaction of the psychosocial and psychophysiologic factors with the physiologic factors which provides for a good or a poor prognosis.

Dying Behavior

All subjects when asked to participate in a study of dying, while in the process of dying, were very willing. One of the patients summed up the prevalent attitude, "I think it is high time we throw some light on the subject and study it together. I can face anything I understand much easier than something I do not."

Subject 4 was a congenial 82-year-old

223

TABLE 4. DECEASED SUBJECTS COMPARED TO LIVING, HOSPITALIZED, AND DISCHARGED SUBJECTS
(18 MONTH FOLLOW-UP; 40 SUBJECTS)

	Deceased (16)	Living (24)	Hospitalized (10)	Discharged (14)
%VC	63	66	69	65
%MBC	36	44	45	43
pH	7.42	7.42	7.43	7.41
Pa_{CO_2}	48	42*	40*	43
Pa_{O_2}	58	63	62	64
Berle I	12	12	13	12
Berle II	20	20	19	20
Berle III	18	22	17	25*
TOTAL	50	54	49	57†
Berle Index total plus %MBC	86	98†	94	101†

Means differ by Mann Whitney U test (one-tailed).
* p < 0.01.
† p < 0.05.

widowed white male who had lived a comfortable, relatively solitary life and had entered the hospital because of

TABLE 5. Deceased Subjects Compared to Living Subjects (4 Year Follow-Up; 40 Subjects)

	Deceased (29)	Living (11)
%VC	62	72*
%MBC	39	45
pH	7.41	7.43
Pa_{CO_2}	45	43
Pa_{O_2}	61	59
Berle I	13	11
Berle II	18	23*
Berle III	18	26†
Total	49	60*
Berle Index total plus %MBC	88	105†

Mann Whitney U test (one-tailed).
* $p < 0.05$.
† $p < 0.01$.

gradually failing health. He considered this hospitalization to be the end of the line since he could not care for himself or tolerate nursing home care. He was ready to die and spent the last few months occupied with sedentary recreational activities. Death to him was consistent with the natural evolution of his life, and he seemed to look forward to it. He was seldom in any kind of physiologic or emotional distress, but was very tired.

Subject 5 was a 44-year-old white divorced male who had no community ties. He was a sensitive, lonely man who was unable to form meaningful personal relationships. He had never been able to stay in one spot and face responsibilities and had therefore been continually on the move. He initially entered the hospital with severe DOPS, which made it impossible for him to continue his peri-

TABLE 6. The Additive Effect of Physiologic and Psychosocial Variables Using the χ^2 Analysis (40 Subjects)

Subjects	MBC < > 41%	Berle < > 60%	MBC + Berle < > 101%
Deceased compared to living (18 mo)	$p < 0.05$	$p < 0.70$	$p < 0.02$
Deceased compared to living (48 mo)	$p < 0.05$	$p < 0.10$	$p < 0.01$
Deceased compared to discharged (18 mo)	$p < 0.20$	$p < 0.20$	$p < 0.02$

patetic ways. He was frightened, hopeless, and had little confidence in the hospital or its doctors. His primary goal appeared to be to die, as he could not see readjusting to a new life style. His increasing respiratory difficulty generated intense fear, and he referred to this as "fear of death itself." The fear appeared more related to what would be done to him in the process of dying, and the possible pain involved, than to the actual fact of dying, which did not appear as threatening as continuing to live in his current status.

Physiologic measurements made during the periods of fear showed an elevation in ventilation, oxygen consumption, carbon dioxide production, and respiratory quotient (Fig 3). The arterial blood gases taken up to the time of death did not correspond to the days on which the other physiologic variables were measured. The dying process appeared to have been associated with a decreased pH and Pa_{O_2} and an increased Pa_{CO_2} (Fig 4).

At autopsy, the cause of death was thought to be pulmonary insufficiency, congestive heart failure, and acute upper gastrointestinal hemorrhage of undetermined etiology.

Subject 6 was a 62-year-old white married male, who entered the hospital with severe DOPS (after being treated for a depressive illness at another hospital). On entering the hospital, he had no place to go, and was unable to work. He was a deeply sensitive, rigid, bitter man. His wife could no longer care for him or tolerate him, and he was determined to die regardless of the doctors' efforts. During the course of his hospital stay, he became more and more overwhelmed and hopeless as he realized that the medical staff would not permit him to die in peace. He stated that he had "given up," and that he was fighting the

227

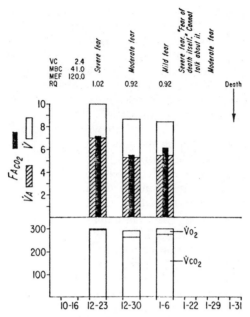

FIG 3. Relative respiratory hyperfunction associated with fear in Subject 5.

doctors and consciously not cooperating. He stated that he was a "burden to himself and his family," and could not see that living was a reasonable course of action.

Despite his feelings about the staff, he remained polite until his life was almost ended, when he became abusive. His clinical course appeared stable until he developed increasingly severe feelings of hopelessness during the last several months of his life. With the onset of these feelings, his clinical course deteriorated, and he soon died. The process of dying did not appear uncomfortable; however, the power struggle with the staff and relatives was very distressing to all concerned.

As shown in Fig 5, the patient's increased feeling of hopelessness was associated with relatively low ventilation, oxygen consumption, and carbon dioxide

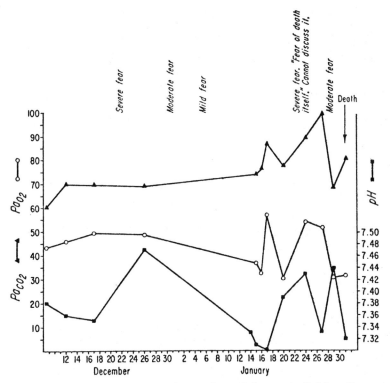

FIG 4. Blood gas values during dying behavior in Subject 5.

output. The respiratory quotient fell when his hopeless feelings were at their maximum. As with Subject 5, the blood gases taken prior to death showed a low pH and Pa_{O_2} and a high Pa_{CO_2}.

The immediate cause of death was not determined, but was associated with confusion and grand mal seizures. At autopsy, cerebral atrophy was an unexpected finding.

Subject 7 was a 60-year-old widowed Catholic female who had been almost continually hospitalized for 16 years with drug-resistant tuberculosis and DOPS (Group IV). For the preceding several years, she had been largely confined to her room and to bed because of her DOPS. Approximately 1 month prior to the start of the study, she had decided to

229

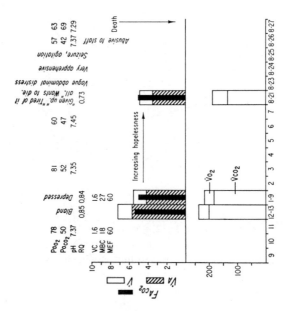

FIG 5. Blood gas and respiratory variables in Subject 6 during dying behavior. Unlike Subject 5, the period preceding death was characterized by increasing hopelessness and relative respiratory hypofunction.

230

die. This decision had followed mass staff resignations because of the threat that the hospital might be closed. New personnel were hired and she said, "They don't know the procedures and are not awfully efficient. This is nerve-wracking."

Although she recognized that she could stay alive if she chose, she said that she was "ready to die" and had "given up." She was comfortable with this decision but was worried that it might be interpreted as suicide. She felt that although her mind was ready to die, she did not know how to stop her body. In the process of dying, which she maintained was very comfortable, she feared that someone would reverse the process or that she would lose her mind. Although she feared death, the struggle to live was so difficult that the greater fear was that of life under the present circumstances. Her fear of having the dying process reversed was very practical, as she said that having this done was one of the most uncomfortable things that had ever happened to her. In her words, "I felt like screaming." This was in a woman who had an enormous tolerance to pain and discomfort. During the process of dying, she was concerned that she continue to contribute to the research project she had joined, and that those around her understand what was happening to her. Above all she wanted to "die with dignity."

She was followed with daily psychiatric interviews during the last 2 weeks of her life. The sequence of events was as follows:

OCT 5. "I have given up. I am ready to die." She was willing her body to die, but said she had not found the right combination yet. She felt that she was withdrawing from the world and refusing to take sustenance from it. She became nauseated easily, and her food did not digest well. She noted that people seemed to avoid her since she had made it plain that she was going to die.

Oct 6.   She was being taught relaxation techniques since she refused to have medications to decrease anxiety or pain because she feared it would interfere with her intellectual functioning. She refused hypnosis for the same reason.

Oct 7.   No change.

Oct 8.   She stopped breathing and was started on an automatic breathing machine through a tracheotomy. The patient said that she "felt like screaming" during the revival procedure. Being unconscious was comfortable, and it was the change to consciousness which was perceived as uncomfortable. Received the last rites.

Oct 9.   She still could not breathe unassisted but did not want the automatic breathing machine discontinued. It was kept going for the remainder of her life. She would have preferred that it had not been started. She said she had been able to utilize relaxation techniques to keep discomfort at a minimum. She wanted to stay alert and refused medications which might impair her reasoning ability. She was very much in the driver's seat and wanted to stay there.

Oct 10.   She remained alert and stated that this was the way she wanted to die. Appetite was almost gone.

Oct 11.   Thirst and appetite were almost completely gone. She was still alert, and no intravenous fluids were to be given. Some of the nursing staff thought we were willing the patient to die which, they concluded, we had no right to do. They stayed with the patient continuously to make sure she did not die. Explanation and reassurance to the staff did nothing to decrease this concern.

Comatose in the afternoon, but she awakened after mild external stimuli. She felt she would have died if left alone. The comatose period was peaceful and relaxing. Again, awakening was very painful.

Oct 12.   She wanted to be sure we had all the data we needed. Wanted to know if her impending death depressed me. When I said yes, she consoled me and said she was glad she did not have my job. She now felt she had been successful in completely shutting off her body, and death was just a matter of time. She did not want the automatic breathing device shut off, but on the other hand, she did not want any other "devices" used to keep her going. Except for suctioning and some pain on swallowing, she was comfortable and relaxed. She stated that death was a natural biological event, and she was ready for it. "Somewhat of an adventure." She feared last-minute resuscitation attempts on the part of the medical staff.

OCT 13. Weakness was increasing, and she now had short comatose periods when she could not move or talk, but could hear. She felt like sleeping continuously. She was pleasant and had a keen mind, although she felt it was deteriorating. When not sleeping, she was constantly uncomfortable because of the suctioning and the tracheotomy tube. She denied fear at this point. She stated that the process she was experiencing was very much like "getting prepared for something." The closest she could come was that it was a natural biological process which prepared you for something—"like getting ready for a long winter nap." Again she stated that being revived made her feel like screaming, and she preferred not going through it.

OCT 14. Consciousness was fading. Almost no intake or output for the past 24 hr. BP was 30/0 and pulse was 130. She stated that she was ambivalent about dying now, but that there was no fear and she was comfortable. She was very cold to the touch and felt cold herself.

OCT 15. A mild increase in thirst and appetite developed along with numerous moist rales in the left chest and occasional pain in that area. She was much more alert than any time over the past several days. She was very upset to learn that it was Sunday as she thought it was still Wednesday. At this point, the "giving up" process appeared comfortable. Again she stated that attempts to revive her made her feel like "screaming," and she feared this more than anything.

OCT 16. Appetite and thirst were

gone again. She was still in control but appeared to be losing her will to remain so.

Oct 17. She was confused and disoriented and knew it. Her time sense and ability to recognize common objects were gone. She was frightened that she might be losing her mind and needed much reassurance and support.

She wanted to give up control and wanted the doctors to use their own judgment with medications and treatment because she felt she was too confused to make adequate decisions. She was very relieved when this was done.

She said she did not fear dying, but that the confusion was frightening, and she felt she needed help in facing it. I informed her that I would have to leave the state for several days and she was very upset.

Oct 18. I said good-bye to her. She was very weak and could barely summon enough energy to smile. She slept most of the time and said that everything was all right and that she was comfortable.

Oct 19. She slept deeply all night. She awoke at 8:00 AM, alert and not confused. She had a comfortable day and required no medication. At 9:45 PM she coughed several times and died.

Measurements of NMA, MA, VMA, creatinine, blood pressure, pulse rate, and body temperature were made during the last 10 days of her life. Due to the necessity for constant ventilation on an intermittent positive pressure breathing apparatus through a tracheotomy tube, measurements of respiratory variables were not made. As illustrated in Fig 6, the patient was excreting massive amounts of NMA, MA, and VMA. The high level of catecholamines was not associated with changes in blood pressure, pulse rate, or body temperature (Fig 7). The patient began excreting small to moderate amounts of ketones* on Oc-

*Ketostik—small to moderate represents approximately 15–20 mg acetoacetic acid per 100 ml of urine.

tober 11 and continued this to the time of her death. Medications, with the exception of small amounts of morphine or codeine and small amounts of Neo-Synephrine aerosol, were discontinued several days prior to the onset of the study.

COMMENT. Dying behavior in these subjects was not in itself uncomfortable. The subjects seemed to regard death as part of the natural evolution of life, and the dying behavior itself was experienced as comfortable and even pleasant. However, the interaction of the patient with the environment in which dying occurred often produced extreme feelings of discomfort in both the patient and the staff. The patient's discomfort did not appear to be related to the dying behavior, although that was the interpretation of those observing the patient. It was related to the inability of those surrounding the patient to come to terms with his death and to painful medical procedures. One patient summed up the feelings of those around her as follows: "They are resentful. They do not want to face facts. They prefer to hang onto hope. I do not really blame the poor dears. They have all worked very hard—above and beyond what they needed to do."

Mention should also be made of the fact that very few patients wanted to die alone. Most needed the same or more human contact during the process of dying as they did while functioning in society.

Discussion

The chronic lung disease patient is seen as using repression, denial, and isolation to insulate himself from inputs which increase disability and discomfort. These defense mechanisms are seen as necessary to survival, and their failure

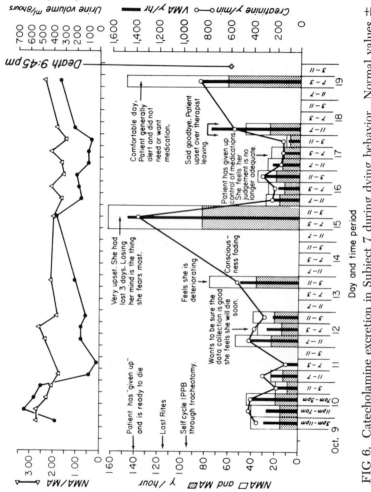

FIG 6. Catecholamine excretion in Subject 7 during dying behavior. Normal values ± SD in young college males: (1) VMA 4.65 ± 1.22 μg/min (279 μg/hr); (2) MA 4.94 ± 3.18 μg/hr; (3) NMA 6.36 ± 2.78 μg/hr.

236

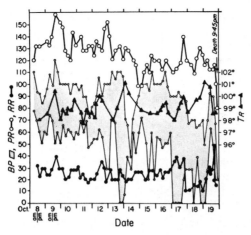

FIG 7. Variations in blood pressure (BP), pulse rate (PR), respiratory rate (RR), and rectal temperature (TR) associated with dying behavior in Subject 7. Excretion of massive amounts of catecholamines was not reflected in changes in these variables.

leads to physiologic and psychologic decompensation.

Psychosocial and psychophysiologic variables are very important in the prognosis and treatment of clinical emphysema. Patients with many psychosocial assets are more effective in protecting themselves from dangerous symptoms or behaviors and are more likely to proceed with a realistic, appropriate treatment program. They therefore are better able to cope with an unprotected (nonhospital) environment. Psychosocial assets are as important as the physiologic assets in treatment and prognosis of severe airway obstructions.

The importance of being able to deal effectively with the environment cannot be overemphasized in these people. The respiratory system is very reactive to environmental and emotional inputs. People who have a great number of affective changes of any kind also have great variation in the dynamics of res-

237

piration. This variability almost always is associated with increased disability (dyspnea) and insufficiency.[12] People with few psychosocial assets or a limited number of coping behaviors experience more affective changes than subjects with many psychosocial assets. People who do not know how to adapt are more likely to get angry, anxious, or depressed when confronted with life change. It should be noted that depression, anxiety, etc were not a part of the Berle rating and that psychiatric disability does not result necessarily in a lower score.

Once dyspnea is present, however, a feedback mechanism appears to operate which intensifies and extends the incapacity produced by the original stimulus. The dyspnea precipitates affective changes, frequently manifested clinically by depression and anxiety, which, in turn, produce increased dyspnea and more physiologic change. The mechanism is self-perpetuating and is seen as being responsible for a large part of the disability in many of the patients.

Many of the patients recognize the role of emotional change in producing symptoms and go to great lengths to avoid experiencing change of any kind. When emotional change is experienced, their attempts to readapt depend on whether activation or inactivation has been induced. If activation has occurred, they try to slow down everything— thoughts and action. If inactivation (withdrawal) has occurred, they try to speed things up and become more activated. Only by successfully counteracting the induced changes in activation are they able to remain comfortable. Many patients view changes in energy levels as wasted energy, which they need to avoid.

Patients with few psychosocial assets also have difficulty understanding what is expected of them or complying when they do understand. This is particularly so when some change in behavior or occupation is required during rehabilitative procedures. Social changes of any kind are tremendous threats since these patients have few or no alternative behaviors. Lack of compliance to a therapeutic program seems to be directly proportional to the amount of behavioral and vocational change required. Learning to deal with the patient with few psychosocial assets is important since they seem to constitute the great majority of problem patients or those needing rehabilitation. In general, patients with high psychosocial assets do not need rehabilitation or can rehabilitate themselves with little or no assistance. The utilization of defenses is seen as varying from patient to patient in both the degree and effectiveness of their use, depending on the psychosocial assets available to the patient. Attacking the patient's defenses directly can be highly destructive and can result in cardiopulmonary decompensation and death.

The significance of common social changes to the patient can be quantified with the Schedule of Recent Experience.*[13, 14] Initial experience has shown that patients with low psychosocial assets remain medically stable as long as they have minimal life changes as indicated by the above test.

Dying behavior is seen as a realistic response on the part of the patient to his total life situation. It is usually triggered by specific social events which are difficult or impossible for the patient to accept. Dying is seen to be a goal-directed behavior which is accompanied by a variety of emotions and their physiologic counterparts. These emotions are usually related to environmental situa-

---

*Additional data can be obtained by writing Thomas H. Holmes, MD, Department of Psychiatry, University of Washington School of Medicine, Seattle, Wash 98105.

tions and not to the dying behavior itself. Dying is described by the articulate patients as comfortable and relaxing and is exceedingly difficult to give up once it is started. As described by one verbal patient: "It's like getting ready for something. Like curling up for a long winter's nap." This patient also described her feelings when this behavior was halted by the doctors as among the most uncomfortable she had ever had: "I felt like screaming."

Although the biologic process of dying seemed comfortable, the emotions generated by their interaction with those around them can be very distressing. Interestingly, these emotions are sometimes related to fear of what would happen to them in terms of resuscitative procedures and to power struggles between the patient who insists on dying and the hospital staff and relatives who refuse to grant the patient the right to die or even talk of death.

It is recognized that death from an acute disease or injury presents as more of a crisis situation. However, it is thought that the giving up of life is no more uncomfortable in those situations to the one who is experiencing death than it is to the patient with chronic lung disease. In this series of case studies, the trauma of death seems more in the eyes of the beholder than in the actual experience of the dying person.

The limited physiologic data that could be collected during dying behavior does not point to any particular pattern of ventilation or metabolism being associated with dying. This is evident despite the fact that respiratory acidosis appeared to be associated with the terminal event in Subjects 5 and 6. Subject 7, who had the most insight and was able to give an excellent description of her feelings during the dying process, had very high levels of catecholamine excretion. This pattern of excretion is consistent with Cannon's hypothesis[15] and conflicts with Richter's observations.[16] However, their observations were on sudden death and are perhaps not applicable to naturally occurring death. Since the dying patients do have in common a unique kind of behavior which precedes death by weeks and perhaps months, they also probably have certain unique physiologic changes which set the stage for death. This unique dying behavior is best described as psychologic and physiologic hibernation. It represents an adaptive response to stimulus inputs and is not necessarily related to organ failure. The behavior is resorted to as the best or ultimate solution to an intolerable situation. This is in keeping with the formulation recently presented by Wolf.[17] Aside from the above generalizations, hypotheses regarding the actual mechanism of death are not warranted with the limited physiologic data available on these subjects. Physiologic studies in progress may provide additional insight.

Summary

Forty subjects with debilitating clinical emphysema requiring hospitalization were studied over a 4-year period. As a group, they were found to utilize denial, repression, and isolation to protect their failing respiratory system from environmental inputs. Failure of these defenses led to physiologic and psychologic deterioration.

During the observation period, 29 subjects (73%) died. The probability of death was increased in the presence of low psychosocial and physiologic assets. Dying was seen to be a specific goal-directed adaptive behavior, which was comfortable and relatively devoid of threat. Emotional upsets accompanying death were seen to be related to problems with family, friends, and hospital staff. The fear and trauma of dying were largely in the eyes of the beholder.

References

1. MARTIN, C. J., PARDEE, N., and DOMINICK, J. The diffuse obstructive pulmonary syndrome: I. Natural history. *Amer Rev Resp Dis 93*:383, 1966.
2. COMROE, J. H. *Physiology of Respiration.* Y.B. Pub., Chicago, 1965.
3. GOLDSMITH, J. R. A simple test of maximal expiratory flow in detecting ventilatory obstruction. *Amer Rev Tuberc 27*:180, 1958.
4. MARTIN, C. J., and HALLETT, W. Y. The diffuse obstructive pulmonary syndrome in a tuberculosis sanatorium: II. Incidence and symptoms. *Ann Intern Med 54*:1156, 1961.
5. BALDWIN, E. DEF., COURNAND, A., and RICHARDS, D. W., JR. Pulmonary insufficiency: I. Physiologic classification, clinical methods of analysis, standard values in normal subjects. *Medicine (Balt) 27*:243, 1948.
6. LOEW, P. G., and THEWS, G. Die altersabnangigkeit des arteriellen sanerstoffdruckes bei der berufstatigen bevolkerung. *Klin Wschr 40*:1093, 1962.
7. DUDLEY, D. L., HOLMES, T. H., MARTIN, C. J., and RIPLEY, H. S. Changes in respiration associated with hypnotically induced emotion, pain and exercise. *Psychosom Med 24*:46, 1964.
8. DUDLEY, D. L., MARTIN, C. J., and HOLMES, T. H. Psychophysiologic studies of pulmonary ventilation. *Psychosom Med 26*:645, 1964.
9. FOWLER, W. S. Lung function studies: II. The respiratory dead space. *Amer J Physiol 154*:405, 1948.
10. MASUDA, M. Differing adaptive metabolic behaviors. *J Psychosom Res 10*:239, 1966.

11. BERLE, B. B., PINSKY, R. H., WOLF, S., and WOLFF, H. G. A clinical guide to prognosis in stress disease. *JAMA 149:* 1624, 1952.
12. DUDLEY, D. L., MARTIN, C. J., and HOLMES, T. H. Dyspnea: Psychologic and physiologic observations. *J Psychosom Res 11:*325, 1968.
13. HOLMES, T. H., and RAHE, R. H. The social readjustment rating scale. *J Psychosom Res 11:*213, 1967.
14. RAHE, R. H., and HOLMES, T. H. Life crisis and disease onset. I. Qualitative and quantitative definition of the life crisis and its association with health change. Unpublished data.
15. CANNON, W. B. "Voodoo" death. *Psychosom Med 14:*182, 1957.
16. RICHTER, C. P. On the phenomenon of sudden death in animals and man. *Psychosom Med 14:*191, 1957.
17. WOLF, S. The turned off heart. *Med Times 96:*132, 1968.

AUTHOR INDEX

KEY-WORD TITLE INDEX